THE POST-WAR HISTORY OF
THE BRITISH WORKING CLASS

THE
POST-WAR HISTORY
OF THE
BRITISH WORKING CLASS

by

ALLEN HUTT

author of
The Condition of the Working Class in Britain
This Final Crisis

.

LONDON
VICTOR GOLLANCZ LTD
1937

Printed in Great Britain by
The Camelot Press Ltd.   London and Southampton

CONTENTS

PREFACE

THIS BOOK has a simple aim. It is to tell the story of the British Labour movement from the World War of 1914–18 up to the present day. No history is so important, or so neglected, as recent history, the history which forms the immediate background and conditioning of current events; and in the case of the working class and its movement this applies with particular force. It is my hope, therefore, that the present work will help to fill an acknowledged gap and will be of some service to all those who seek guidance for action, present and future.

What the reader will find here is a plain narrative of events, which I have tried to document accurately and to set down objectively. My concern has been to let men and parties speak for themselves, to recount the facts without arguing about them. Though when one has spent nearly twenty years of life, from youth onwards, in active association with the Labour movement it is natural to feel passionately about the issues involved; and I certainly have long had strong views on the need for unity of the working class, for a consistent forward policy—views which have been reinforced by the writing of this book.

The available material for the period covered is naturally boundless; and no one can be more conscious than I of the incompleteness of this study. For the earlier years I owe much to the standard works of the Webbs and Mr. G. D. H. Cole (particularly his *Short History of the British Working-Class Movement*). Extensive use has been made of the admirably compiled official reports of the annual Trades

Union Congresses and Labour Party Conferences, as well as of newspapers and the ocean of pamphlets and other ephemeral literature produced by all sections of the movement. Particularly helpful have been the *Labour Monthly* and *Labour Research* (the Monthly Circular of the Labour Research Department), whose files I always find indispensable.

G. A. H.

London, April 1937.

CHAPTER I

THE REVOLUTIONARY YEARS

WHEN THE MAROONS split the silent air on that November morning in 1918 they signalled much more than the ending of the World War. Those detonations, hailed with heartfelt relief as harbingers of peace, ushered in the most troublous and stormy age of profound social crisis ever known by this country and that overwhelming majority of its people who toil to live. The increasing acuteness of social problems in Britain had, it is true, been a dominant feature of the years immediately preceding the war. From the turn of the century real wages had declined while profits had risen. The rich were waxing fat on the wealth newly drawn from overseas. The working men began to deploy their forces for a frontal attack on the system that condemned them to want and frustration, and to refashion their organisations for this purpose.

The strikes of the miners and railwaymen stood out in the general movement of working-class revolt. They were the biggest strikes Britain had seen; and they were actuated by a new, aggressive spirit. Trade unionism was being forged into something very different from a mere instrument for collective bargaining, into something whose " object and purpose " wrote the Webbs, " cannot be attained without the transformation of British politics and the supersession of the capitalist profit-maker as the governor and director of industry." The same authorities observe that while the number of recorded industrial disputes was only 399 in 1908, it " rose in 1911 to 903, and culminated in the latter half of 1913 and the first half of 1914 in the outbreak of something like a hundred and fifty strikes per month.

British trade unionism was, in fact, in the summer of 1914, working up for an almost revolutionary outburst of gigantic industrial disputes, which could not have failed to be seriously embarrassing for the political organisation to which the movement had committed itself, when, in August 1914, war was declared."

This pre-war movement was essentially a trade union, and within the unions a rank-and-file, affair. There was, as the previous quotation implies, a divergence between this movement and the Labour Party, whose leadership, as typified in the tactics of Mr. Ramsay MacDonald, had spread much disillusionment as a result of its preoccupation with parliamentary manœuvrings and its coquetting with the ruling Liberals. No revolutionary political party of the working class stood at the head of this essentially political, and implicitly revolutionary, movement; for no such party existed. Of the active spirits in the movement some were members of one or other of the existing Socialist sects; some were members of none.

War overwhelmed the movement, but the recovery was not long in coming. The clamping down of an iron dictatorship on the country did not dissipate the ingredients of the " revolutionary industrial outburst " that had been preparing. Pre-war wage demands became even more imperative with the rapid rise in the cost of living. Profiteering pointed even more sharply the contrast between rich and poor. The abrogation of trade union conditions and the drive for dilution of labour, dictated by munitions needs, seemed to increasing numbers of workers to menace the whole future of the trades by which they lived. Since the Labour Party and the trade unions had officially gone over to support of the war, the union machine becoming in effect the State's labour department, it was only natural that, as the movement raised its head again, its industrial and rank-and-file character should be still more pronounced. This was the feature of the first big wartime strikes, those of the South Wales miners and the Clyde engineers in 1915. The men on the job were organising on the job. In engineering, the shop stewards, already existing as card inspectors and reporters to their union district committees, were transformed into workshop representatives and leaders. They formed the core of the apparatus of shop and works committees which was rapidly established, cutting across old craft divisions and in the new strength and solidarity which it engendered mobilising the workers for action with an effectiveness not previously known.

It was on the Clyde that this wartime movement reached its greatest height. Out of the strike of 1915 arose the Clyde Workers' Committee, pledged to resist the Munitions Act, support of which by the union officials its initial manifesto stigmatised as " an act of treachery to the working class." Directly representing the mass of workers in the engineering works and shipyards of the vast industrial area centring on Glasgow, the Committee was concerned with wider issues than the immediate one of control of the conditions of dilution. Its proclaimed objects were " to obtain an ever-increasing control over workshop conditions, to regulate the terms upon which workers shall be employed, and to organise the workers upon a class basis and to maintain the class struggle, until the overthrow of the wages system, the freedom of the workers, and the establishment of industrial democracy have been attained." The idea of workers' control was potent in the coalfields too; at the 1918 conference of the Miners' Federation, Secretary Frank Hodges declared that " unless accompanied by an effective form of working-class control, I do not believe that nationalisation will do any good for anybody."

Trade union membership mounted rapidly as the war continued. In 1913 the Trades Union Congress counted less than 2¼ million affiliated members; in 1918 over 4½ million were in its ranks. There were extensive moves for federation and amalgamation, the statutory restrictions on the latter being modified by an Act of 1917. In that year also the constitution of the Triple Alliance of miners, railwaymen and transport workers, planned in the spring and summer of 1914 on the initiative of the first-named, was finally ratified.

At the same time the employers set about a serious unification of their forces on a national scale, establishing the Federation of British Industries in 1916.

The social atmosphere was already lowering and thunderous when the lightning of the March Revolution in Russia blazed across the heavens. A people grown weary of war rejoiced that the traditional citadel of European reaction had been overthrown. Enthusiasm for the Russian example produced a widely-attended convention at Leeds in June 1917, which aimed at establishing a nation-wide network of Workers' and Soldiers' Councils on the model of the Soviets, though the attempt came to nothing. Meantime the Clyde, Sheffield, Barrow, London and other munition centres were swept by a wave of strikes (in May). The hitherto solid pro-war front of the Labour Party began to crack. Tense excitement marked the acceptance of the Soviet invitation to an international Socialist peace conference at Stockholm. Henderson resigned from the coalition Cabinet. It was decided to draft a new constitution and a Socialist programme for the Party.

Not many Socialists in Britain sensed the real significance of the events in Russia. Redoubtable John McLean, superb agitator and educator, revered leader of the Clyde workers, Britain's outstanding genuine revolutionary Marxist, declared in the summer of 1917 that Russia's freedom would only be secure if the workers took power; he added that the workers in Britain needed to do likewise, by throwing all their forces into the struggle against the war, for the overthrow of the ruling capitalist class. In November came those days that shook the world, shook it to its uttermost depths. The flood of distorted news and scare propaganda could not conceal the simple fact that for the first time in history those of low degree had captured the seats of the mighty—and were sitting tight. Of Clyde sentiment the moderate P. J. Dollan wrote: "There is general discontent in Socialist and Labour circles at what seems to be the apathy of the official Socialist and Labour bodies in this country towards our Bolshevik comrades. Their methods may not be genteel, but they get there, and their aim is our aim." Litvinov, plenipotentiary of the new Soviet Republic, received an ovation at the Nottingham conference of the Labour Party in January 1918. Simultaneously the Clyde representatives of the engineering and allied trade unions threatened the Government with a political strike if its new Man-Power Bill (the final stage of the " comb-out ") was not withdrawn, and also demanded the immediate calling of an international conference to discuss peace terms. Sir Auckland Geddes, hastily despatched to overawe these turbulent engineers, retired in disorder as his patron Mr. Lloyd George had done two years before.

Throughout the last desperate year of war the tide of unrest flowed stronger. A monster May Day demonstration closed down the Clyde and electrified its people. Never had the shop stewards and the Workers' Committees been so firmly rooted; contact between the different districts was developing and the movement was reaching out to co-ordination on a national scale. In August the police strike, out of which the Government hastened to blarney its way, came as a threat from an unexpected and highly significant quarter. It coincided with intelligence of mutinous preparations at a number of South Coast naval bases, where lower-deck committees had been elected. Since the winter of 1917 disturbances had likewise been multiplying in the army; there were mutinies at base camps (Etaples), shootings of military police;[1] even the Brigade of Guards—if Mr. Stephen Graham is to be believed—were not wholly immune from the prevailing disaffection.

The breaking of the great German offensive preluded the collapse of the Central Powers and the armistice. Hapsburg and Hohenzollern followed Romanov into the dust. The sorry scheme of things entire had certainly been shattered to bits; would it be remoulded nearer to the heart's desire of toiling humanity? In this country, as a disinterested chronicler has noted, the working class as a whole had been

[1] A documented account will be found in T. H. Wintringham: *Mutiny*, ch. ix, pp. 305–27.

sustained during the war by its " hope for some great social deliverance arising out of the ashes of world conflict." The ruling class, replete with " the enormous and even unprecedented profits made throughout the whole range of business enterprise " (Webb), possessed of a vast accumulation of artificially enhanced capital values (in the summer of 1918 the sixpenny shares of the leading cellulose concern were quoted at £14 10s.), fortified by an unparalleled growth of combination and monoply, sought to exorcise the demon of revolution with a Ministry of Reconstruction and Whitley Councils. Meanwhile, within three days of the armistice an emergency conference of the Labour Party met in London. It dragged the Labour ministers out of the coalition and recorded its " protest against any patching up of the old economic order." For the General Election, a " call to the people " was issued under the headings of " a Peace of Reconciliation; Hands off Democracy; Land for the Workers; a Million Good Houses; a Levy on Capital," demanding more specifically:

> " The immediate nationalisation and democratic control of vital public services such as mines, railways, shipping, armaments, and electric power; the fullest recognition and utmost extension of trade unionism . . . the national minimum . . . the abolition of the menace of unemployment . . . the universal right to work or maintenance, legal limitation of the hours of labour and the drastic amendment of the Acts dealing with factory conditions, safety and workmen's compensation."

On a poll of less than 60 per cent of the newly-enlarged electorate, and with a platform that Mr. Keynes described as a " concoction of greed and sentiment, prejudice and deception," the Government of the " hard-faced men who look as if they had done very well out of the war " was victorious. Yet in comparison with the previous election (1910) the Labour Party had increased its poll from half a million to $2\frac{1}{4}$ millions and with its 57 seats became in effect the Opposition. It soon appeared, however, that this meant little. Great things were toward in the country, but they found neither reflection nor inspiration in the activities of the Parliamentary Party under the pedestrian leadership first of the late Mr. William Adamson and then of Mr. J. R. Clynes.

During the first three months of 1919 British capitalism was skating on thin ice. The " revolutionary outburst " that was threatening in 1914 now seemed likely to materialise in a far more acute form and in circumstances vastly more menacing to the existing social order. Not only was the mass of the working class in a state of ferment; for the first time millions of working men had been trained to the use of arms, great numbers indeed were still under arms. Britain had a huge conscript army, clamouring stridently for demobilisation—heroes who wanted to get to the fine new homes they had been promised. Between the armistice and the turn of the year was a period of preparation. Demands were being formulated on the one hand, temporary concessions made on the other. In practically every trade the unions were pressing for shorter hours, for wage advances that had been forgone during the war, for the restoration of trade union conditions. The Government hastily introduced an Act to prevent any reduction of wages for a stated period and also provided for a system of out-of-work donation for demobilised servicemen and discharged munitions workers.

In the opening days of 1919 it seemed that an explosion was inevitable. Demobilisation was proceeding far too slowly to satisfy the war-weary, army-weary, troops; and this was intensified by the drafting of men for the new war that Britain had begun in North Russia, the anti-Soviet intervention at Archangel. There were mutinies in a whole series of camps and depots, especially in the London and Southern Commands.[1] Thousands of Army Service Corps men commandeered lorries and poured into London to place their grievances before the Government. Unfortunately the self-imposed isolation of most English Socialists from the armed forces and their problems meant that this

[1] T. H. Wintringham, *op. cit.*

movement remained spontaneous and undirected. It was in some degree symptomatic that in one case the rebellious soldiers turned for guidance, not to any working-class body but to the egregious Bottomley. Nevertheless, the situation was sufficiently critical for the historian to assert that the development at this stage of a general forward movement by the workers in industry, and the co-ordination of this movement with the revolt that had begun to blaze among the troops, could have brought about the downfall of the régime.

What actually happened was that the movements that occurred were independent of each other. There was no concerted action, no co-ordinated attack. The leaders either did not clearly realise the strategic and tactical problems they were facing, or else sought to hold back their forces, who were straining at the leash. It was therefore possible for the Government, by skilful manœuvring, by employing force (meaning mainly the threat of force) or fraud as required, to dispose of its adversaries one by one.

First indication of the trend of events was the Forty-Hour strike on the Clyde which lasted from January 27th–February 11th. Of the unanimity and determination of the Clyde engineers, shipyard and other workers in this strike to shorten their working week there could be no sort of doubt. The local union officials were at one with the shop stewards and the Workers' Committee in preparing the strike. Even at the height of its wartime struggles the atmosphere of Britain's storm centre had not been so supercharged. Demonstrations surged through Glasgow. The Red Flag was hoisted on the municipal flagstaff. Better than anything the " Battle of George's Square " showed the temper of the workers; when a demonstration in the city centre was attacked by the police, and its leaders—William Gallacher, David Kirkwood and others—mercilessly beaten up, the crowd did not disperse but fought back and showed that it could more than hold its own. Everywhere men sensed that this was no ordinary strike and the authorities frankly feared a rising. Selected reinforcements of young and fresh troops, unwearied by war and lavishly provided with tanks and machine-guns, were rushed to the Clyde, which they duly occupied the day after the George's Square battle and the arrest of the strike leaders. No reliance was placed on the strong garrison already in Glasgow. They were veteran troops who were regarded so dubiously that they had been rigorously confined to their barracks at Maryhill since the commencement of the strike. Yet the strikers had no contact with, made no approach to, their potential allies behind Maryhill's dour walls.

It appears that, as William Gallacher has since said of himself and the other strike leaders, " we were carrying on a strike when we ought to have been making a revolution." Imbued with the conviction that industrial organisation and action alone counted, the shop stewards' movement, says Gallacher, regarded " politics " with contempt, and their " failure to realise the need of continuous and consistent leadership embracing all phases of activity represented a fatal weakness that was to lead to our complete eclipse." At the same time the Clyde strike was isolated, the national officials of the unions opposing it. Their influence was sufficient to prevent the men in other engineering and shipbuilding centres (with the exception of Belfast) from joining their Clyde brethren. Union discipline was invoked; the Amalgamated Society of Engineers' Executive, for instance, suspended its district officials on the Clyde.

Even before the clash of the Clydeside conflict resounded through the country the million-strong army of the coalfields was preparing for battle. In conference at Southport on January 14th the Miners' Federation had resolved to demand a 30 per cent increase in wages, a six-hour working day, and nationalisation of the mines with a measure of workers' control. These demands were rejected—the mines were still under the Government control imposed as a wartime measure—whereupon the Federation referred the whole question to its members. An exhaustive ballot returned an overwhelming majority in favour of strike action (the voting was 615,164 to 105,082), and notices were duly

tendered. Presented with this ultimatum in the latter days
of February the Government found itself in a hazardous
position. All the advantages were on the side of the miners.
Coal stocks were at famine level, London having only three
days supply. At the same time the other members of the
Triple Alliance (railwaymen and transport workers) were
in consultation with the miners, and had themselves tabled
demands for which they were in negotiation. In short, Mr.
Lloyd George and his colleagues were confronted with the
alarming prospect of a general strike fraught with revolutionary implications.

The Government's reaction was to pull a two-fold bluff;
and this bluff was not called. On the one hand they made
it clear to the miners' leaders that they would use troops
to suppress a strike; on the other hand they promised a full
and free investigation into the affairs of the mining industry,
with the implementing of any recommendations, if there
were no strike. The Federation leaders, headed by President
Robert Smillie, thereupon exerted themselves to secure the
acceptance of the Government's offer. Mr. Smillie was
justly held in universal respect, but it required every scrap
of his influence and persuasion in hour upon hour of
vehement debate at the delegate conference on February
26th–27th to obtain by a narrow majority what was only a
provisional acceptance. Strike notices were not withdrawn.
Their operation, scheduled for March 15th, was simply
suspended for a fortnight to see what would be the result
of the initial labours of the Royal Commission presided over
by Mr. Justice Sankey in which the miners (being allowed
to nominate or approve no less than half the members)
agreed to participate. The effect of this Commission's proceedings was sensational. Newspapers compared it with a
revolutionary tribunal. Coal capitalism was in the dock
and—it seemed—on trial for its life. An interim Report,
presented punctually on March 20th, conceded a wage
advance of 2s. a shift, a reduction of working hours from
eight to seven, and added that " even upon the evidence
already given, the present system of ownership and working

in the coal industry stands condemned and some other system must be substituted for it . . . we are prepared to report now that it is in the interests of the country that the colliery workers shall in the future have an effective voice in the direction of the mines."

Were the miners to accept this instalment of their demands on hours and wages, reckoning that the already unmistakable indication of the Commission's attitude on nationalisation was a sure guide to its final recommendations ? Could they rely, that is to say, on the Government's assurances ? On the very day of the presentation of the interim Report Mr. Bonar Law, speaking in the name of the Cabinet, repeated those assurances in the House of Commons; he repeated also the threat to use the full powers of the State to break a miners' strike. Confirming these verbal assurances there came on the following day this categorical written pledge, addressed to the Secretary of the Miners' Federation:

11 Downing Street,
Whitehall, S.W.
21st March, 1919.

DEAR SIR,—Speaking in the House of Commons last night I made a statement in regard to the Government policy in connection with the Report of the Coal Industry Commission. I have pleasure in confirming, as I understand you wish me to do, my statement that the Government are prepared to carry out in the spirit and in the letter the recommendations of Sir John Sankey's Report.

Yours faithfully,
A. BONAR LAW.

On the strength of the Bonar Law letter the resumed delegate conference of the miners on March 26th virtually ended the crisis by accepting the interim Report and by taking a ballot which resulted in the final withdrawal of the strike notices.

The Government could now breathe again. The moment of greatest danger was past. The bluff had worked. That it was nothing but bluff was soon to be shown. On June 23rd the Coal Commissioners presented their final Reports. Proposals for nationalisation and the granting to the miners of a share in control were common to the Reports of the Chairman and the six miners' spokesmen, which thus constituted in effect a Majority Report. Five of the employers' and coalowners' representatives opposed any change in ownership. The sixth, Sir Arthur Duckham, produced a scheme of his own for the trustification of the industry, retaining private capitalist ownership and control, with elaborate district profit-pooling and regulating arrangements. Confidently the miners called on the Government to carry out its pledged word to implement Sir John Sankey's proposals which, though falling short of their own plans as regards control, their delegate conference in July was prepared to accept. But pledges were now a thing of the past. From anxious placation of the miners the Government turned to insolent provocation. Negotiations in the various coalfields for piece-rate adjustments consequent on the introduction of the seven-hour day were thrown into confusion by an unjustified order from the Coal Controller prohibiting any increase in piece-rates in excess of 10 per cent. This caused a stormy and bitter strike in the Yorkshire coalfield lasting from the middle of July to the middle of August. Troops were sent in and naval ratings put to manning the pumps. Nothing daunted, the men held firm and the misconceived prohibition had to be withdrawn, after a struggle that had cost the powerful Yorkshire Miners' Association £356,000 in strike pay.

Then the Government spoke, in the very week of the resumption of work by the Yorkshiremen. On August 18th Mr. Lloyd George announced in the House of Commons that the Government rejected nationalisation, thus throwing overboard Sir John Sankey's Report, and propounded instead a vague and diluted version of Sir Arthur Duckham's trustification scheme. Derisively dubbed " Duckham and water " this proposal was taken seriously by no one and passed quickly into limbo. Five months, almost to the day, had passed since the giving of the Government's written pledge. Too late the miners' leaders realised how, and why, they had been bluffed. Mr. Smillie himself, in a subsequent survey, put the issue with his accustomed candour:

" The miners were very reluctant to submit their claims to a Commission, for their previous experience of such bodies had led them to believe that Commissions were usually appointed to get rid, for the time being, of some ugly question which it was not the intention of the Government to deal with seriously. Mr. Herbert Smith, Mr. Frank Hodges and I were mainly responsible for the acceptance by the miners of the Government's offer of a Commission, and I can sincerely and honestly declare that had we not fully believed that the Government would act on its findings we should have taken a very different course. We should have advised the men to reject the Commission and to carry out the decision arrived at by ballot vote of the members of the Federation."[1]

No wonder Mr. Vernon Hartshorn asked indignantly during the debate of August 18th: " Why was the Commission set up ? Was it a huge game of bluff ? Was it never intended that if the reports favoured nationalisation we were to get it ? . . . That is the kind of question the miners of the country will ask, and they will say ' we have been deceived, betrayed, duped.' "

It is time to add here certain considerations on that other aspect of the Government's February bluff—their threat to use the armed forces to the limit in suppressing a strike. This, magnified into a fatalistic anticipation of violence and bloodshed deluging the coalfields, weighed heavily with the Federation leaders, notably with Mr. Smillie. From this anticipation the dour President recoiled, saying privately to his colleagues " if there is a strike they will use the soldiers. My people will be shot down. Anything rather than that ! " Now in the first place the Government simply

[1] *Daily Herald*, December 2nd, 1919.

had not at its disposal sufficient reliable troops to suppress by violence a movement that would have embraced the whole country. We have seen how extremely shaky the military situation was at the beginning of 1919. Even six months later, when demobilisation was almost complete and the situation was far more stable, the employment on a wide scale of troops against a strike was shown to be at once a futile and highly risky operation; for during the railway strike, say the Webbs, " it was reported that in some cases the soldiers fraternised with the pickets and were promptly withdrawn to barracks; and the Cabinet was certainly warned, by high military authority, against attempting to use the troops." In the second place it may be pointed out that at such a time of extreme social tension the first volley fired would have sounded the death-knell of the régime even more surely than the volleys of Bloody Sunday in Petersburg introduced Russia's 1905 upheaval.

At all events the experience of the miners had shown one thing with classic clearness. No longer could it be supposed that the working class had grounds for reposing any confidence in the word, be it never so solemnly pledged, of a Government of its rulers. Henceforth it was beyond doubt that such a Government in times of crisis would invariably feel itself wholly free of any moral considerations in dealing with the workers.

Parallel with its bluffing of the miners during those critical months of February and March 1919, the Government had to employ the same species of confidence trick on a wider front, gaining the needed respite, as Mr. Cole puts it, " at the cost, not of actual concessions, but merely of setting up the machinery which encouraged the trade unions to believe that substantial concessions would subsequently be given." Employers' organisations and trade unions were invited to take part in a National Industrial Conference which met in London on the same day that the miners first agreed to participate in the Sankey Commission. The engineers, and the unions associated in the Triple Alliance, boycotted the Conference, which proceeded to elect a joint committee whose deliberations resulted in the presentation to a resumed Conference in April of a unanimous report recommending legislation for a general forty-eight hour week, and for a minimum wage commission. An elaborate and ably drafted memorandum on the causes of and remedies for Labour Unrest was submitted by the trade union representatives on the joint committee; it spoke plainly of the " growing determination of Labour to challenge the whole existing structure of capitalist industry." That challenge was hardly to be carried any further by the National Industrial Conference. Bills were indeed drafted by the Government, but in such a form that they were totally unacceptable to the union representatives. The Conference had served its purpose though the committee lingered futilely on for another couple of years.

The Government's successful efforts to stave off the day of reckoning won not exposure but applause from some people in high position in the Labour movement. In his Chairman's address to the annual conference of the Labour Party at Southport in June 1919, Mr. J. McGurk, a well-known Lancashire figure, said:

" During the past few months industrial unrest has been more deep-seated and widespread than ever before. It seemed inevitable at one time that the nation would be plunged into a national stoppage, with disastrous results to the whole of the people. Fortunately, the Government soon realised that the state of feeling among the workers was so serious as to demand instant and effectual attention. The Miners' Federation had already handed in notices. . . . The railwaymen, transport workers, engineering and shipbuilding workers, and practically all skilled and unskilled workers were in a state of ferment. Recognising the extreme danger of delay, the Government acted promptly [setting up the Sankey Commission and convoking the National Industrial Conference] . . . Both these inquiries have exerted a considerable influence in allaying, at any rate temporarily, the widespread feeling of industrial discontent which was so serious and threatening a factor in our national life in recent months."

Against this may be set the considered judgment of an eminent historian of the movement like Mr. G. D. H. Cole, who says that " the entry of Labour into the Industrial Conference and the Coal Commission—the latter acclaimed at the time as a great Labour triumph—was the determining factor in tiding over the critical industrial situation of the first half of 1919. . . . Recommendations which the Government had pledged itself to honour . . . were disregarded when the time of the most urgent danger to capitalism had gone by. Views will differ as to the most probable results of a persistence in the militant spirit which seemed to be gaining the upper hand at the beginning of 1919, but there can be no doubt that the Industrial Conference and the Coal Commission both gave the Government time to pass the point of most urgent danger without the development of a general militant policy on the part of Labour."

The Government could congratulate itself on having avoided the necessity of giving battle to the miners at a critical time. Content to leave them for a season (every ton of coal was a precious source of rich profit with the famine prices then ruling), it turned its attention to the railwaymen. These had been marked down as the object of the counter-attack which the governing class, alarmed by the events of the early part of the year, conceived it politic to deliver. In those hot summer days of 1919, the industrial outlook continued thunderous. The largest movement was that of the Lancashire cotton operatives, 300,000 of whom struck in June for a forty-eight hour week and a 30 per cent wage increase, which they successfully achieved. Next month the Police Union was provoked into calling its second strike; but the Government was well prepared. the response was poor, all the strikers were dismissed, while substantial concessions in pay and conditions of service enabled trade unionism in the police force to be stamped out.

Negotiations for a series of demands had been entered into by the railwaymen's unions, it may be recalled, simultaneously with the presentation of the miners' demands in February. These demands turned on what was called "standardisation" of wage rates, involving complicated discussions on the combination of basic rates with the war bonuses that had been granted, and aiming also at the removal of the many anomalies in the rates earned by the same grades under different companies. Railwaymen had won the eight-hour day immediately after the war, and expected "standardisation" to mean an upward levelling of wages.

Deliberately the Government set its hand to a policy of procrastination. Negotiations were dragged out from February to August, by which time the railmen's tempers were wearing thin. Obviously it was necessary to avoid an open issue on the railways while the mining crisis was at its height; but there was more in the delay than that. Ministers subsequently boasted that the Government had been holding the men off in order to perfect its secret preparations to smash a railway strike. The "hard-faced men," dizzy with their own success, were talking big among themselves about the inevitability of a "big fight with the unions," who needed to be "taught a lesson," etc. Two of their own were in charge of the proceedings, those fraternal Knights of Big Business, Sir Auckland ("Howled-down-at-Glasgow") Geddes, President of the Board of Trade, and Sir Eric ("Squeeze-Germany-till-the-pips-squeak") Geddes, Minister of Transport.

August arrived, the plot began to gather speed. First the demands of the locomotive-men were fully met, a sop to this key section which it was hoped would keep them out of the coming struggle. For a brief space the general negotiations continued, in an atmosphere of mounting irritation. Then the Government, judging the time ripe, struck. In September it presented the National Union of Railwaymen with a "definite" offer. As if intent on provoking an immediate and angry strike, Sir Auckland Geddes with his own hand altered the word to "definitive"; the terms thus sharpened into an ultimatum were of the most draconic character. Cuts ranging from 1s. or 2s. to 16s. a week were demanded, with a basic rate in the lowest grade of 40s. a week. Aghast, the Executive of the N.U.R. met on September 24th, a Wednesday, and despatched orders to all branches for a strike to commence at midnight on the following Friday.

The " definitive " offer was simply the climax of the most calculated piece of provocation in any Government's record. For the fact that these terms were conditional on a drop in the cost of living index which no one expected to happen, was discreetly hidden—save for a last-minute reference by Mr. Lloyd George, which that normally lucid statesman saw fit to couch in such vague phrases that it was quite unintelligible to the railwaymen's representatives. Indeed, the impression that the Government was in fact demanding these cuts was heightened by the peremptory refusal of Sir Eric Geddes, during the final negotiations after the issue of the strike call, to permit any criticism of the " definitive " offer. Clearly the Government wanted war at any price. There was no vagueness about the Prime Minister's denunciation of the strike as an " Anarchist conspiracy " (the railwaymen being led by that already respectable Privy Councillor Mr. J. H. Thomas), and as a " wanton attempt to hold up the community " (the N.U.R. so little wanted or expected a strike that they had only £3,000 available in ready cash and had not even notified their associates in the Triple Alliance).

These wild words set the tone for the extraordinary Press barrage which burst unitedly upon the country over the week-end of September 27th–28th. They were followed up by a daily strafe supplied to all newspapers from Downing Street under the personal direction of Sir William Sutherland, one of the Prime Minister's principal private secretaries. The quality of the Government propaganda was aptly mirrored in a *Times* leader, which thundered that this, " like the war with Germany, must be a fight to a finish." And, it appeared, a fight with the gloves off and as many punches below the belt as possible. The Government, in defiance of all precedent and without a scrap of legal authority, caused the week's pay due to the strikers to be arbitrarily withheld. It became known that plans were actually being discussed to starve the railwaymen and their families by using the Government's control of food supplies to introduce discriminatory rationing. Large-scale calling out of troops (though this weapon bent in the Government's hands, as has been noted above), and even more the sinister instructions broadcast to local authorities to enrol a "Citizen Guard," conveyed the ugly suggestion that civil war was at hand.

Yet at the end of a week the Geddes brothers had met their Waterloo. The Government, which had seemed to have everything in its favour, was running for its life. The " definitive " offer was explained away. By the settlement of October 5th, there were to be no cuts. Existing rates were stabilised (and the lowest grade even secured an advance in basic rate). Full reinstatement and no victimisation was unconditionally conceded; and the impounded week's arrears of pay was paid. The railwaymen had saved, not only their own wages and conditions, but those of the whole working class, from a successful assault that might otherwise have antedated the slump by fully a year and a half.

Why did the railwaymen win? First, there was unexampled solidarity in their own ranks. The locomotivemen, spurning the August bribe, struck to a man in unity with their comrades of the other grades. Despite the usual tiny trickle of blackleg passenger trains, the mineral and heavy goods traffic was coming to a standstill. Economic paralysis was creeping over the country. By the end of the week 400,000 miners and other workers had been thrown idle; a further week would have seen literally millions out.

Second, the railwaymen sought and found powerful allies. The Co-operative movement rose magnificently to the occasion. Emergency arrangements made through the Co-operative Wholesale Society and its Bank enabled the necessary £500,000 of strike pay to be made available at every N.U.R. branch in the country. The local Co-operative Societies agreed to accept vouchers from strike committees in exchange for food. Keen sympathy from the railwaymen's comrades in the Triple Alliance, especially the transport workers, strengthened the hands of the Mediation Committee appointed by the Transport Workers' Federation Executive, with representatives of the miners, the Trades Union Congress and the Labour Party (the Committee, as the Webbs say, was much concerned with " restraining their own members from impetuous action in support of the railwaymen "). Not least important was the attitude of the compositors and machine-men on the London newspapers, whose chapels soon made it clear that there would be neither setting nor printing in Fleet Street unless the railwaymen's case was given a fair show. An informed Liberal observer, Mr. C. F. G. Masterman, could write that " before the strike had ended the railwaymen had rallied nine-tenths of the industrial workers to their side; that—partly, indeed, through the strongest provocation—they were increasing sympathisers from the middle classes by hundreds of thousands a day."

Third, the railwaymen answered the flood of Government propaganda with propaganda of their own, not defensive, not apologetic, but a determined counter-attack which struck home with deadly effect. This was no amateurish effort, but an expert job. Entrusted by the N.U.R. Executive to the Labour Research Department it showed for the first time how skilfully handled publicity could be a weapon of prime importance in a great labour struggle. Enlisting the services of a host of voluntary helpers, including a number of the most noted writers and journalists associated with the Labour movement, the Department was able to get going within twenty-four hours a publicity machine which roused the admiration of " various persons with experience in war administration in France, one of whom stated that he had not at any time during the war witnessed so rapid and effective an improvisation to meet a crisis."[1] But there was much more here

[1] This, and the other quotations in this paragraph, are taken from the report made by the Department to the N.U.R. after the strike.

than a piece of technical virtuosity. The Department, accustomed from its position as the independent research organ of the movement to review facts and situations realistically, saw that its task was not to explain things away, but to defeat the enemy. Therefore it " pursued the policy of taking every means to break up the solidarity of the Press with the Government. By the end of the week most of the papers were hampering the Government if they were not helping the railwaymen " ; in this its stated intention was not so much to create any atmosphere of conciliation " as that the morale of the other side should be weakened by divided counsels."

Of the details of the work done, through signed articles and statements, cartoons, a daily news service, the cinema news-reel, circulars to clergy and other bodies, it is not possible to speak here. Most vivid in the memory is the campaign of advertisement in the Press which the Department initiated, the N.U.R. Executive authorising an expenditure of £2,000 a day under this head. They had the advantage of the Government, who only came in a day later ; and the challenging and unchallengeable presentation of the facts of the railwaymen's case forced the Government publicists to plunge more and more heavily and to retreat day by day from their initial positions. The Department did not use a fact or a figure that had not been checked and verified on the basis of an elaborate information service that took account of every change in the situation. The Government had no defences capable of withstanding such well-served publicity artillery, whose range-finding and sighting were always so witheringly accurate.

Working-class opinion was more profoundly stirred by the railway strike and its substantial success than by any previous event of that first stormy post-war year. And with good reason ; for it was seen that the oft-threatened frontal attack with all the forces of the State could be repulsed. It may seem surprising that the railway strike was not the starting-point for a big forward movement in industry. That it might have spread to other industries is conceded ;

it did not do so because Mr. Thomas and the railwaymen's leaders took pains to prevent any such eventuality, pointedly refraining from calling on the Triple Alliance for sympathetic strike action. Yet one positive and permanent effect the strike did have on the wider movement. It gave decisive impetus to the growing demand for a General Staff for Labour; but the discussion of this falls more properly to the next chapter.

During the autumn and winter of 1919–20 there were sufficient signs of continued activity on individual sectors of the Labour front, though there was no large-scale action. Of a crop of smaller strikes some ended in significant victory (the shop assistants at the Army and Navy Stores), some in failure (the ironfounders). Political advance accompanied industrial militancy and the sense of unity on vital issues. In November the municipal elections, the first held since before the war, resulted in sensational Labour Party successes, especially in mining areas like Durham and South Wales and in London. Whereas in 1912 there were only 46 Labour councillors among the 28 Metropolitan Boroughs, the 1919 elections returned no less than 572, giving a Labour majority in twelve Boroughs. In similar fashion the Parliamentary by-elections showed the Labour tide running strongly. Between the General Election and the summer of 1920 there were 30 by-elections: the aggregate votes showed a Government decline of 4,406 and a Labour increase of 135,816.

In the spring effective use was made by the dockers of the inquiry clauses of the new Industrial Courts Act. A Court of Inquiry, presided over by Lord Shaw, hit the headlines to a degree second only to the Sankey Commission itself. Mr. Ernest Bevin won national repute, earned himself the title of the Dockers' K.C., by his powerful advocacy of the case for wage increases and decasualisation of dock labour. The high profits of the port employers were exposed, and the attempt to base a low-wage argument on the cost-of-living index utterly destroyed. As a result the Court awarded a national minimum wage of 16s. a day, and recommended that a scheme for decasualisation be at once prepared and applied. The onset of the slump gave the employers the pretext for putting paid to all that; and dock labour to this day remains casual, though some of the worst evils have been mitigated by the registration scheme operated jointly by the employers and the union, simply in the sense that the total labour force has been drastically reduced.

It is time to revert to the story of the miners. After the Government's double-cross in August 1919, the Miners' Federation decided not to take industrial action itself but to remit the case to the Trades Union Congress which, at its annual gathering in September, decided by a 55 to 1 majority in favour of " compelling the Government to adopt the scheme of national ownership and joint control recommended by the majority of the Commission." Provision was made for the summoning of a Special Congress in the event of the Government failing to surrender at discretion when interviewed by the Parliamentary Committee of the T.U.C. In December the Special Congress was duly called. It launched a " Mines for the Nation " campaign; but the Government seemed still unmoved. The campaign, to be brief, was generally allowed to have produced no concrete result. Complaints, not unjustified, that national leaders of the movement were conspicuously absent from the campaign could not conceal the fact that the miners had been led into an impasse through the policy pursued in the critical early months of 1919. The position was reconsidered at a recalled special T.U.C. in March 1920. Two methods of achieving the miners' aims, and compelling the Government to honour its pledge, were propounded in the resolution laid before the Congress: " (a) Trade Union action in the form of a general strike; (b) Political action in the form of intensive political propaganda." By 3,870 votes to 1,050 the general strike was negatived; by 3,732 votes to 1,015 the second proposal, which in effect meant shelving the whole question, was adopted. A month later the Parliamentary Committee and the Labour Party Executive met the Miners' Federation Executive to discuss future action. The meeting adjourned without taking any decisions. Nothing remained of the Sankey Commission save those thick blue volumes of its Report and Minutes of Evidence.

These developments naturally did not allay the miners' discontent. In July 1920 the Federation put forward a dual demand for wage increases coupled with a reduction in the price of household coal. A ballot showing heavy majorities for strike action, notices were tendered, to expire on September 25th. For the first time the miners directly appealed to their associates in the Triple Alliance for aid. The appeal did not have the anticipated result. The railway and transport union leaders fought shy of a sympathetic strike and limited themselves to the rôle of conciliators. Suspending their strike notices the Miners' Federation resumed negotiations, new wage proposals were drafted (the price point had been dropped, since it had seemed to arouse no interest), but these were unsatisfactory. The strike began on October 16th. At this late hour the railwaymen's leaders took a ballot which showed a significant majority for sympathetic strike action on October 24th; but the moment had passed when this threat might have won the miners' demands and the miners' leaders themselves agreed to the cancelling of what was in the circumstances little more than a formality. A few days later the strike was settled inconclusively, on a temporary agreement (to expire in March 1921) which conceded a wage advance related to output—the so-called *datum line* which has given this strike its usual name.

So as 1920 ended, the Triple Alliance had emerged discreditably from its first actual test; while the Government seized the opportunity to equip itself, its heirs and successors, with unlimited dictatorial powers to deal with any great industrial upheaval. The Emergency Powers Act, rushed into law in five days (October 22nd–27th), for the first time in peace made freeborn Englishmen liable at any Government's arbitrary discretion to all the rigours of

that ancient Junker-Tsarist device the " state of siege."
Yet this year 1920 saw the most significant of all the
varied movements of the British working class during the
close-packed period under review. The account of it will
conclude this present chapter; and it has seemed best to
treat it so, rather than within the chapter's general chronology, because it represented the highest level of achievement of the movement in those critical post-war revolutionary years. I am referring to the fight against the general
war, or rather wars, of intervention against the young Soviet
Republic, in which imperialist Britain played a leading part.

The general sympathy, the instinctive solidarity, displayed by working people in this country for the land where
folk like themselves had taken power and were seeking to
lay the foundations of Socialism, have already been mentioned. That sympathy was, in the early days at any rate,
a spontaneous, elemental sort of thing that welled up from
the depths; it was not a matter of conscious and precise
understanding of the issues save among a small minority and
in certain more advanced areas (the Clyde, for example).
Nor did informed guidance come from the leadership of the
movement. Alike in the Independent Labour Party (still
the largest and most influential Socialist organisation) and
the Labour Party there was a dead set against the Bolsheviks. In the *Herald* Mr. Brailsford condemned their
" reckless and uncalculating folly " in seizing power and
declared later that " they have shown no trace . . . of
statesmanship." The *Labour Leader* carried denunciations by
Philip Snowden and others. At the Labour Party Conference in July 1918 Kerensky was introduced by the
platform to plead for anti-Soviet intervention in the name
of " democracy." But the forces at work were too strong
to be held back by doubts and quibbles and ill-informed
attacks on this New Thing that had arisen in the East. At
the Inter-Allied Socialist Conference in September 1918,
it was already evident that the honeyed phrases used to
cover the reality of intervention had begun to lose effect.
In December of that year the Labour Party Executive

BT

asked the Government to define its intentions with regard .
to Russia; the request was acknowledged—and ignored.

Nineteen-nineteen saw the movement against intervention steadily gathering strength. In the spring, news of
increasing assistance to Generals Denikin and Wrangel
caused much disquiet; at a special joint conference on
April 3rd, representing both the political and industrial
Labour movements, called to discuss the proposed League
of Nations Covenant, the Miners' Federation took the lead
in pressing through a resolution demanding an end to
intervention and the immediate withdrawal of the new
Conscription Bill then under discussion by the Government. This same resolution proposed the calling of a
special conference to organise resistance to intervention;
but the proposal was not operated.

By the summer it was clear that the general sentiment
was unmistakably in favour of action to stop the assault
on the Workers' Republic. At the Labour Party Conference in June there was a discussion on the need for direct
action to stop the war on Russia. Mr. William Brace,
shortly to surprise the movement by retiring to a secure
Government post, described direct action as a " slippery
slope "; Mr. Clynes observed that the conference was
" threatening a blow at democracy," adding that the
General Election had shown that " working men were not
ready for their appeal "; Sir James Sexton did not believe
in letting mad dogs loose. These views animated the
majority of the Executive, to judge from its report to the
conference. But they received the following broadside
from Mr. Smillie:

> " It was rather strange that the Executive Committee
> of the Labour Party should have taken up exactly the
> position of every exploiter and capitalist and politician in
> this country at the present time. They feared more than
> anything else what had come to be called direct action.
> But he wanted to put it that direct action might be con-
> stitutional action. . . . They were told their action was

unconstitutional. He would like to follow Mr. Williams' statement as to whether the action of the Government of this country was constitutional. Had they not deceived the people ? Were they not returned to power under false pretences ? Did not every member of their Committee believe that the present Government was sitting in its place through fraud ? If they believed that the Government deceived and lied to the people in order to get returned, if that was true, was the great Labour Movement not to take any action to get rid of a Government that was sitting there through fraud and deceit ? "

From another angle Mr. Herbert Morrison voiced this searching criticism:

" He wanted to know what the Party had done in the matter of the war on the Socialist Republic of Russia . . . They had got to realise that the present war against Russia on the part of this country, France and the other Imperialist Powers, was not war against Bolshevism or against Lenin, but against the international organisation of Socialism. It was a war against the organisation of the Trade Union movement itself, and as such should be resisted with the full political and industrial power of the whole Trade Union movement. But what had the Parliamentary Party done ? They had done so much that the matter was not worth a single reference in the report which was under discussion. This report was an insult to the energy, the intelligence and the vigour of the whole Labour movement of the country."

There was no mistaking the conference's temper. By 1,893,000 votes to 935,000 it carried a resolution demanding an immediate end to intervention, prescribing Labour Party and T.U.C. co-operation " with the view to effective action being taken to enforce these demands by the unreserved use of their political and industrial power."

When autumn came there were further signs of the extension of the movement. Glasgow Trades Council proposed a twenty-four hour general strike. Impressive demonstrations paraded the streets of London. On the second anniversary of the Revolution, November 7th, 1919, a National " Hands Off Russia " Committee was established, representing the united forces of the industrial and political working-class movement, without distinction of opinions or tendency. While this Committee energetically undertook a national campaign, both throughout the Labour movement and in public meetings and demonstrations, determined little bands of militant Socialists were spending themselves without stint to get action in key areas like London's dockland. Here members of the British Socialist Party (like boilermaker Harry Pollitt) and of the Workers' Socialist Federation, two of the later constituents of the Communist Party, strove unceasingly.

Meantime the tide in Russia had begun to turn. The Red Army had rolled back the Whites on front after front. British troops were evacuated from Archangel. The Soviet Government hopefully set about the great tasks of peaceful economic reconstruction. Suddenly the tension was renewed with the unprovoked Polish invasion in the spring of 1920. It was soon realised that Poland was being heavily backed by Britain and France. Around the question of the despatch of munitions from this country to the Poles, who were now over-running the Ukraine, the campaign against intervention naturally turned. The agitation was redoubled; but ships laden with munitions continued to clear for Poland. Yet the leaven was powerfully at work. On the very day, May 10th, 1920, that the newspapers blared forth the tidings of the Polish capture of Kiev, carrying also a congratulatory message of his late Majesty George V to Marshal Pilsudski, a cloud no bigger than a man's hand appeared on the horizon of triumphant reaction. The dockers engaged in loading the London freighter *Jolly George* with munitions for Poland had been getting very restive; they had taken the matter up inside their union and had been assured of support; and on that day they struck work. The coal-trimmers refused to coal the vessel. And the owners could do nothing but have the munitions unloaded again. The *Jolly George* incident electrified the whole movement. A week later the conference of the Dockers' Union, in session at Plymouth, decided to put a general ban on the loading of any munitions for use against Russia. Mr. Ernest Bevin, in a moving speech, exposed the war intrigues of capitalist interests in Western Europe. At the same time a manifesto denouncing the war was issued by a number of prominent " moderates " among the Labour leaders.

Repercussions were still vigorous in June, when the Labour Party Conference met at Scarborough. To a resolution condemning the Peace Treaties and demanding peace with Russia, the British Socialist Party advanced an addendum proposing the immediate summoning of a national conference " having for its object the organisation of a General Strike that shall put an end once for all to the open and covert participation of the British Government in attacks on the Soviet Republic," and further recommending " that unions should support their members in refusing to do work which directly or indirectly assists hostilities against Russia." This addendum was opposed, rather surprisingly, by Mr. Bevin, who said that " he was a tactician after all " and " wanted the Movement to be free to take the requisite action at the proper moment when circumstances determined "; he thought that, rather than prescribe direct action, it would be better to raise a special union levy to pay for the despatch of commissions of investigation to the various countries of Central Europe. However, this was not the end of the matter. Within two months the threat of open war by Britain on Russia compelled the carrying into effect of the principles of the defeated addendum, while Mr. Bevin was proud to claim the part of a pioneer in the action that ensued.

What had happened was a sensational reversal of the fortunes of war in the Russo-Polish conflict. The Poles had over-reached themselves. Whipped out of the Ukraine by a series of brilliant Red counter-thrusts, their armies were sent reeling back to the gates of Warsaw. Hurtling across the plains of Southern Russia in the most amazing forced cavalry march in history, Budienny's famous *Pyervaya Konnaya* (the 1st Cavalry Army) was in hot pursuit of the fleeing Poles. A few more kilometres and the red flag would be flying over the city on the Vistula; that, the statesmen of Old Europe well knew, meant that the floodgates of revolution would be open. At once the British Government showed its hand. In the House of Commons on July 21st Mr. Lloyd George plainly hinted at war, and contingent orders were given to the British fleet in the Baltic. British troops were used to break a strike of dockers at Danzig against the landing of munitions for the Poles. On August 3rd Lord Curzon, Foreign Secretary, despatched a peremptory Note to the Soviet Government threatening war if the advance of the Red Army was not stayed.

Six years to the day after the War to End War had begun here was the threat of a new war—to end the workers' hopes of Socialism. As one man the working-class movement of Britain rose. On August 4th, 1920, a Wednesday, Labour Party headquarters telegraphed all local Labour Parties and Trades Councils urging that demonstrations against war on Russia be held on the following Sunday, August 8th. The demonstrations broke all records, and there were literally hundreds of them. A flood of telegrams of protest poured in on the Government. It was indeed, as the Labour Party Executive later reported, " one of the most striking . examples of Labour' unanimity, determination and enthusiasm in the history of the movement." Strength came because on this fundamental issue there was complete unity. It was noteworthy that the special edition brought out by the *Daily Herald* on that Sunday gave prominence to the call for action against the war issued by the newly-born Communist Party.

In this atmosphere the Parliamentary Committee of the T.U.C., the Labour Party Executive and the Parliamentary Party assembled in the House of Commons on Monday, August 9th. Unanimously this joint meeting decided to warn the Government that " the whole industrial power of the organised workers will be used to defeat this war," notified the Executives of all affiliated organisations " to hold themselves ready to proceed immediately to London for a National Conference," advised them " to instruct their members to ' down tools ' on instructions from that National Conference," and constituted a representative Council of Action with full powers to implement these decisions. The conference met in the Central Hall, Westminster, four days later and fully endorsed these decisions. It " pledged itself to resist any and every form of military and naval intervention against the Soviet Government of Russia," mandated the Council of Action to remain in being until it had secured recognition of the Soviet Government and the establishment of normal trading relations, and authorised the Council " to call for any and every form of withdrawal of labour which circumstances may require to give effect to the foregoing policy."

The tone of the speeches at this great conference, boldly facing the issues involved, was significant. Mr. Ernest Bevin told the delegates that " this question you are called upon to decide to-day—the willingness to take any action to win world peace—transcends any claim in connection with wages or hours of labour." Mr. J. R. Clynes said that " no Parliamentary or political measures, we felt, could be effective in themselves to save the country from being committed to war against its will." " No Parliamentary effort could do what we are asking you to do," urged Mr. J. H. Thomas, adding bluntly, " when you vote for this resolution do not do so on the assumption that you are merely voting for a simple down-tools policy. It is nothing of the kind. If this resolution is to be given effect to, it means a challenge to the whole Constitution of the country (Cheers)." Mr. Thomas was that year's president of the Trades Union Congress. Mr. A. G. Cameron of the Woodworkers, chairman of the Labour Party Executive, was even more outspoken. Declaring that " Constitutionalism can only exist as long as it does not outrage the conscience of the community," Mr. Cameron said that power was needed for " a united Council to declare action at a given moment." " If the day should come when we do take this action," he concluded, " and if the powers that be endeavour to interfere too much, we may be compelled to do things that will cause them to abdicate, and to tell them that if they cannot run the country in a peaceful and humane manner without interfering with the lives of other nations, we will be compelled, even against all Constitutions, to chance whether we cannot do something to take the country into our own hands for our own people."[1]

There was no war with Russia. The Lloyd George–Curzon partnership had arrogantly cried " Check ! " to the advancing Red Army. " Mate ! " riposted the united working class of Britain, turning the tables in one move. The wielders of power had been met with power—power expressing the will of the decisive majority of the working people of this country, power based on the solid phalanx of $6\frac{1}{2}$ million trade unionists, power residing not merely in a central directing body but in the network of local Councils of Action that had sprung up, 350 of them, covering every important centre of population. That the Council of Action did not proceed further, although it received many requests to deal with other urgent matters (the war in Ireland and unemployment, for instance), does not affect its positive historical achievement. For here was the manner of instrument, very practical, very familiar, British-made throughout, by which the working class could exercise power.

It is interesting to note Lenin's comment that:

" This Council of Action, independently of Parliament, presents an ultimatum to the Government in the name of the workers—it is the transition to the workers' dictatorship. . . . The whole of the English bourgeois Press wrote that the Councils of Action were Soviets. And it was right. They were not called Soviets but in actual fact they were such."

[1] Speeches quoted from the official *Report of the Special Conference on Labour and the Russo-Polish War*, pp. 12–18.

CHAPTER II

A MOVEMENT IN LABOUR

THE NATURAL ACCOMPANIMENT of the critical period
that has been described in the preceding chapter was an
intense process of change in the working-class movement
itself. Old forms and old methods no longer corresponded
with the forces actually at work. New circumstances prescribed new values in every sphere of thought and action;
and the movement as we know it to-day took shape.

Attention has already been drawn to the contradiction
between the militancy, enthusiasm and solidarity shown
on the individual sectors of the workers' front and the isolation of each sector one from another. An army in the field
whose component divisions operate as they think fit, without any sort of central co-ordination or direction, is not
going to win battles. This, after all, is a very elementary
fact, whose application to the working-class struggle the
events of 1919 brought speedily home. It was realised that
the Army of Labour, too, must have its General Staff or
it could not hope for victory. The railway strike made this
realisation a peremptory urge to action. The Mediation
Committee which had functioned during that strike, the
trade union side of the National Industrial Conference, and
the Trades Union Congress accordingly participated in the
establishment of a Co-ordination Committee which
examined the whole problem and presented a detailed
report and recommendations to the special T.U.C. which
met in December 1919.

Examining frankly the existing situation the report
observed that " again and again the lack of co-ordination
has resulted, not only in the overlapping of administrative

work, but also in unnecessary internal and other disputes, involving vast financial and moral damage to the whole Labour movement. To do away with some of this over-lapping and to provide means of co-ordinating the work of certain sections was the object with which the Triple Industrial Alliance was founded by the miners, railway-men and transport workers, and the same object is behind the numerous steps towards closer unity which have been taken in various industries and groups. The Negotiating Committee, hastily improvised to deal with the situation created by the railway strike this autumn, was generally felt to have fulfilled, however imperfectly, a vital need of Labour; but it is clear that it ought not to have been necessary to create a new and temporary body to do this work; the necessary machinery should have been already in existence in the form of a really effective central co-ordinating body for the movement as a whole."

Two problems required solution. The first was to secure central direction of the trade union forces in their specific industrial activities. The second was to co-ordinate the whole movement—political, industrial, and Co-operative. Both problems were appreciated by the Co-ordination Committee, whose view was that " the body which is required should and must be developed out of the existing organisation of the Trades Union Congress and out of its closer co-operation with other sections of the working-class movement." Here the difficulty was that the T.U.C. had never been an effective confederation of trade unions, a national trade union centre. Originating as, and remain-ing, a voluntary association of fully autonomous con-stituents—who were liable to withdraw from Congress in a huff if a ruling were given against them in some petty demarcation dispute—it had for many years increasingly exasperated enlightened trade union opinion by its failure to tackle the new issues arising from social and economic changes. Instead of being a legislative organ for the trade union movement, the annual meeting of Congress was little more than a combination of holiday parade and talking-shop. There was no leadership, either at or between Congresses, from a responsible executive body; for the Parliamentary Committee, as the name implies, had merely the administrative function of lobbying Ministers with Congress resolutions, a proceeding that had become as futile as it was formal.

Clearly the Parliamentary Committee, whose very functions were " in great measure a survival from a previous period," could not fill the bill. The special T.U.C. accordingly directed, on the basis of the report presented to it, that the Standing Orders of Congress be revised in order " to substitute for the Parliamentary Committee a Trades Union Congress General Council " as " a central co-ordinating body representative of the whole trade union movement." A scheme was duly prepared, ratified at the Portsmouth Congress in 1920 and operated at the Cardiff Congress in the following year. In place of the Parliamentary Committee of sixteen members there arose the General Council of thirty-two members. For the purpose of representation on the Council the affiliated unions were divided among seventeen industrial groups (an eighteenth *ad hoc* group being formed for the representation of women workers), and these were allotted from one to three representatives, according to their numerical strength. Any union could nominate candidates for the representation of its group; but these candidates then had to submit to a ballot of the whole Congress in which the union block vote operated. The members of the General Council were divided among six Group Committees, each embracing a number of the separate industrial groups; in this way it was intended to concentrate attention on the problems of specific industries.

The establishment of the General Council did not, however, solve even the first of the main problems already indicated. While the new Standing Orders mandated the Council to " promote common action by the trade union movement on general questions, such as wages and hours of labour," to assist unions in the work of organisation and propaganda and to secure united action with the trade union and Labour movements abroad, they left the Council without the necessary powers to enforce decisions upon the unions. The traditional and baneful sectionalism of the trade union movement in Britain remained intact.

This gave weight to the criticism that came from the Left, voiced in a Communist appeal to the delegates at the Cardiff T.U.C. Here it was suggested that the current talk about a General Staff of Labour might amount to no more than " a new alliance of old leaders, who have already shown how incapable they are of really leading the workers against the Bastilles of capitalism. They will leave the old sectionalism of Labour intact, and this means the same old chaos and confusion hidden under a new and high-sounding name." It was urged that the T.U.C. should turn itself into something wider—a real Congress of Labour, based not on the trade unions alone but on a whole system of shop and works committees, grouped around the local Trades Councils. Thus reinforced the Trades Councils could function as the authoritative local agencies of a genuine General Staff. It may be added that though this suggestion evoked no official response at the time the Trades Councils were subsequently (1924) brought within the orbit of the General Council by the formation of a Joint Consultative Committee. This arrangement, which provided the General Council with local machinery, though not in the transformed sense suggested above, followed the establishment in 1922 of an independent National Federation of Trades Councils, a body whose militant outlook and growing strength constituted a challenge to orthodox complacency.

What of the wider problem of co-ordinating the movement as a whole ? In 1921 the previously existing Labour Joint Board, representing the Trades Union Congress and the Labour Party, was reorganised as the National Joint Council—now called the National Council of Labour—representing equally the T.U.C. General Council, the Labour Party Executive, and the Parliamentary Labour Party. Among its specified duties the National Joint Council was to "*endeavour* to secure a common policy and joint action "; the word I have italicised suitably expresses the consultative and conciliatory, rather than executive, character of the Council. In its 1919 report the Co-ordination Committee had stressed the need " to take into account the relation of the reorganised Central Industrial Committee to the other sections of the movement, and especially to the Labour Party and the Co-operative movement." But even the limited proposal to associate the new General Council with the Labour Party and the Co-operative movement in the joint control of extended research, legal, and publicity departments was not fully operated. The immense resources of Co-operation remained unharnessed, though wartime experiences had driven that movement to abandon its traditional non-political attitude and to establish (in 1917) the Co-operative Party, which worked in association with the Labour Party while preserving its independence.

Parallel with the developments described, there took place a whole series of union amalgamations. British trade unionism was transformed in five years. Nowhere was this more marked than in the field of transport and unskilled labour. In 1921 the numerous unions of dockers and road transport workers of all kinds, which since 1910 had been loosely grouped in the Transport Workers' Federation, combined to form the Transport and General Workers' Union. This remarkable organisation, dominated by the forceful personality of its general secretary, Mr. Ernest Bevin, was highly centralised but combined with this an ingenious system of administrative devolution through a vertical division of its members by industrial groups and a horizontal division by areas. It subsequently absorbed the Workers' Union and has become the largest single union in the country, concerned in scores of industries and sharing the general labour field with the National Union of General and Municipal Workers. The latter body drew into one the considerable number of previously separate general labour unions.

Other amalgamations, though important, have not had

the same influence on the movement as a whole. The expansion of the old Amalgamated Society of Engineers into the Amalgamated Engineering Union in 1920, by the absorption of half a dozen of the leading craft unions in engineering, still left that industry honeycombed with craft societies of varying strengths. A similar picture was presented by the building trade, even after the fusion of the old Bricklayers and Stonemasons in the Amalgamated Union of Building Trade Workers, and that of the two historic unions of Carpenters and Joiners in the Amalgamated Society of Woodworkers; true, the various craft societies in the trade had in 1918 allied themselves in a strong National Federation, but secession was not to be unknown. None the less the general consolidation of forces through amalgamation in the distributive trades, woollen textiles, iron and steel, clothing, the Civil Service (especially the Post Office), to name but a few, was of undeniable importance.

What has so far been said can be regarded as a prelude to the discussion of the deep changes that were effected in the political movement of the working class. These fall under three main heads: the transformation of the Labour Party, the changed rôle of the Independent Labour Party, and the assembly of the scattered revolutionary forces in a united Communist Party.

For the first time the Labour Party assumed the aspect of a definite political party, with a stated Socialist programme and individual membership, while still retaining its initial character of a political federation of trade unions. Discussions and draftings in 1917-18 produced a new Party Constitution, which set forth as the Party's objects:

" To secure for the producers by hand or by brain the full fruits of their industry, and the most equitable distribution thereof that may be possible, upon the basis of the common ownership of the means of production and the best obtainable system of popular administration and control of each industry or service;

"Generally to promote the Political, Social, and Economic emancipation of the People, and more particularly of those who depend directly upon their own exertions by hand or by brain for the means of life."

The detailed programme, prepared in the first place as a report on Reconstruction after the war, and significantly titled *Labour and the New Social Order*, declared that:

"We need to beware of patchwork. The view of the Labour Party is that what has to be reconstructed after the war is not this or that Government Department, or this or that piece of social machinery; but, so far as Britain is concerned, society itself . . . We of the Labour Party . . . recognise, in the present world catastrophe, if not the death, in Europe, of civilisation itself, at any rate the culmination and collapse of a distinctive industrial civilisation, which the workers will not seek to reconstruct . . . The individualist system of capitalist production . . . with the monstrous inequality of circumstances which it produces and the degradation and brutalisation, both moral and spiritual, resulting therefrom, may, we hope, indeed have received a death-blow. With it must go the political system and ideas in which it naturally found expression. We of the Labour Party, whether in opposition or in due time called upon to form an Administration, will certainly lend no hand to its revival. On the contrary, we shall do our utmost to see that it is buried with the millions whom it has done to death."

Here was a straightforward Socialist call. It evoked a striking response, seen both in the flocking of millions to the Labour banner and in the rapid growth of the Labour Party's organisation. The 146 Trades Councils and Labour Parties which were affiliated to the national Party before the war had grown to 389 in 1918–19. By 1920 the total number of divisional and local Labour Party organisations had topped the 2,000 mark—less than half a dozen of the

602 constituencies lacking a local Labour Party—reaching to over 2,350 the following year. Even more spectacular, in many ways, was the spread of organisation among women. In 1919 there were 271 Labour Women's Sections; in 1920 there were over 425; in 1921 there were 650, several having around 800 to 900 members, the aggregate membership figures being 70,000.

Labour and the New Social Order was drafted by Sidney and Beatrice Webb, most august of Fabians; so it was not surprising that the traditionally reformist outlook of the Fabian Society should find expression in the programme, contrasting with the forthright passages already quoted. It was possible for continental critics to point to the programme's inferior theoretical insight and knowledge, and to the defects in the analysis of current events that this induced. The programme constantly reiterated that its proposals were not " class " proposals. The Webbs themselves claimed that the new programme and constitution had " transformed the Labour Party from a group representing merely the class interests of the manual workers into a fully constituted political party of national scope " and that they had " led to a considerable accession of membership, largely from the professional and middle classes." This attitude was also that of the Party Executive. Resisting at the Scarborough Conference in 1920 an attempt to rescind the individual membership clause, Mr. Egerton Wake, national agent and Executive spokesman, asked the delegates " to face the position that the Labour Party was becoming a great corporate body. It had a following in every section of the community and, therefore, their organisation ought to be broad enough to accept all those people."

What was to be the position of the Independent Labour Party in face of these developments ? It was the largest Socialist organisation in the country and the political core of the Labour Party, of which its leaders—notably Ramsay MacDonald and Philip Snowden—were the outstanding politicians. Should it take the view that, with the Labour

Party's acceptance of a Socialist aim and programme, together with the introduction of individual membership, its historic mission had been fulfilled and therefore that it should disband, merging itself in the wider body? That would have been perfectly logical and understandable; but it was not till years later that this was to be advanced, by Snowden, as an argument against the continued existence of the I.L.P. Alternatively, should it renounce its political heritage and step out as a frankly revolutionary party? That too would have been a perfectly logical step, corresponding to what many (including numbers of I.L.P. members themselves) thought the critical times required.

In the event the I.L.P. adopted neither of these clear-cut alternatives. It steered a middle course; and when that is done in politics it sows confusion, usually redounding to the advantage of reaction. Nevertheless this centre position was a natural outcome of the whole history of the I.L.P., which had always lacked the firm and consistent theoretical foundation of Marxism, tending ever to regard Socialism as a matter of the heart rather than of the head. The tendencies implicit here were enhanced when, largely as a result of its pacifist attitude during the war, it became from 1918 onwards " the refuge of all those men and women of influence, reputation and learning, who had lost faith in the Liberal Party " (Max Beer)—or, as a less urbane commentator put it, was " over-run with ex-Liberals." These people were not the only recruits, however. There was a significant increase in the working-class membership and a concurrent growth of opposition to the MacDonald leadership.

The battle was fought out upon the issue of international affiliation, which summed up the questions of principle that all Socialists then had urgently to decide. The Second International (the international federation of Labour and Socialist Parties, founded in 1889) had collapsed at war's impact. Provisionally, and unstably, reconstituted at the Berne conference in February 1919, it was making very heavy weather by the turn of the year. The new Third

(Communist) International, which had held its constituent Congress in Moscow in March, was gathering support at a rate which for a time bid fair to leave the Berne adherents little more than a rump of Right-wing leaders. In the I.L.P. the new current set in strongly; at its conference in January 1920 the important Scottish Division of the Party went on record in favour of affiliation to the Communist International by 158 votes to 28; when the annual Party conference took place at Easter the National Administrative Council, which had expressed its own general view in a special memorandum against Communism, faced a difficult position. Withdrawal from the Second International was overwhelmingly carried. The N.A.C., however, avoided a straight vote for or against affiliation to the Communist International, by counterposing the plan they already had in hand for a " unity " conference organised by parties outside both Internationals. To many delegates this plan naturally proved attractive, the more so since it was coupled with a promise to make an exploratory approach to the Communist International. It secured 472 votes as against 206 for the direct motion for affiliation.

That actually settled the matter. R. C. Wallhead, the Party chairman, and Clifford Allen, N.A.C. member (now Lord Allen of Hurtwood), visited Moscow and propounded twelve questions to which the Executive Committee of the Communist International tendered a detailed and famous reply, drafted by Lenin himself. But it is not unfair to the majority of the I.L.P. leadership at that time to say that the Moscow trip had only an academic interest for them. Snowden fulminated loudly in the *Labour Leader* against the Soviets and the Communists. The N.A.C. went ahead with the " unity " conference scheme, which eventually led to the conference in Vienna at the beginning of 1921, when the International Working Union of Socialist Parties was formed. This facing-both-ways body, better known as the Two-and-a-Half International, was to reunite with the Second in 1923, when the revolutionary tide had ebbed. One word may be added on a curious personal reflection

of the lack of reality—or more properly lack of principle—
in the I.L.P.'s attitude on these international issues. The
fact that it had withdrawn from the Second International
did not prevent MacDonald, the Party leader, shortly
becoming one of the secretaries of that International, nor
did it prevent him making the principal speech at the
Labour Party Conference in 1920 against a motion to
secede from the Second International which was lost by
1,010,000 votes to 516,000.

Now to the third and last phenomenon demanding
review: the founding of the Communist Party of Great
Britain. It is difficult without a survey of the history of
Socialism in this country since its rebirth in the eighteen-
eighties to convey the full meaning of this event.[1] Here it
must suffice to say that while the efforts of the great pioneers
—William Morris, Tom Mann, John Burns, Eleanor Marx
and the others—had been directed towards the establishment of a powerful revolutionary Socialist Party of Britain's
working men, of which every trend in social development
argued the urgent necessity, this had remained an un-
realised aim. The soil of Britain certainly proved fruitful
for revolutionary sects, the colour of whose ideas ranged
from a not so deep pink to an ultra-revolutionary red. But
none of these small groupings was able to develop into the
entirely new kind of Party that was required. From the
standpoint of the theory and practice of Marxism, the
scientific Socialism of Marx and Engels, Britain was a
benighted and a backward country. In the pre-war rank-
and-file movements, among the shop stewards, through
the revolutionary sects, new elements were taking shape:
but it needed the shock of the Russian Revolution and the
establishment of the Communist International—together
with the prolonged and painstaking personal intervention
of Lenin himself—to fuse them into a Party.

That this outside shock had to be imparted was a
historical necessity that need cause no surprise. In similar

[1] The interested reader may refer to my *This Final Crisis*, pp. 79–130,
206–18.

fashion Marxist ideas came from outside into the Russian workers' movement in the 'nineties or the French workers' movement in the 'seventies. The only difference in the case of this country was that the ideas were in truth coming home to roost in their native land. Marxism was being brought back to its country of origin. As the Communist International said in its reply to the I.L.P., Marxism " did not proceed from the imagination " of Marx and Engels, who " defined the aims of the Labour movement by the study of capitalism and the experience of the first great revolutionary movement of the working class, the Chartist movement of the British workers."

Following the constituent congress of the Communist International in March 1919 the British revolutionary groupings began exerting themselves to form a united Party. A referendum of the British Socialist Party, incidentally the only one of the Socialist sects that was affiliated to the Labour Party, favoured affiliation to the Communist International by 98 branches to 4. Communist unity was supported by the most influential section of the Socialist Labour Party and by the Workers' Socialist Federation, the East End organisation led by Sylvia Pankhurst. Yet the movement for unity was being slowed up by divergent views on questions of principle and tactics; and here Lenin stepped in. Writing to Sylvia Pankhurst in August 1919 he pointed out that these divergences (for example, on the attitude to Parliament) should never be allowed to " delay the formation of a vigorous workers' Communist Party in England." He sought to make the revolutionary sectarians of Britain understand the Communist conception of *Party*, and how widely it differed from anything in their tradition or practice, in a celebrated passage:

" It is essential for the Communist Party that it should be intimately and continuously associated with the mass of the workers, that it should be able to carry on constant agitation among the workers, to take part in every strike, to answer all the questions that agitate the minds of the masses. This is above all necessary in a country like England, where so far (as, indeed, in all imperialist countries) the Socialist movement and the Labour movement in general have been exclusively guided by cliques drawn from the aristocracy of labour, persons most of whom are utterly and hopelessly corrupted by reformism, whose minds are enslaved by imperialistic and bourgeois prejudices."

It is worth noting that it was specially in relation to Britain that Lenin answered in advance the allegation—it is still common form in some quarters—typically voiced by Ramsay MacDonald at the Scarborough conference of the Labour Party in June 1920, when he said that the Communist International " proposed to apply Russian conditions to international policy." Discussing the problems of the Communists in Britain in *Left-Wing Communism*, written in April 1920, Lenin observed that " the problem here, as everywhere, consists in the ability to apply the general and fundamental principles of Communism to the specific relations between classes and parties, to the specific conditions in the objective development towards Communism—conditions which are peculiar to every separate country, and which one must be able to study, understand and point out." Or again: " unity of international tactics in the Communist workers' movement everywhere demands, not the elimination of variety, not the abolition of the national peculiarities (this at the present moment is a foolish dream), but such an application of the fundamental principles of Communism—Soviet power and the dictatorship of the proletariat—as will admit of the right modification of these principles in their adaptation and application to national differences."

At a convention in London over the week-end of July 31st–August 1st, 1920, the Communist Party of Great Britain was formed, as a fusion of the B.S.P. with the main part of the S.L.P. and with the South Wales Socialist Society. Simultaneously, at the Second Congress of the Communist

International in Moscow Lenin had led the discussions on the problems of the Party in Britain with the representatives of the various British groupings who were present. " We want new Parties, and not parties like the British Socialist Party of to-day," said Lenin, " we want parties that are in close touch with the masses and understand how to lead them "; at the same time he set himself to convince of their errors those extreme " Lefts " who opposed working in Parliament on principle and who were hostile to any attempt to link up with the masses by seeking affiliation with the Labour Party.

These discussions cleared the way for completing the union of the Communist forces. In January 1921 two small sections that had stood outside, the Communist Labour Party and the Communist Party (British Section of the Third International) united with the main body, to be followed two months later by the pro-Communist Left wing of the I.L.P. Yet in these early days the Party was still far from being one of the " new Parties " demanded and defined by Lenin.

Sectarianism marked the Party's first approach to the Labour Party, evidenced in its letter of August 10th, 1920. Here three points were set forth—first a statement that the Communist Party accepted Soviets and the Dictatorship of the Proletariat; second, the repudiation of Parliament as a means of revolution (making Mr. Henderson's flesh creep by declaring that all Communist representatives " must be considered as holding a mandate from the Party and not from the particular constituency for which they happen to sit "); third, and last, the request for affiliation. Only in later correspondence, after the Labour Party Executive had rejected this application, was the wider angle emphasised, namely that the Labour Party was surely " so catholic in its composition and constitution that it could admit to its ranks all sections of the working-class movement that accept the broad principle of independent working-class political action." This raised the whole question of democracy within the Labour Party, which was already an issue. For these were days when Mr. Herbert Morrison was fighting the Executive at conference after conference on this point, urging that the local Labour Parties should have a wider voice in the selection of the Executive and not be steam-rollered by the trade union block vote.

While the Communists sacrificed debating points (there was hardly much purpose in asking " does the Labour Party Executive decisively and categorically reject the Dictatorship of the Proletariat ? ") it became clear that on its merits their case held good. When the Communist Party stated that it " intends to conform to the Constitution of the Labour Party, without prejudice to its right of criticism on policy or tactics in common with all affiliated bodies," it seemed a little strange for the Labour Party Executive to say " the Communist Party again refuses to give an unqualified promise to become a loyal constituent of the Labour Party." When charged with violating a " fundamental principle " of the Labour Party through its membership of an International which contemplated the use of " unconstitutional " means in certain circumstances, the Communist Party replied by pointing out that the affiliated I.L.P. was a member of an International (the Vienna Union) which envisaged circumstances when " the working class will be able to become the ruling power only by direct action of the masses (mass strikes, armed rebellion, etc.)." The Labour Party Executive's assertion that this statement was " irrelevant to the present issue " hardly carried conviction.

The line-up of forces was interesting. The secretary of the London Trades Council seconded affiliation when, for the first but not the last time, the question came before a Labour Party conference (at Brighton in 1921). He was supported by A. J. Cook and Herbert Smith for the miners. The Glasgow Trades and Labour Council intervened with the Labour Party Executive at the end of that year to secure a discussion between them and Communist Party representatives. On the other hand the principal supporters of the

Executive were men who have long since deserted the Labour movement.

The big anti-Communist speech at the Edinburgh conference in 1922, for instance, was delivered by Mr. Frank Hodges, then secretary of the Miners' Federation. Appealing to the delegates as " lovers of the working class, believers in the aspirations of the people," Mr. Hodges denounced the Communists as " the intellectual slaves of Moscow . . . taking orders from the Asiatic mind, taking the judgment of middle-class Russia—the residue of the old régime . . . the same type of intellectual whom they despised in this country " (!)—a singular reference to Lenin, Stalin, and such great figures. But of Mr. Hodges, director of the Bank of England, the movement has these many years dispossessed itself even of the residue. At the same conference this gentleman was followed by Mr. MacDonald, who declared that the Communists were approaching the Labour Party only in order to stab it in the back. Unfortunately those who swung the big block votes behind Mr. MacDonald and the Executive—who won by 3,086,000 to 261,000—could not foresee the future. If they could have done so it might have given them pause. Had they looked forward only nine short years they would certainly have seen the Labour Party stabbed in the back, but not by the Communists. In 1931 the man behind the knife was to be none other than James Ramsay MacDonald.

CHAPTER III

CAPITALISM'S ASSAULT

In the summer of 1920 came the first sign that the artificial and temporary post-war " replacement " boom in British industry was shortly to break. Wholesale prices stopped rising, sagged, began to fall steadily. By winter, severe depression had set in and was spreading from month to month, with mounting unemployment figures as its index. This was something deeper than the usual periodic slump; it signalised, finally and irrevocably, the ending of the once privileged position of Britain in world economy; it showed that capitalism here was stuck fast in the slough of economic and social retrogression. The very depth of the crisis ensured that the men of property would stop at nothing to find some sort of way out for themselves and their system. Hence a general attack on the workers' standard of living, aimed at the abrogation of all the gains of the war and post-war period, was inevitable.

The first blow was struck at the miners, a natural consequence of that dominating position of the coal industry which has already been stressed. Falling prices, reparations coal deliveries, and the re-emergence of competitive suppliers combined to knock the bottom out of the fantastic export price racket which had been that industry's post-war mainstay. Nowhere was the crisis sharper than in coal. At the same time the miners were the vanguard of the workers' army; their defeat meant, not only respite for the coal-owners, but the clearing of the road for successful wage attacks in every other industry.

It will be recalled that the datum-line strike of 1920 had been settled by a temporary agreement. This was due to

expire on March 31st, 1921. Negotiations were proceeding
between the miners and the owners for a permanent agreement when, on February 15th, 1921, the Government
suddenly announced its intention to introduce a Bill providing for the termination of the existing State control of
the mines five months earlier than had been prescribed by
statute the previous year. The appointed day was to be that
on which the temporary agreement ended. Obviously the
choice of date was no coincidence; and the collusion of the
owners with the Government was made evident by their
immediate announcement of sweeping wage reductions.
Lock-out notices were posted at all collieries while Parliament was still debating the Decontrol Bill, which became an
Act on March 24th. Seven days later the lock-out had
begun.

Drastic is hardly the word for the owners' demands. They
were out for the ending of national wage regulation, the
annulment of the uniform national increases that had been
awarded, and resumption of the old system of district agreements. Their concrete wage proposals meant a return to a
level vastly below pre-war earnings, for they prescribed the
1914 rate plus 20 per cent when even the official cost-of-
living index was 141 per cent above the 1914 basis. Cuts
ranged as high as 42s. a week in some cases. The miners,
for their part, stood firm for the maintenance of their wages
by national agreement. Admitting that there were differences in profitability between district and district, they proposed that a National Pool should be established, so that
the richer coalfields might assist those less fortunately
placed to maintain a reasonable nationally determined
rate of wages.

From the start the issue was rightly seen as one involving
far more than the fate of the miners. The whole Labour
movement roused itself to meet what the *Daily Herald* called
" a frontal attack on the whole working class by the
capitalists and their Government." It was only nine months
since the triumph of the Council of Action; and the spirit
of unity and determination which had swept the country

then was still very much alive. In retrospect those early days of April 1921 leave one indelible impression on the mind—that of a giant, pulsating with energy, straining impatiently for the word " go." No active participator in, or even observer of, the Labour movement in those days could fail to sense the way in which the working people of this country were stirred to the roots of their being, eagerly awaiting the call to action.

The miners had appealed to their associates in the Triple Alliance, the railwaymen and transport workers, whose leaders assembled in London and, after failing to get negotiations resumed, issued on April 8th a call for a general railway and transport strike. This was timed for Tuesday, April 12th. The tremendous response may be gauged from the pages of reports, covering all industrial centres, which the *Daily Herald* featured during the ensuing days. It was immediate and decisive. The Government's response was also immediate. The new Emergency Powers Act was at once invoked to declare a " state of emergency." Military preparations were extensive. Reservists were called to the colours and a special corps, the Defence Force, embodied. Machine-guns were posted at pitheads. Troops in full battle order were despatched to the big working-class areas. Supply depots were established in public parks, commandeered for the purpose.

Meantime the pits had been closed down by the most complete stoppage on record. The Miners' Federation was at full strength, and the men in fine fighting trim. Even the " safety men " were all out. And Mr. G. D. H. Cole, one of the best informed contemporary observers, says that " public opinion was coming round to the miners' side." These facts, however, did not weigh much with the Triple Alliance leaders, in anxious and permanent session at Unity House, the railwaymen's headquarters. They had issued the strike call but their concern appeared to be to get negotiations restarted at all costs. At last, by persuading the Miners' Federation to notify its districts that essential safety work, such as pumping, should be permitted, they were able to get the miners and the Government in conference again —this was on the morning of the 12th—and accordingly the strike date was postponed to Friday, April 15th. Inevitably the delay played into the hands of those who desired to call the strike off.

The tone of the discussions at Unity House became " chaotic and panicky " (to quote Mr. Cole) as the Alliance chiefs grew more alarmed by the Government's provocative preparations for civil war, more susceptible to the propaganda suggestions in the enemy Press that the rank-and-file—with whom the leaders were markedly out of touch—were wavering. Then, on the night of Thursday the 14th, Mr. Frank Hodges, who happened to be in the House of Commons, was invited to speak to an unofficial but influential committee of M.P.s (mainly Conservative) which had been set up because of the general dissatisfaction with the Government's handling of the situation. Speaking impromptu, and without the authority of the Miners' Executive, Mr. Hodges proposed a scheme for a temporary settlement of the wages issue, leaving over the miners' other demands (the National Pool, etc.). The committee at once communicated the sense of these proposals to the Prime Minister; but next morning the Executive flatly disowned their secretary, very properly reprimanding him for his unauthorised personal action in a matter of such moment. Yet the incident gave the Alliance leaders a pretext for throwing in their hand, on the plea that the miners had rejected a possibility of settlement. At three o'clock that afternoon—it was only seven hours before the railwaymen and transport workers were due to strike—Mr. J. H. Thomas emerged from the conference room at Unity House, ran down the steps to the waiting reporters, handed them the bald announcement that the strike was off. Such was " Black Friday."

It is not necessary to describe the confusion into which these words plunged the movement throughout the country. The baldness of the announcement naturally heightened its stunning effect. Equally natural were the reactions that immediately followed—cries of " betrayal ! " and bitter gibes at the " Cripple Alliance." But the débâcle called for a more objective explanation than that. Though it is not without interest to note that three out of the four men who drew public attention as its principal figures were later to find themselves outside the Labour movement. They were Mr. Hodges, Mr. J. H. Thomas (who has gone even further—outside public life) and the late Mr. Robert Williams, then secretary of the Transport Workers' Federation, who ended his days as a National Government propagandist.

Fourth on the list was Mr. Ernest Bevin, now (1936–7) chairman of the Trades Union Congress General Council and for many years the biggest single figure in the trade union movement. At the conference of the Transport Workers' Federation at Edinburgh in June 1921 he said that if he had to live Black Friday over again he would repeat his action. The débâcle, he said, was due to lack of preparation and to the fact that each union was autonomous; he further claimed that " there was also weakness among their own members." Following him the late Mr. Havelock Wilson, most notorious racketeer the movement has known (under him the Seamen's Union openly functioned as the labour department of the Shipping Federation and was at one time expelled from the T.U.C.), heaped praise upon the leaders for their action and told them there was no blackness about the day at all. It should, he declared, be called " Glorious Friday."[1]

Mr. Bevin, however, had put his finger on the spot; though he might have probed a little deeper. Truly preparation was lacking, sectionalism was rampant, aim and method alike were obscurely conceived, if conceived at all. But are these not the responsibility of leadership? Mr. Cole has told how, when the movement was bounding upward in 1919–20 the union leaders " took things easy, or busied themselves with small affairs, when they should have been straining every nerve to prepare for the

[1] *Daily Herald,* June 10th, 1921.

coming struggle. The result was that the slump towards the end of 1920 took them altogether unprepared." So, in the critical days of April, " conscious of their own helplessness and lack of ideas for dealing with the situation, and of the panic which was laying hold of them, they attributed helplessness and panic to the rank-and-file in an even higher degree." That they projected their own shortcomings on to the rank-and-file can hardly be held to absolve the leaders of responsibility.

Black Friday had crumpled up the centre of the workers' front; all that remained was a series of sectional rearguard actions, stubbornly fought but doomed to defeat. At the end of June the miners resumed work on the owners' terms, demonstrating their unending hostility by a small adverse majority on a ballot vote. A Government subsidy temporarily eased the wages slash, and it proved necessary in the case of the lower-paid grades to fix a slightly higher minimum than the bare percentage on basis rate would give. This was significantly called the " subsistence " wage.

Throughout industry the employers' attack was pressed home. Reductions were enforced on engineers, shipyard workers, builders, seamen (the ships' cooks and stewards unsuccessfully struck), cotton operatives (after a general lock-out). By the end of 1921 wage-cuts averaging no less than 8s. a week had been suffered by 6,000,000 workers. The wage attack continued during 1922, involving some stoppages (the provincial printers, for example); but the greatest dispute of the year was the engineering lock-out, lasting from March to June, directed mainly against the powerful Amalgamated Engineering Union but intermittently involving the 47 separate small craft unions in the industry. The employers re-established their claim to undivided authority in the matter of overtime working and all questions of " managerial functions," draining dry the immense funds of the A.E.U. in the process. Meantime the Government majority in Parliament had repealed the legislation guaranteeing the agricultural labourer a minimum wage: once more the countryside was plunged into the depths of brutish poverty.

Defeat struck hard at the unions. The big post-war gains in membership melted away. Between 1921 and 1923 there was a drop of over 2,000,000 in the affiliated membership of the Trades Union Congress, representing rather more than the increase registered since 1918. With ranks thus thinned the unions found the financial burdens imposed by a prolonged period of bad trade a grave menace to their solvency. How did trade unionism react to this crisis? In a very conservative way, to judge from the action or inaction of its leading representatives. This was made clear at the Southport T.U.C. in 1922, when a full-dress debate took place on the question of the powers of the new General Council. From the previous discussion of this problem the reader will have appreciated how much turned on its solution; but it was apparent at Southport that even the chastening experiences of Black Friday's aftermath had not brought that solution nearer. One after another the most influential leaders rose, each speaking from a different angle and yet each making the same speech. Obviously no one could openly damn the proposals to give the Council wide powers over-riding union autonomy. Yet no one wanted, or had faith in, these proposals, not even the members of the General Council itself, who were " still in spirit representatives of their trades," as Mr. Frank Hodges illuminatingly put it during the Southport debate. The old sectionalism was still dominant.

A year later things had certainly not improved. Indeed the whole movement was shocked by the proceedings of the Plymouth T.U.C., where the principal note was an undignified and petty squabble, with much mutual re-crimination, over a series of inter-union demarcation disputes. Coming as it did on top of a wide revival of the movement, witnessed in a whole array of industrial conflicts, this exhibition of sectionalism at its worst only served to strengthen the marked trend to a new and forward-looking policy. Between February and July 1923 there were strikes of builders in the Eastern Counties (and a narrowly averted national stoppage), of the agricultural labourers in Norfolk, of the seamen (unofficial: the union, which had agreed to the heavy wage cuts which provoked the strikes, supplied the shipowners with blacklegs), of the boilermakers and of the dockers (unofficial). The dockers' strikes, significantly, were not defensive; the men were demanding wage increases and were only persuaded to return when the Transport and General Workers' Union agreed to set on foot a national wage movement.

The employers' offensive has now been traced to the point at which there were the first signs of a counter-attack from the workers' side. It is time to revert to the issue whose emergence preceded the attack on wages—unemployment. In the early autumn of 1920 there were 250,000 unemployed; by the end of the year the number had risen to 700,000; it passed the million mark in February 1921 and the two million mark in June. There is no need to argue the importance of these facts, which afforded the most striking example of the failure of capitalism and its governmental policies, and presented the Labour movement with a clear-cut political issue on which it could score heavily. The Council of Action had shown how the mobilisation of the whole movement around an issue which united all working-class opinion was able to bring victory. Since the movement had, during the war, foreseen the emergence of large-scale unemployment at its close and had drafted an elaborate series of proposals for combating it, there was reason to expect big developments.

Those developments did not take place. Urged to include unemployment in the scope of its agitation, as recorded in Chapter I, the Council of Action excused itself on the ground that this was beyond its mandate. However, it proposed an emergency resolution, demanding adequate maintenance for the unemployed and " warning " the Government, at the special Labour Party conference which met on December 29th, 1920, to consider the Irish situation. The Government thereupon invited Labour representatives to serve on an official inquiry into unemployment whose terms of reference were so circumscribed that its deliberations would have been meaningless. Refusing the invitation, a joint meeting of the Labour Party Executive and the Parliamentary Committee of the T.U.C. decided to appoint their own committee of inquiry, which duly reported to a joint national conference on January 27th, 1921. In a lengthy resolution this conference adumbrated the policy of " work or maintenance," making concrete proposals for " enlarging employment "; it added a protest against the attacks on wages and pledged the two national Executive bodies to " give their united assistance to the unions whose wage standards are threatened."

How was this admirable policy to be enforced? An adjournment till February 23rd was ruled so that the unions could secure a mandate from their members. When the conference resumed, however, it was seen that no serious effort had been made to do this. What the results might have been may perhaps be inferred from the example of the Boot and Shoe Operatives, a union well known for its moderation, whose members on a ballot vote had declared in favour of a twenty-four hours protest strike. This proposal the conference decisively defeated. Instead it " invited the Executive Committee of every trade union to secure the affiliation of all its branches to the local Labour Parties and bring all its members actively into political work, in order to take the earliest possible steps to promote a Labour candidate for every constituency in which this has not yet been done."

Since the leadership of the Labour movement thus failed to rise to the occasion on unemployment as an issue it was not surprising that the unemployed themselves should be cold-shouldered. Instead of the movement going out to organise and lead them they were left to organise themselves, taking their leadership from the militant element in their own ranks, of whom the principal representatives were members of the Communist Party. A London District Council of Unemployed was formed in October 1920,

CT

based on the local committees which had sprung up with the onset of mass unemployment. This body asked the conference of February 23rd to hear a speaker; but this was refused, the late Arthur Henderson claiming that the delegates assembled already represented the unemployed through their unions. Amid uproar the Council's organiser, Wal Hannington, made a brief speech of protest; and thereafter the separate organisation of the unemployed took further shape. National conferences of unemployed committees were held in the spring and autumn of 1921 and the National Unemployed Workers' Committee Movement was born. Membership naturally fluctuated, but during the next couple of years the movement showed that it was able to maintain a pretty stable minimum of 300–400 local branches. The strength that the unemployed could bring to the general movement was shown by their active picketing in a number of disputes (notably the engineers' lock-out in 1922) and by their election work (at the Southwark and Camberwell by-elections in December 1921 and February 1922 they helped to turn the scale in Labour's favour).[1]

The official policy turned unemployment from a potential source of strength for the movement into a source of weakness. The unions, which had evaded their responsibilities in February 1921, found themselves by the end of the year bled white by unemployment benefit payments which had totalled some £7,000,000. It hardly mended matters to plead that in so doing the unions had served as a bulwark against revolution. This plea, implicit in the official attitude, was voiced in the House of Commons by Mr. T. E. Naylor, M.P., the astute secretary of that powerful craft union the London Society of Compositors. " I want the Government to realise, if they can," he said, " what would have happened in this country, supposing there had been no trade unions to stand between the working class of this

---

[1] A full-length account of the inception and growth of the unemployed movement is now available in Wal Hannington: *Unemployed Struggles, 1919–36.*

country and the revolution which would have undoubtedly broken out, had it not been for the fact that the trade unions were looking after their own members in time of stress and thereby saved the country from disturbance time and time again."

In sharp contrast stood the phenomenon of " Poplarism." The extension of the system of unemployment insurance in November 1920 did not offset the large demands that were made on the Poor Law. In Poplar the Labour majority on the Borough Council withheld the payments due to the County Council and other authorities as a protest against the saddling of impoverished local bodies with the whole burden of relief. Legal action was taken against the Council, but they remained firm. On September 1st, 1921, a majority of the Councillors, headed by George Lansbury, were accordingly imprisoned for contempt of court. The sensation was immense and the Government had to give way. After six weeks legislation was rushed through which did something to even up the anomalies in Poor Law finance as between the rich and the poor Metropolitan Boroughs. " Guilty—and Proud of It ! " the Poplar Councillors had headed the statement of their case; they had won a famous victory, incidentally giving the Labour Party a hold both on the municipality and the two Parliamentary seats of Poplar that long remained unshaken. Unfortunately the most influential circles in the Labour Party leadership did not feel quite so proud of such " unconstitutional " action. Poplar fought alone and its victory was local.[1]

Why was it that, as the preceding exposition has suggested, the Labour Party chiefs did not produce the forward policy that the times demanded, did not counter the challenge of united capital, operating in conjunction with the Government, by organising united working-class action ? The answer lies in the further development of those processes of change in the Party whose beginnings were described in Chapter II. From this angle the year 1922 may

---

[1] " Poplarism " was attacked, e.g., by Mr. MacDonald: see below, p. 92.

be regarded as a turning-point, marking as it did the return of Mr. Ramsay MacDonald from the wilderness and his confirmation in that extraordinary and fatal supremacy over the Labour Party that was predestined to lead to the catastrophe of 1931. There were very few who realised that Mr. MacDonald was, as Lenin had written of him three years before, simply a supreme master of " that smooth, melodious, banal and Socialist-seeming phraseology which serves in all developed capitalist countries to camouflage the policy of the bourgeoisie inside the Labour movement."

It was as leader of the fight against the Communists (re-member the Edinburgh Conference) that Mr. MacDonald resumed the Labour Party leadership. His most admiring biographer has said that the part he played in this " big controversy . . . ultimately proved the means by which he at once saved and conquered the Labour Party." In whose interest was that conquest may be deduced from the com-ment of *The Times* after Edinburgh, which asserted that " the Labour Party was wise to set itself right with public opinion on the first principles of British polity," defined as private property and the monarchy. Nor was the uncom-promising hostility to the Communists a matter of caprice. The Communist Party advocated a consistent working-class policy. Mr. MacDonald and the dominant group of Elder Statesmen of the Labour Party at whose head he now stood (I.L.P.ers like Snowden, trade union politicians like Thomas, Henderson, and Clynes, Fabians like Sidney Webb) could not tolerate such " dangerous thoughts." They believed that the policy of the Labour Party should be neither consistent nor working class. It became clear, indeed, that for them the Socialist sentiments in the new programme and constitution of 1918 were but the guinea stamp; the real gold lay in the emphasis on the " national " character of the Labour Party, in the repudia-tion of " class " outlook, in everything that presented Labour as the up-to-date equivalent of Liberalism.

Quite understandably this MacDonald line connoted a curious timidity, an apologetic, passive, confused handling of the tactics of the political battle. This was noticeable in the General Election of 1922. That election was in no sense forced by the Labour Party, though the stock of few Governments has stood lower with the mass of the people—and especially with the working class—than did that of the Coalition Government in 1921–22. The initiative was allowed to pass into the hands of the Tory caucus at the famous Carlton Club meeting. Then the Labour programme was presented as the " best bulwark against violent upheaval and class wars . . . This is Labour's alternative to Reaction and Revolution." A responsible political journal of the standing of the *New Statesman* was able to say that on the main issues of home and foreign policy there was " no serious division of opinion between the Liberal and Labour Parties."

Of all the demands in the programme the Capital Levy was the one which the enemy exploited as the signal of red ruin (though it was nothing of the kind). It was also the one which aroused the keenest popular response. A book on the subject by Dr. Hugh Dalton had rapidly sold 17,000 copies. So warm was the regard for it in the Party that even in 1923—when it was in process of being pushed in the background—Mr. Ammon had to say on the Executive's behalf at the Party conference that the " Capital Levy was the centre stone of the whole fabric of their policy . . . They still intended to keep it as an integral part of their programme no matter what criticism might be brought against it." Yet the leaders treated the issue very gingerly, obviously wishing they had never been saddled with it. Catching the infection, one candidate in a Labour seat publicly dissociated himself from the demand; his majority slumped to a bare two figures. Candidates who plumped strongly for the Levy got the biggest majorities. This was most marked in the industrial North. Indeed, the most sensational victories of the whole election—the triumphant Labour sweep through Glasgow and its satellite Clydeside towns—were won by abandoning the mildness and caution of the official programme in favour of an aggressive policy expressed in a series of leaflets and manifestos drafted by John Wheatley.

After the election it was the votes of the " Clyde Brigade " which turned the scale in MacDonald's favour at the first meeting of the Parliamentary Party, enabling him to oust Clynes from the leadership. Like most others they were dazzled by the aura which Mr. MacDonald's attitude during the war had, rightly or wrongly, cast about him. They had forgotten the pre-war MacDonald, central figure in the notorious Leicester by-election intrigue, supporter of Liberal industrialists, more anxious to consort with the Great Ones than with working men—with whom he was quite out of touch and of whose views, especially if they were critical views, he was entirely intolerant. It is recalled that in those days Mr. MacDonald lunched with the Kaiser and was unmoved by Party protests, while it was with the greatest difficulty that he was persuaded to meet representatives of the dockers then on strike.

The Clyde men soon found out their mistake. Mr. MacDonald, now Leader of the Opposition (the Labour Party's seats had jumped from 75 to 142) showed from the start that he intended to play the Parliamentary game according to the most exalted traditions, accepting it as an end in itself, and moulding the Party accordingly. The spirit of working-class revolt which had pushed the Labour vote up in four short years from 2,370,000 to 4,250,000 was to be refined away until not even an aroma was left. Opposition was to be no more than polite exercise in the art of parliamentary fencing; on fundamentals there was to be assimilation. The Labour Party had to function as a pillar of society, in both senses of the latter word. No detail escaped attention, not even the grooming of Labour members' wives to fit them for decorous association with the nobility and gentry; this task was genteelly fulfilled by the ladies of the Half Circle Club.

The Elder Statesmen showed themselves hypersensitive to upper- and middle-class opinion and very insensitive to the workers' viewpoint. In the builders' and agricultural labourers' strikes of 1923, Mr. MacDonald intervened; and the manner of his intervention clearly showed that he was all too conscious of his position as the leader of a great party of State. Meantime, the fight to keep the Labour Party clear of revolutionary infection was continuing. Yet at the Annual Conference of the Party in 1923, the renewed application of the Communist Party for affiliation had gathered somewhat more support. It was rejected by 2,800,000 votes to 366,000. Harry Pollitt was able to point out that there were 38 Communists duly delegated to the Conference compared with a mere seven the previous year. It may be noted that the principal anti-Communist speaker, as before, was Frank Hodges, who affirmed that " Russia had nothing to teach the political democracy of the western world " and that " of all the Labour movements the British was the best . . . the nearest to power and the most capable of maintaining power." It was significant that the Executive had to announce the withdrawal of a clause, passed on a show of hands at the Edinburgh Conference, whose intention was to exclude Communists from eligibility as delegates. There was strong trade union support for this withdrawal, it being intimated that all that concerned the unions was that delegates should accept the constitution of the Labour Party, which the Communists did.

The 1923 conference was the occasion of Sidney Webb's celebrated presidential speech on the theme of the " inevitability of gradualness." Mr. Webb declared that " the whole nation has been imbibing Socialism without realising it," proclaimed the " futility of violence " and deposed Marx in favour of the " spirit of fellowship preached by William Morris." Unfortunately Mr. Webb forgot that Morris was a believer in the inevitability, not of gradualness, but of civil war (see his *News from Nowhere*). Mr. Webb ventured on some electoral mathematics, announcing with satisfaction that " a continuation of the rising curve of Labour votes . . . would produce a clear majority of the total votes cast in Great Britain somewhere about 1926." It was to produce something rather different.

During the whole period that has been discussed in this

chapter, the revolutionary forces had been slowly and painfully consolidating themselves. Since 1921 a number of militant trade unionists had come together to form the British Bureau of the Red International of Labour Unions, founded at Moscow in the summer of that year. Particularly among the miners' unions (Fife and South Wales, for instance) strong support for the R.I.L.U. developed. It was among the miners that a wider militant grouping, the Minority Movement, began to take shape during 1923, and was next year the backbone of the campaign which carried A. J. Cook to power as Secretary of the Miners' Federation following the resignation of Frank Hodges on his election as M.P. Foremost in this growing militant movement were veterans like Tom Mann and younger fighters of the calibre of Harry Pollitt, who was already winning high repute as one of the Boilermakers' delegates to the T.U.C. and Labour Party Conferences, and whom a hostile critic (a German Social Democratic observer) described as " a highly gifted man who towers head and shoulders above the average trade union leader."[1]

Something of the shortcomings of the youthful Communist Party may be gauged from a letter written in August, 1921, by Lenin to Thomas Bell, then the Party's representative in Moscow. " I am afraid," Lenin said, " we have till now in England few very feeble propagandist societies for Communism (inclusive the British Communist Party) but no really *mass* Communist movement."[2] The news had just been received that the South Wales Miners' Federation had decided by a two to one vote to affiliate to the Red International of Labour Unions. On this fact Lenin seized, stressing that " perhaps it is the beginning of a new era . . . *the beginning* of the real proletarian mass movement in Great Britain in the Communist sense."

The important thing was, he continued:

---

[1] Egon Wertheimer: *Portrait of the Labour Party* (2nd edition), pp. 36-7.

[2] " I beg to apologise for my bad English," ran a modest postscript. The language and emphasis in the quotations here given are as in the original.

" 1. To create a very good, really proletarian, really mass *Communist Party* in this part of England—that is such party which will *really* be the LEADING force in *all* Labour movement in this part of the country. (Apply the resolution on organisation and work of the party adopted by the 3rd Congress [i.e. of the Communist International] for this part of your country.)

" 2. To start a daily paper of the working class in this part of the country. To start it not as a business (as usually newspapers are started in capitalist countries) not with big sum of money . . . but as an *economic* and *political* tool of the *masses* in their struggle."

It was interesting to notice how Lenin emphasised that without the starting of a daily newspaper in this way " there is no BEGINNING *of the really Communist mass movement in this part of your country*." But his advice was not heeded, was in fact never made known till years afterwards when it was published as a document of historical interest. He had certainly put his finger on the spot. In those first critical years of the Communist Party's life, the striking thing was the continuance of the traditional methods of the old B.S.P. The organisation was that of a purely propagandist body. The party organ was a weekly propaganda journal of the familiar type, only its name being changed from the *Call* to the *Communist*. It was characteristic that the South Wales miners' decision which so excited Lenin left the *Communist* entirely unmoved, being dismissed in an indifferent and obscure reference of three lines. Despite the devotion and energy of the Party members in face of heavy persecution (there were many arrests and imprisonments and a raid on the Party headquarters), it was clear that unless it achieved a thoroughgoing break with old traditions the Party was rapidly approaching a standstill.

So serious was the situation by the spring of 1922 that a conference was called which set up a special commission to review the whole organisation and work of the party. The report of this body, whose principal members were R.

Palme Dutt and Harry Pollitt, was adopted by the annual congress in the autumn of the same year. It followed out the essential ideas indicated by Lenin in the letter quoted above. Taking the resolution of the Communist International to which he had referred, the Commission's report worked out a detailed application of its principles to the British party. Complete reorganisation was planned in order to have, as the report said, " a party organised for the task of revolutionary leadership . . . our task is not to create some ' propagandist ' society or revolutionary club but to create an efficient machine of the class struggle." The new conception meant that " every party member would have to be a working member." The party organ, it was laid down, " should be a *newspaper* of the working class and not a small magazine of miscellaneous articles with a Communist bias," and should aim at becoming a daily paper. These transformations were effected. The party began to make headway. Early in 1923 the *Communist* gave place to the *Workers' Weekly* (captioned " The Forerunner of the Workers' Daily "), which shortly achieved a circulation outdistancing that of the other Socialist weeklies.

CHAPTER IV

"IN OFFICE BUT NOT IN
POWER..."

Since the war our world has been in a chronic state of crisis. Sometimes the manifestations are less acute than at others, but the crisis is never resolved. And there are periods when tension becomes so agonising that an eruption, threatening to overwhelm the whole social fabric, appears imminent. When such periods mature, and the fate of Europe trembles in the balance, it is always Britain that holds the key to the situation. This was the case in 1923. Here has to be sought the principal determinant of the General Election at the close of that year and the consequent formation, in January 1924, of Britain's first Labour Government.

The Continent was enmeshed in the tightening net of the Versailles Treaty. German economy had been shot to pieces; the autumn of the year that had begun with the occupation of the Ruhr and that witnessed the frightful crash of the mark saw the desperate country on the verge of revolution. Reparations were recoiling violently on the heads of their authors, the victor countries, who in their turn found themselves faced with an imperious creditor in the United States. Europe was being drained of gold to swell the already overflowing coffers of Wall Street.

In Britain the Baldwin Government was placed at a serious disadvantage in the endeavour to tackle this menacing situation. Clearly Anglo-American co-operation in securing some new stabilisation in Europe was essential or capitalism might be doomed. How could it be achieved other than by reversing the flow of gold across the Atlantic, cleansing the German plague-spot by liberal and repeated applications of the salve of American capital investment, with the City profitably assisting in this sanitary operation? To devise an appropriate plan an international commission of experts was mooted, under the presidency of General (" Hell 'n Maria ") Dawes. The mere name of that Yankee politician-militarist, bitter foe of organised labour, was enough to suggest that the plan he sponsored would be of a character to merit, and receive, determined working-class opposition. Would it be possible for a Tory Government in Britain to carry such a plan through ?

Calculation of the probabilities here involved had to be related to other considerations of internal politics. There was the intractable problem of unemployment; in industry the workers were beginning to take the offensive once more; the rapid rate of increase of the Labour vote presaged a Labour majority at the next General Election, assuming that Parliament lived out its legal term to round about 1926–7. Thus to the risk of failure in achieving the stabilisation of capitalism in Europe there was added the certainty of a worsening of the home situation. Nor could Mr. Baldwin and his friends extract comfort from the satisfactory way in which Mr. MacDonald's leadership of the Labour Party had been shaping up. A Labour majority, arriving under the conditions forecast, was bound to produce results highly disagreeable to the men of property; for either Mr. MacDonald would have to carry out some sort of Socialist programme or other leaders would be found in his place; should they fail, Kerensky-like, the revolutionary forces would make rapid headway. It had not escaped notice that the Labour Party chiefs, while hurling anathema at the Communist Party, had in 1923 abandoned the attempt to exclude individual Communists in their capacity as affiliated trade unionists.

All these problems seemed to point to one solution— forestalling a Labour majority by the immediate translation to office of a Labour minority, governing by grace of the

Liberals. It was a daring solution, requiring all the skill in political manœuvring in which the British governing class has so long excelled. Even if it was not conceived in these clear terms the point remains that no other hypothesis explains the turn of events. Mr. Baldwin dissolved and appealed to the country, playing up the one issue, tariffs, calculated more than any other to damage his own Party and hand seats by the score to both Labour and Liberal. The General Election of 1923 left the Conservatives the strongest Party, but in a minority of 89 against the combined forces of the Liberals and the Labour Party, the former counting 158 M.P.s and the latter having jumped from 142 to 191. After some delay Mr. MacDonald formed a Government on January 22nd, 1924.

Tory and Liberal leaders alike made no concealment of their aims. Speaking at the meeting of the Conservative Party after the election, Mr. Baldwin said:

" It was on unemployment that the Labour Party relied on coming to power within two or three years. Their calculations were that the discontent in the country coupled with want of action on our part would have swept them into power and us out by 1926. And I believe myself that that would have happened, and believe that in spite of the losses in this election we shall emerge all the stronger and able to bring to pass a great victory about the time when in my view nothing but disaster could have overtaken us."

(Mr. Baldwin's prophetic soul did not lead him astray in his presentiment of a " great victory " in 1926 !) To the National Liberal Federation, Mr. Asquith (as he then was) explained that the installation of a Labour Government " with its claws cut " was the best insurance against a fighting Labour Government. " The experiment," he opined, " could hardly be made under safer conditions," adding blandly that " we still sleep more or less comfortably in our beds. Capital steadily pursues its old routine of continuous and on the whole prosperous investment." Significantly

remarking that " their foreign policy is the same as ours,"
Lord Grey, architect of the war of 1914, declared: " I
regard the advent of a Labour Government under these
circumstances with no apprehension at all." Responsible
capitalist circles generally echoed these sentiments.

Our rulers, to put it briefly, were speculating on the
successful carrying through of a double process of dis-
rupting the working-class advance of which the Labour
Party's growing strength was the reflection. One side of this
process was the disillusionment which a Labour Government in leading strings was expected to produce ("Mr.
MacDonald's Government cannot attempt to continue in
office too long . . . as a Ministry on sufferance without dis-
rupting the Labour Party itself both in Parliament and in
the country," said the *Observer*); the other side was the
governing-class assimilation of the leading circles of the
Party (" The great and manifold tasks of the Empire must
in the end subdue these new forces to their purpose," said
The Times).

At the time, however, this skilful manœuvre was scarcely
perceived, except by those on the extreme Left whose powers
of political analysis had been made keen by an understanding of Marxism that was then far rarer than it is to-day. I
remember—for I was one of them—the milling crowd in
Trafalgar Square cheering itself hoarse in the small hours
of a clammy November night as " Lab. Gain " flashed
repeatedly across the illuminated sign (those were the days
before broadcasting had turned polling night into an affair
of the individual fireside). That enthusiasm symbolised the
general reaction of the Labour movement. There was a
universal sense that we were all very lucky, for we were
about to see great things.

Now it would be mistaken to deduce from what has been
said above that in this the movement was deceiving itself.
The fact that the governing class found it necessary to give
the Labour Party the chance of taking office, even as a
manœuvre, was a sign of the further break-up of traditional British politics, was a sign that our rulers' grip was

weakening. Indeed their whole calculation would have been brought to nought if Mr. MacDonald and his colleagues had regarded themselves as a Labour Government —that is to say a Government acting in the interests of the labouring majority of the population and therefore opposing the interests of the privileged minority.

This was the crucial point; it was unfortunately obscured by the arguments that had proceeded for some time on the issue of Minority *versus* Majority Government. At the 1923 Labour Party conference Mr. MacDonald had stated categorically that " no sane person would undertake to form a Government with a majority of about half a dozen. . . . They had to get an absolute majority of the House of Commons before a Labour Government would stand a ghost of a chance of pleasing its people with its work, and a Government that did not please its Party with its work had better remain in opposition." Next year, as Prime Minister, he told the Party conference that " when the opportunity came, so far as I was concerned I never had a moment's hesitation as to what we should do. To have shirked responsibility would have been cowardly. . . . It would have shown the spirit of shivering fear rather than that of trustful gallantry, and the latter is the spirit of the Labour Party."

Now this was an entirely abstract presentation of the issue. To imply, first, that no minority Government could " please its people " and then to assert that " trustful gallantry " dictated the formation of such a Government was merely MacDonaldite word-spinning. Nor was discussion brought to earth by the not surprising tendency on the Left to contrast unfavourably the Labour Government's legislative achievement with its election pledges (on nationalisation, for example). In the nature of things a major programme of legislation cannot be looked for from a minority Government. Because most men realise this the Great Alibi —" in office but not in power," " a Socialist Government but not a Socialist Parliament "—proved such an effective weapon in the hands of the Elder Statesmen and their apologists. But that seemingly omnipotent apologia shatters to bits when set against the real issue, which was one of *administration*. Even a minority Government has wide administrative powers. Mr. J. H. Thomas made a big point of this at the 1925 Labour Party Conference in arguing against those who thought that only a majority Government should be envisaged. Referring to the two fields of foreign policy and unemployment insurance, Mr. Thomas claimed that the Labour Government had shown it possessed ample powers to act administratively. Mr. Thomas was quite right; and the same point was actually stressed by Mr. MacDonald himself, who in a speech to the I.L.P conference at York in the spring of 1924 said bluntly, " we are in office with power."

Once this vital point is conceded it is evident that the fact of a Government having a majority or only a minority is a secondary consideration. The action of political leaders is determined by their policy, by their outlook, and not by their majority or minority position. Is politics immune from the ordinary criteria of everyday life, according to which one judges a man's integrity and capacity rather by how he conducts himself in adverse conditions than when all the advantages are on his side ? Politicians who cannot do the right thing when they are in a minority, it has been said, are scarcely likely to do it when they are in a majority.

There can be no question that in 1924 the Labour movement as a whole supported the decision to form a Government. That support set an acid test before the Government. Would it stand openly by the masses of the population in their daily struggle to maintain their existing conditions of work and life, and to advance to better conditions ? Would it recognise that, in a class society, it existed to act in the interests of a class, the working class ? From the previous chapter it will have appeared that the omens were not auspicious. The Elder Statesmen had made it all too plain that it was to the " community," not to their class, that they paid allegiance. Mr. MacDonald declared in a speech in his constituency of Aberavon that he did not care for the name of " Socialist " and opined that it was his privilege " to be regarded as a sort of non-party Party leader." The responsibilities of office were assumed to the refrain—" the King's Government must be carried on." When Cabinet-making was over Mr. MacDonald was seen to have produced a very odd mixture; but there was significance in the oddity. Names of beloved Socialist veterans like Lansbury, which men had expected to see enjoying pride of place, were conspicuously absent. On the other hand there were included Lord Chelmsford, ex-colonial governor and ex-Viceroy of India, put at the Admiralty to pacify those senior naval officers who uttered dire threats of what would happen if any Labour cad tried to boss them, Lord Haldane, the philosopher who was a master in the art of war-preparation, and Lord Parmoor, aged Liberal lawyer. The Labour men in the Cabinet were " safe," as the saying goes, with the single exception of John Wheatley; and Mr. MacDonald had first tried to fob off the intellectual leader of the Clyde Brigade with an under-secretaryship.

Turning now to review the Labour Government in action, it might be suggested that the task of appraisal is superfluous, since the criticisms that were voiced by the Government's most intimate supporters after its fall really tell the whole story. Nevertheless, some recapitulation of the main facts will be suggestive. Take the " acid test " already indicated; how would the Government act on the home front ? The main positive achievement came from the Cabinet's one consistent Socialist member. Wheatley's Housing Act was a major measure of social reform, and with its projected auxiliary legislation (such as the Building Materials Bill) would have struck a shattering blow at monopolistic vested interests in one of their worst forms. Nothing else compared with this in its scope. The restoration of the legal minimum wage in agriculture redressed a wrong perpetrated by the Coalition Government. The abolition of the " gap " or waiting period for the receipt of benefit removed an anomaly in the functioning of the unemployment insurance system. The raising of Old Age

Pensions was a recognition of the need to adjust these payments to the increased cost of living. Mr. Snowden's " Free Trade " Budget was an orthodox Liberal essay, " vindictive against no class and against no interest " as he himself said; the unchecked operation of profiteering monopoly rapidly offset its removal of the taxes on food.

It is instructive to compare the actions and attitude of Britain's first Labour Government thirteen years ago with those of France's first Labour Government in our own day. The difference is striking—all the difference, in fact, between a disunited Labour movement with a confused and timid policy capitulating to Liberalism, and a united Labour movement with a clear and militant policy able to draw Liberalism in its wake. Unemployment, for instance ; where the MacDonald Government, apart from the abolition of the " gap," confessed its helplessness (Labour Minister Tom Shaw's confession that solutions for unemployment could not be produced like rabbits out of a hat), the Blum Government introduced its 1,800,000,000 francs public works scheme, announcing that it would nationalise those concerns failing to assist in this common effort. Take the case of the Civil Service; where the MacDonald Government aroused keen protest throughout the service for its failure to sever the strangling bonds of red tape and to grant civil rights, the Blum Government restored the cuts in civil servants' salaries and added an allowance for living expenses.

Outstanding in this comparison, however, was the different attitude to the struggles of the workers in industry. Immediately it took office the Blum Government was confronted with the tidal wave of stay-in strikes, without parallel in the history of France or any other country. What did it do ? Talk cant about the " community " and try to secure peace at any price ? No; it intervened decisively on the side of the workers, brought the employers sharply to heel, and transformed French industrial conditions by enacting the principle of a legal minimum wage, a compulsory 40-hour working week, annual holidays with pay, and the full recognition of trade unionism (which speedily led to a general rise in wages of from 7 to 15 per cent). The MacDonald Government likewise took office at a time when the strike wave was rising, even though it was not at all of the same order of magnitude as the 1936 strikes in France; still the recorded strikes rose from 628 in 1923 to 710 in 1924 and the numbers involved from 405,000 to 613,000. How did the Government react?

A railway strike was in progress when the Government was formed. The issue lay in awards of the National Wages Board imposing wage reductions and unfavourable adjustments in conditions, especially at the expense of the loco-motive-men. These had been accepted by the National Union of Railwaymen but rejected by the Associated Society of Locomotive Engineers and Firemen, organising the bulk of the locomotive grades. Eventually the Associated struck and gained certain concessions. Many N.U.R. drivers and firemen came out with their mates of the Associated, but many others remained at work, the division between the two unions naturally imparting much bitterness to the struggle.

The attitude of the Government to this strike was authoritatively recapitulated by Mr. Tom Shaw in a later House of Commons debate on industrial disputes. He said: " In that emergency the Government was asked what its position was, and its position was quite plainly stated. The House was told we had no sympathy with this un-official [*sic*] strike, and that all the resources of the Government would be used to prevent the four essential services— light, water, food, and power—from being stopped." Mr. Shaw averred that on the merits of a trade dispute " it would be unwise in the highest degree for a Minister, who may be called upon at any moment to act as impartial chairman for the parties, to express any opinion whatever." He was followed by Mr. Clynes, who claimed proudly that in its handling of strikes the Labour Government " played the part of a national Government, and not a class Government, and I am certain that any Government, whatever it might be, could not in the circumstances have done more than we have done to safeguard the public interests."

In February came a national strike of dockers, following up the unofficial stoppages of the preceding year. It was keenly fought, the men showing unshakable solidarity, and some wage advances were secured. The success was in no sense due to the Government, on whose behalf Mr. MacDonald had hastened to declare that " the Government will not fail to take what steps are necessary to secure transport of necessary food supplies, and has already set up the nucleus of an organisation." Extreme pressure was brought to bear upon the dockers' leaders, as they publicly bore witness. " I wish it had been a Tory Government," said Mr. Ernest Bevin, " we would not have been frightened by their threats. We were bound to listen to the appeal of our own people." He had never heard from Tory or Liberal " the same menacing tones or the same expressions of fear," Mr. Ben Tillett told the Labour Party conference the following year.

Throughout the spring and summer a series of stoppages, official and unofficial, were symptomatic of the general forward movement among the workers which could have been turned into a tremendous reinforcement for the Labour Government if that Government had been prepared to regard itself as an instrument of working-class advance and not as a " national Government." In April there was a shipyard lock-out, following on the unofficial strike of the underpaid ship-repairers at Southampton. The same month saw a dramatic unofficial strike of the workers at the Wembley Exhibition. Railway shopmen, divided among many unions, have always been regarded industrially as a conservative element; but in June on the London Tube railways they too struck unofficially. A big builders' strike in July led immediately to a six weeks' national lock-out.

A national coalfield strike was narrowly averted in April–

May. The Government, which had set up a committee of inquiry under Lord Buckmaster, offered the miners a Minimum Wage Bill as an inducement to hold their hand. The Bill, however, ran aground in committee and the Miners' Federation had to make the best terms it could in negotiation with the coalowners. Wage advances were conceded in the compromise agreement that ensued, but it was only to run for a year and was a direct forerunner of the conflicts of 1925–26.

Of all the industrial disputes the London traffic strike at the end of March threw most light on the Government's attitude. The tramwaymen struck for higher wages and the busmen joined them. The Tube men were considering sympathetic action. In face of the chaos that resulted the Government was urged by the union leaders to take over and reorganise the traffic services of the metropolis, improving them and securing a decent standard for their workers. The Government duly intervened but hardly in the sense suggested. There was an unpleasant strike-breaking ring about Mr. MacDonald's statement that " the major services must be maintained, and the Government . . . must give protection to those engaged in legal occupations." At the same time the Government went to the length of invoking the hated Emergency Powers Act. To many this seemed scarcely credible; the fact remains that the *London Gazette*, No. 32923, of April 1st, 1924, carried the official notification of the Proclamation by the King of a State of Emergency under the Act. Colonel Wedgwood was appointed Chief Civil Commissioner. Only the speedy ending of the strike, coupled with a strong private protest from the General Council of the T.U.C., who were said to have hinted at the possibility of a general strike if the State of Emergency were enforced, smoothed the matter over.

The complacent calculation of *The Times* that the " great tasks of the Empire must subdue these new forces to their purpose " was working out only too well. In an after-luncheon speech at Wembley Mr. Clynes told his gratified hearers that Labour was " being converted from its former grooves to the wider view." Mr. J. H. Thomas proudly proclaimed that " men faced with these responsibilities can never again be the indifferent propagandists that they were in the past. They must remain for all time responsible politicians keeping only in mind the greater interests of a great country."

The " propagandists " had for a generation opposed war, supported disarmament. The " responsible politicians," while suspending work on the Singapore naval base (hardly a matter of urgency while Japan was facing years of reconstruction after the disastrous earthquake) laid down five new cruisers—" we have placed first and foremost the needs of the Navy and the need for replacement " explained Mr. MacDonald. Simultaneously the Air Force was substantially strengthened, estimates increasing by £2,500,000. " They have shown a real largeness of view," purred *The Times*, " in rising above the deep-rooted prejudices of many among their adherents . . . and a degree of moral courage not common in any party in acting upon what the interests of the State demand against the known wishes of large sections of their supporters." This same readiness to act " in the interests of the State against the known wishes of their supporters " was seen in such things as the Government opposition to back-bench amendments designed to prevent the armed forces being used in industrial disputes.

It was a melancholy spectacle. For upon men with a long and honourable reputation as pacifists, even as conscientious objectors during the war, fell the task not only of justifying increased armaments, but of justifying their use. Thus Mr. William Leach, Under-Secretary for Air, announcing that " we have not made any change in the policy of the late Government in Iraq," had to repeat the conventional defence of the aerial bombing of tribesmen as a measure for maintaining order. And in general the colonial policy of the Government registered " no change." This was true of Egypt, where indeed the conversations between Mr. MacDonald and Zaghlul Pasha were so

animated on the British side that they were used by Mr.
MacDonald's Tory successor as the beginning of the policy
of coercion that he was carrying out. To India, uplifted by
the hope of a new spirit of friendship and sympathy, Mr.
MacDonald telegraphed in true Curzon vein—" no party
in Great Britain will be cowed by threats of force or by
policies designed to bring Government to a standstill." In
earnest of this determination not to be cowed the Bengal
Ordinances were decreed, permitting detention without
trial, and widely operated; troops were called out in the
Bombay cotton strike and volleys at Jaito accounted for
fifty casualties; at Cawnpore Indian Communists were put
on trial for " conspiracy to deprive the King-Emperor of
sovereignty "—that is to say, for embarking on Communist
propaganda and activities of a kind that are entirely legal
in this country—and received jail sentences of four years
apiece.

Foreign policy was the field in which perhaps bigger
results were anticipated than in any other; it was also that
in which subsequently even the ranks of those otherwise
critical of the Government could scarce forbear to cheer.
Why those cheers persisted, as they did, is one of the un-
solved mysteries of politics. The most that can be said is
that they were another symptom of that almost eerie
domination exercised by Mr. MacDonald over the movement until the final crash. Any informed observation of
Mr. MacDonald's diplomacy is bound to conclude that it
was alien to the whole purpose and spirit of the working
class and its movement. Since history has so mercilessly put
paid to Mr. MacDonald's account, and since his doubling
of the Foreign Office with the Premiership meant that the
Labour Government's foreign policy was peculiarly his
personal affair, it is scarcely necessary at this time of day
to go into great detail. The curious may be referred to a
brilliant contemporary indictment, entitled *The Diplomacy of
Mr. Ramsay MacDonald.*[1] Under the pseudonym " U.D.C."

[1] Printed in the *Labour Monthly*, January–February 1925, and separately in pamphlet form.

(which considerably agitated the Union of Democratic Control) one of the movement's most expert writers on foreign affairs subjected Mr. MacDonald to a fire so withering, timed and aimed with such perfection, delivered with such cold ruthlessness, that to get any sense of the nature of the onslaught one would have to hark back to the grand days of swingeing political polemic.

Here it will suffice to survey the Labour Government's foreign policy in the barest outline. Central problem in Europe was, of course, the Versailles Treaty and Reparations. Treaty revision in the widest sense (including the reparations clauses) had been a Labour election pledge and had also long featured in Mr. MacDonald's personal pronouncements. " Pursuing the will-o'-the-wisp of reparations is the great curse of every country," he had cried. " There will never be peace," he said in a speech at Leicester in 1923, " so long as the Versailles Treaty is in existence." Certainly the translation of those sentiments into reality would have meant working hard and fighting hard; but it could have been done. Mr. MacDonald did not do it. When Mr. Henderson made a speech in which he referred to the desirability of revising the Versailles Treaty, Mr. MacDonald categorically repudiated him. He flung himself at the head of the arch-reactionary M. Poincaré, the Treaty's dourest and most obdurate defender, absurdly wooing that discredited statesman on the very eve of his electoral defeat by M. Herriot and the *Bloc des Gauches*, achieving nothing by such antics except, as the French Socialists tartly observed, the presenting of M. Poincaré's *Bloc National* with election capital worth at least 100,000 good solid votes.

As to Reparations he himself now became the principal pursuer of the will-o'-the-wisp. In private he is said to have gone so far as to declare that a heavy Reparations burden on Germany was necessary in order to prevent German industries becoming too dangerous competitors. In public he flung himself heart and soul into the job of getting the Experts' Report (the Dawes Plan) adopted and operated.

" Here," he exclaimed to the I.L.P. conference at York, " is Europe's chance. Put it into operation all at once. Finish the job and bring peace and security to the Continent." In the course of the same speech he admitted that " there are things in the Dawes Report that I do not like. But if I begin to raise this detail and that detail, France, Belgium and Germany would do the same." In other words, to tackle the " things I do not like " (meaning the mortgaging of Germany's resources and the intensified exploitation of the German workers ?) would mean a job of work. It was so much easier to let the whole thing go through. That it had nothing whatever to do with " peace and security," being intended simply as a more efficient means of squeezing Reparations out of Germany than had yet been devised, was just nobody's business. Nor was it of moment that the policy of which the Dawes Plan was the essential part—the Anglo-American financial colonisation of Europe—was bound, by the enormous rationalisation of industry and uneven development of productive capacity to which it led, to pave the way for world economic crisis in five short years; was bound also, by continuing the national oppression of vanquished Germany, to aid in engendering Hitlerism.

Mr. MacDonald might gush effusively in his approaches to a reactionary statesman like M. Poincaré. In his relations with Governments where a little extra warmth might have been looked for he remained frigid, even hostile. He treated the Labour Government of Mexico to a gratuitous display of sham Palmerstonian fireworks because the Mexicans had the temerity to suggest that Mrs. Evans, a wealthy English ranch-owner and resident in their country, was subject to its laws. He proceeded to offend the Mexicans mortally by proposing to appoint as the head of a special mission to their country Sir Thomas Hohler, who had been British Minister to Hungary under the Horthy Regency, and was therefore perhaps hardly a tactful appointment.

Worse still, he applied a similar technique to the relations between Britain and the Soviet Union. For years Mr. MacDonald had been as anti-Soviet as the most hard-shell continental Social-Democrat. Georgia was his King Charles' Head. And here he was, the unchallenged controller of British foreign policy. True, the looked-for recognition was not long in coming; but it only came because of outside pressure. The first Cabinet meeting came and went without a decision on the point, though it was confidently expected to be one of the earliest made, in view of the Party's pledges and of the keen and unanimous feeling throughout the movement. It was bruited about that Mr. MacDonald was deferring to Foreign Office opposition. Reaction was immediate. Neil MacLean, M.P., opened a campaign of polite remonstrance in the columns of the *Daily Herald*. Duncan Carmichael advised the Government that the London Trades Council (of which he was then secretary) saw no option but to organise a protest meeting. Mr. MacDonald yielded.

Even so recognition had something grudging about it. No ambassadors were exchanged, though Mr. MacDonald had previously, in writing, promised the Moscow Embassy to his old friend James O'Grady (later Sir James) " when we recognise the Soviet Government." There was a pledge to take immediate steps to stimulate Anglo-Soviet trade by making the stroke of the administrative pen necessary to bring the U.S.S.R. within the scope of the Export Credits scheme. It was not honoured. When Mr. MacDonald came to open the Anglo-Soviet Conference in London he did so in a speech that was warmly hailed by Tory newspapers for its " firm " tone. Instead of noting that these were negotiations between two Governments that both, according to their lights, took the name of Socialist, he delivered an allocution on the difference between the British and Soviet systems of government, dilated on the wickedness of propaganda with special reference to the Communist International's criticisms of himself, and generally behaved as if he were an accredited plenipotentiary of the Council of Foreign Bondholders and the Association of British

Creditors of Russia. His dominating influence was to be seen later in the General Election appeal's sections on relations with Russia; these, in addition to a general proclaiming of "equitable treatment for all interests," specifically stated that negotiations for a guaranteed loan to the U.S.S.R. could only be carried through "when compensation has been secured to British subjects for their losses in Russia."

There remained only the problem of the Foreign Office itself. For many years the Labour movement had been convinced of the need for a thorough purge of this preserve of reaction. In August 1923 Mr. MacDonald himself wrote in the *New Leader*: "We propose to end the bureaucracy of the Foreign Office, with its queer mentality and selection of subversive agents."

"That proposal" (wrote "U.D.C." in the work already cited) "went the way of all the others. He ended nothing and changed nothing. He left every 'queer mentality,' every 'subversive agent' where he found it. He refused even to reinstate in the service men of Labour sympathies who had been driven from it. Herriot the Radical transformed the personnel of the French diplomatic service. MacDonald the Socialist left ours untouched. . . . He came to the Foreign Office, he saw, and was conquered. Those skilled dealers with men took his measure swiftly. . . . 'He is the easiest Foreign Secretary I have ever had to manage,' was the complacent summing up of one of the most powerful of them. . . . He has written his own epitaph in that amazing article in the *Spectator* in which he boasted naïvely how he—who had been sent to Downing Street to change the whole current of our foreign policy—had preserved its continuity."

By the early autumn of 1924 a profound and growing divergence between the Prime Minister and the organised workers was making itself felt. In a new preface to his little work *Socialism, Critical and Constructive*, Mr. MacDonald announced that the working class was "infected" with the

" evil of profiteering," that workers " in their struggles to secure their ends are tempted to forget that they are all dependent members of a social unit," that " public doles, Poplarism, strikes for increased wages . . . not only are not Socialism, but may mislead the spirit and the policy of the Socialist movement." These Whig sentiments (Liberal would be too Left a description of them) contrasted strongly with the now swiftly running tide of militancy in the world of labour, evidenced in the strikes which have already been described, and finding organised expression at the Hull Trades Union Congress in September.

At the Plymouth Congress in 1923 it had been agreed to set up a Joint Advisory Council between the General Council and the National Unemployed Workers' Movement. Trades Councils were advised to co-operate locally with the unemployed movement and a national campaign was carried through, culminating in country-wide demonstrations on Sunday, June 1st, 1924. An Unemployed Workers' Charter was drafted, embodying six points " for immediate attainment by united action "; these covered the demand for work or maintenance, Government work schemes under union conditions, State workshops to supply the needs of Government departments, reduction in hours to absorb the unemployed, occupational training centres, and the provision of houses at appropriate rents. This Charter the Hull T.U.C. endorsed, at the same time adopting a wider Industrial Workers' Charter (including the demand for nationalisation, etc.), and instructing the General Council to report to each annual Congress on the progress made in relation thereto. A step forward in regard to General Council powers was taken, unions being obliged to notify the Council of all disputes and the Council being authorised in certain circumstances to intervene. By a nearly two to one vote the principle of organisation by industry was endorsed and the Council instructed to draw up a scheme for linking up the unions in " a united front . . . for improving the standards of life of the workers." The Council was likewise instructed " to call a Special Congress

to decide on industrial action immediately there is danger
of war."

The Hull Congress also recorded progress in the affairs
of international Labour. For the first time a fraternal
delegation from the Soviet trade unions was received, and
it was decided to reciprocate by the despatch of a T.U.C.
delegation to the U.S.S.R. At the Vienna Congress of the
International Federation of Trade Unions, in June, the
British delegates had succeeded in keeping the door open for
negotiations with the Soviet trade unions when the I.F.T.U.
majority, full of anti-Soviet spleen, wished to shut it tight.
Referring to the Vienna proceedings, the late Mr. A. A.
Purcell, presiding at Hull, spoke of the need " to bring every
national trade union centre within the four corners of a
genuinely united and avowedly anti-capitalist International
Federation of Trade Unions." Congress unanimously agreed
to Mr. Purcell's statement that they should empower the
General Council " to take all possible steps . . . in bringing
together the different elements of the Labour movement in
Europe."

These advances were not a spontaneous and sudden manifestation. They had been prepared by the first serious
rallying of militant trade unionists on a wide scale in the
shape of the Minority Movement, whose beginnings in the
coalfields have been noted in Chapter III. At a conference
in London in August 1924 the National Minority Movement was launched. Attended by 270 delegates, representing
200,000 trade unionists, this conference attracted wide
notice. Presided over by Tom Mann, and with Harry
Pollitt as general secretary, the new Movement organised
a nation-wide series of district conferences, added Metal
and Transport sections to its initial Miners' section. Pollitt
stated the Minority Movement's aims as follows:

" We are not out to disrupt the unions, or to encourage
any new unions. Our sole object is to unite the workers in
the factories by the formation of factory committees; to
work for the formation of óne union for each industry; to

strengthen the local Trades Councils so that they shall
be representative of every phase of the working-class
movement, with its roots firmly embedded in the factories
of each locality. We stand for the creation of a real General
Council that shall have the power to direct, unite and
co-ordinate all the struggles and activities of the trade
unions, and so make it possible to end the present chaos
and go forward in a united attack in order to secure,
not only our immediate demands, but to win complete
workers' control of industry."

Alike in the Labour Party and the trade unions it was
obvious that the conflict of policy and outlook between the
militants and MacDonaldism was coming to a head. To
these problems of the relationship of forces within the
Labour movement the concluding days of the MacDonald
Government have particularly to be related.

Everyone knows that the Government finally fell because
the Liberals turned against it over the Campbell case and
the Anglo-Soviet Treaty; and it is generally recognised that
both these matters symbolised the growing urgency of those
working-class issues which it had been Mr. MacDonald's
whole purpose to deny. Why, though, did Mr. MacDonald
choose to dissolve precisely at this point? It was not the
first time the Government had been defeated on a vote of
the House. Nor were any of the Party leaders desirous of
an election; quite the reverse. Certainly the Liberals
(greatly irritated by Mr. MacDonald's peevish mishandling
of them, policy questions apart) were not displeased when
the Government put itself in their hands by the Campbell
blunder. It may be recalled that J. R. Campbell, acting
editor of the *Workers' Weekly*, was arrested and his prosecution ordered for the publication of a " don't shoot ! " appeal to the troops. In face of a storm of protest from all
sections of the Labour movement the prosecution was
dropped. Challenged, as it was bound to be, the Government prevaricated, first stating that the prosecution could
not have succeeded, then alleging that Campbell was not

really responsible and that if the responsible person could be found he would be prosecuted, the whole welter of evasion being served up with a thick sauce of sentimentalities about Campbell as a crippled and decorated ex-serviceman (which he was). The fact was that the Campbell case reflected just that critical balance of forces in the movement to which reference has been made. While the prosecution symbolised the hardening MacDonaldite attitude, its withdrawal symbolised the power of those elements which were inevitably moving towards a clash with Mr. MacDonald and the Elder Statesmen.

For Mr. MacDonald, then, dissolution was a necessary even if desperate step. It meant, as R. P. Dutt penetratingly pointed out in the *Labour Monthly* at the time, that:

" He could rally the whole movement behind him in the unity of the fight, shatter the doubts of his supporters and sweep the Labour Party conference in a wave of enthusiasm. At the same time he could use the very situation to carry the war into the enemy's camp, turn on the Communists as the authors of all his misfortunes and induce the conference in the ardour of electoral propaganda and the wooing of the petty bourgeoisie to carry the most rigorous sounding measures against the Communist working-class fighters. If he were returned to power as a result of the election, he would be in a new and stronger position to face his attackers on either side . . . And if he were returned in Opposition he would be in a still stronger situation. He could then hide the barrenness and sterility of his Government under the glorious tale of what they ' would have ' done. He could become again the leader against capitalism, and restore his tarnished working-class reputation by the heroics of Opposition. And at the same time (while secretly thankful for the relief from a situation he was unable to face), he could turn the deadly finger of responsibility upon his Communist enemies for the wreck of the first Labour Government."

That is precisely what happened. I can recollect no conference so frenziedly at the feet of one man as was the
Labour Party conference in those early days of October
1924 at the feet of Mr. MacDonald. The atmosphere in
the Queen's Hall was so hectic that it resembled more an
American Presidential nomination convention. No need for
the Prime Minister to stand on the defensive; after those
cheers the Government's record could be disposed of with
a wave of the hand (" some of our work had to be frankly
patchwork "). He proceeded to stress that " Communism
. . . has nothing practical in common with us. It is a product of Tsarism and war mentality." The Executive proposed that no Communist should be eligible as a Labour
candidate, though it was noteworthy that the previous
year's decision on the admissibility of Communists as union
delegates was upheld, the Executive stating that " their
energy and enthusiasm are undoubted." In the debate
Mr. Frank Hodges once again functioned as the Executive
spokesman. " Why do the Communists not go out into the
wilderness ? " he asked in a speech that Harry Pollitt
described as the " first open step towards splitting the
Labour movement of this country." Mr. Hodges was supported by none other than Mr. George Spencer, of Notts,
so soon to win notoriety as the founder of the " non-
political " company union in that coalfield. Mr. Spencer
considered that " if there was one outstanding fact in the
world's history it was that nothing substantial had ever been
accomplished by revolution." Mr. Spencer's reading of
history had obviously been desultory.

Three aspects of the Communist issue were presented to
the conference for decision, and the differences in the voting
were notable. The affiliation of the Party was heavily
rejected, by 3,185,000 votes to 193,000. On Communist
candidatures the minority leapt up to 654,000, the majority
falling to 2,456,000. The banning of Communists from
individual membership was only narrowly carried, by
1,804,000 votes to 1,540,000.

One other intervention was made in the debate on the

Executive's behalf. It came from Mr. Herbert Morrison, whom we have already met as a critic of the Executive on the question of Party democracy, and who was in later years to play a leading part as a Communist-hunter. His conclusion was that the Communist Party " has no right to come into the Labour Party . . . for the purpose of putting sand into the machine." Alas, poor Herbert ! Sand was to be put into the machine only too devastatingly, and within a few days of his utterance of those words. The wrecker, however, did not sport the five-pointed star of Communism, though he might have been seen in gold-laced levée dress. He was none other than the conference's ovationed idol, Labour's first Prime Minister.

Recalled in cold blood it seems still an incredible thing. Here was the Executive declaring in advance that the election " will be the most momentous in the history of the Party." Here was Mr. MacDonald sounding a clarion call to the wildly cheering delegates for the Party " to take the field, not to defend itself but to attack its enemies." " Back to your constituencies," he cried in his closing words, for the " greatest fight "—" work, work, work for a majority." And they did fight (with their Communist comrades shoulder to shoulder with them in the front line, incidentally) . . . pushing the Labour vote up to nearly 5,500,000 as against 4,400,000 in 1923, in face of the most ferocious anti-Labour election scare in history. For that scare, the notorious " Zinoviev Letter," main responsibility rested on the shoulders of Mr. MacDonald.

Now that crude and clumsy forgery, purporting to be instructions from the Communist International to the British Communist Party, might in any case have been launched as a scare by the Tory Press, who knew all about it. But such a partisan stunt, however it were put over, would not have had one-tenth the effect that was secured through its official launching by the Foreign Office, the department of State at whose head the Prime Minister himself stood. True, the Note of " protest " to the Soviet Government was signed " in the absence of the Secretary of

DT

State " by a permanent official, Mr. J. D. Gregory, head of the Northern Department—a gentleman whose later resignation from the Foreign Office as a result of the franc speculation episode may be recalled. Mr. MacDonald could have issued an immediate repudiation, exposed the whole affair, taken action against those responsible. Instead he tacitly endorsed the business by preserving a mysterious and unbreakable silence that flung shattering confusion into the Labour ranks and was exploited up to the hilt by the Tories.

Despite its increased vote the Labour Party lost 42 seats. The Liberals were annihilated, losing 119 out of 158 seats. The Tories gained 152. Mr. MacDonald, and no one else, had put in office a Tory Government with an oppressively swollen majority. It was of no consequence that the Executive of the Parliamentary Labour Party later went on record proclaiming the Zinoviev Letter a forgery; for no steps against Mr. MacDonald were proposed. Many thought, and said, that the whole affair, from Mr. MacDonald's angle, was a matter of pathology rather than politics, due to his anti-Communist hysteria. Subjectively, perhaps; but objectively it accorded singularly well with Mr. MacDonald's desire to insure himself against the risks and responsibilities of continued power by making certain his defeat and return to Opposition.

After the débâcle voices of criticism, hitherto held in check, were heard on all sides. " The chief fault of the Ministry," wrote the *Daily Herald*, " was a tendency to be more official than the politicians of the old Parties, and an anxiety on the part of a good many to prove that a Labour Government was no different from any other. That was certainly a mistake." For the I.L.P. the *New Leader* castigated " a record which we disavow," averring that " it was no part of our strategy for winning power to court the confidence of the middle class by seeming to be as sound imperialists as Liberals and Tories are "; while the chairman of that Party sadly reflected that " we " had revealed " a capitalist attitude to power and freedom." Ex-Cabinet

Minister John Wheatley bluntly declared that "a timid 'statesmanlike' attitude makes no appeal to a people struggling to emancipate itself from poverty."

Yet in spite of these signs that a lesson had been learned one thing was missing. There was no apparent realisation that without challenging and changing the leadership of Mr. MacDonald and the Elder Statesmen the prime cause of these errors remained in effective operation. Britain was entering on a critical period with a Government of open reaction firmly in the saddle. And Labour retained as its leader one who, after all he had done and not done as Premier, could say nothing more than that " as an Opposition they would give the State, the people, and the Commonwealth their fullest service. They would serve the nation in Opposition as they served it as a Government. . . . It will still be a fight of gentlemen."

CHAPTER V

RED FRIDAY

AFTER THE FALL OF THE LABOUR GOVERNMENT the opposing tendencies in the movement grew more marked and diverged more sharply. Throughout the ranks there was a lively ferment, finding particular expression in the increasingly Leftward trend in the trade unions, and reflected on the General Council of the T.U.C. itself. At headquarters, however, Emperor MacDonald and his Marshals, still firmly in the saddle, continued to move to the Right. Already, before the Government's fall, and in anticipation of the Labour Party Executive's attack on them at the 1924 conference, the Communist Party had warned that the real issue between them and the Mac-Donaldites was " not the issue of the rôle of violence in the struggle for Socialism, nor the question of dictatorship or democracy," but whether the leadership should be allowed " to continue its present policy of adaptation to capitalism." The movement, claimed the Communists, faced the alternatives of " a new Liberal Party—or a more vigorous Workers' Party."

These developments naturally did not take place in a vacuum. Their background was the prolonged depression and decline in British industry, exemplified in the renewed crisis in coal that followed the temporary fillip resulting from the Ruhr occupation. Official alarm about the state of the coal industry was to reach the point of declaring, in 1925, that the industry was " heading for irretrievable disaster." The miners realised that conflict was certain when the temporary agreement terminated in the summer of the year, and the secretary of their Federation, Mr. A. J.

Cook, was actively campaigning throughout the coalfields urging the need to prepare for resistance. In January 1925 the Miners' Federation took up a suggestion—originally broached by the Amalgamated Engineering Union in the summer of 1924, though without immediate result—for the establishment of an Industrial Alliance. It was proposed that the Miners, Engineers, Railwaymen, and Transport Workers should confer on this project. Developments were slow, and the initial conference did not take place till June 4th. The July crisis intervened before the plan had advanced beyond the stage of preliminary discussion and draft.

This urge for unity found its most dramatic expression in the international sphere. The sentiments voiced at the Hull T.U.C. were further developed by the fraternal delegation from the General Council which in November–December 1924 visited the Soviet Union. A double purpose was fulfilled by the delegation. It attended the sixth All-Russian Trade Union Congress and also made elaborate tours of investigation with a view to preparing a detailed report. The delegation, whose chairman and secretary were the late A. A. Purcell and Fred Bramley (the T.U.C. Secretary), had the opportunity of discussing the whole question of international trade union unity with the Soviet trade unionists. Means of achieving joint action by the British and Soviet movements to this end were canvassed; and in a letter dated November 17th, at Moscow, signed on behalf of the delegation by Mr. Bramley, these aims were agreed by the British representatives: " (1) To request the Amsterdam International to agree to a free and unconditional immediate conference with representatives of the Russian trade union movement. (2) To secure for the Presidium of the Russian movement and the General Council of the British Trades Union Congress, full power to act jointly for the purpose of promoting international unity." On the delegation's return to London the General Council, meeting on December 29th, unanimously endorsed their attitude and the declaration quoted.

It is beyond question that the General Council did not at all suspect how its well-meant and justly motivated efforts to rally the scattered forces of international Labour would at once cause the heathen to rage furiously together. Yet the first telegrams reporting the actions of its delegation in Moscow touched off an amazing explosion of spleen, calumny and misrepresentation of every kind in which the organs of continental Social-Democracy unhappily vied with those of the British governing class. Few propaganda campaigns in recent history have been more sustained or more relentless than the remarkable barrage that was directed unceasingly at the heads of the General Council during the whole period of its sponsoring of the cause of international unity. The Press front here was unbroken, from the *Manchester Guardian's* warnings against " dangerous policy " to the *Daily Telegraph's* amiable references to an " almost incredible record of treasonable mischief." *Vorwärts*, famed central organ of German Social-Democracy (where is that paper now ?) throughout inspired and led the campaign in the European Labour movement against unity and the General Council.

When the British delegation's notable Report on Russia was eventually issued, at the end of February 1925, it was the victim of a similar unscrupulous Press campaign. The Report said that " in Russia the workers are the ruling class." This was held to show " excess of faith and credulity," according to *Robotnik*, Poland's leading Social-Democratic daily ; in almost identical language castigated by the *Daily Mail* as " infantile credulity." " Providing splendid arguments for the counter-revolution " fulminated Friedrich Adler, secretary of the Labour and Socialist International.

In this atmosphere of constant sniping, alike from foes and from those who might have been thought friends, the General Council continued its drive for international unity. It sought to get the International Federation of Trade Unions and the Russian unions together in an unconditional conference, where the many outstanding points of difference could be thrashed out as a first step to the establishment of all-embracing international trade union unity. The I.F.T.U., on the other hand, refused to meet the Russians unless the latter first agreed to affiliate with them on the basis of their existing constitution, which embodied precisely those points of difference upon which discussion was required. At bottom Amsterdam's line was strongly partisan. Its leaders were blinded by hatred of Communism. They would accept the Russians on terms which they hoped would make the Russian unions a lever against Communism in the Soviet Union. They also hopefully anticipated the collapse of the Red International of Labour Unions from the withdrawal of its strongest section. Against any suggestion of an Amsterdam-Moscow *rapprochement* on a world scale they set their faces.

Amsterdam certainly stuck to its guns with a determination worthy of a better cause. The first full-dress discussion took place at the I.F.T.U. General Council meeting on February 5th–7th, 1925; but a powerful speech by Fred Bramley, on behalf of the British delegation, left the majority unmoved. No affiliation, no conference, they repeated. Mr. Bramley, who said plainly that he himself was no Left-winger, urged the Council to set aside prejudice. "We believe," he said, "that the inclusion of Russia would enlarge the influence of our international trade union movement. We believe that the inclusion of Russia in our international movement would strengthen the economic and political position of the working class throughout the world. We believe that the inclusion of Russia in the international movement would also assist towards the establishment of world peace." A blunt Englishman's blunt plea; but it fell on deaf ears. The speaker had put his finger on the spot when he observed bitingly that:

"It appears to me you can discuss any other subject under the sun without getting into that panicky state of trembling fear and excitement and almost savage ferocity which you get into when you are discussing Russian affairs. . . . You can discuss calmly and without excitement the operations of the Fascisti in Italy; you can discuss with great calm the suppression of trade union organisations in other countries; you can discuss the activities of capitalist Governments, and their destruction of the trade union movement in one country after another without this unnecessary epidemic of excitement; but when you begin to discusss Russia, you begin to suffer from some malignant disease. . . . get rid of the panicky fear that seems to invade and dominate your minds in dealing with Russia."[1]

It is interesting to notice how the leading figures among the majority which voted down the British plea for unity in 1925 have since been converted. For one of them was Léon Jouhaux, now leader of the reunited French trade union movement and prominent supporter of the Communist-Socialist united front which is the Blum Government's sheet anchor; the other was Francisco Largo Caballero, to become, eleven years later, Premier of that Government, including Communist and Socialist ministers, which united the whole Spanish people in arms against the Fascist mercenary barbarians. It is our British leaders who have retrogressed while their one-time opponents have moved forward.

Substantially Amsterdam never altered its position. At different meetings there were different formulæ. But when a further full-dress debate took place, at the I.F.T.U. Council meeting in Amsterdam in December 1925, the resolution adopted marked no essential change. Meantime, in April, the British General Council had conferred with the Russians and an Anglo-Russian Joint Advisory Council was finally set up. The key point of these proceedings was to be found in clause (3) subsection (b) of the statement submitted by the General Council, in which the Russians

[1] This speech was published in full at the time, in pamphlet form, under the title *Relations with Russia*.

concurred. Here it was proposed that, in the event of the I.F.T.U. persisting in its refusal to convene an unconditional conference with the Russians " the British Trades Union Congress General Council will undertake to convene a conference, and endeavour to promote international unity by using its mediatory influence as between the Russian trade union movement and the Amsterdam Bureau." This proposal, as part of the whole international line of the General Council, received the unanimous and enthusiastic endorsement of the Scarborough T.U.C. When the Anglo-Russian Council met in Berlin in December, after the further failure to persuade Amsterdam to relent, it was agreed that the implementing of this clause was " one of the first practical steps to be taken " and that the Council should meet again early in 1926.

Yet the clause was not implemented, and the Anglo-Russian Council did not meet as prescribed. Perhaps the incessant stream of propaganda had had its effect on the more orthodox members of the General Council. They had heard from *The Times* that their actions " may cause irreparable injury to the trade unionism of the Continent, which, though with difficulty, is maintaining a bulwark against the westward spread of Communism among the workers." Lord Birkenhead had told them that their deeds were " gravely mutinous " (and Galloper Smith was surely an authority on mutiny). The *Daily Telegraph* had declared their efforts to be a " matter of national humiliation." " Perhaps bourgeois, but certainly apt," purred *Vorwärts* of a *Times* leader praising the " sound sense " of Amsterdam and denouncing the " fatal error " of the British General Council. And when *Vorwärts* attacked the Berlin meeting of the Anglo-Russian Council as " a two-faced game " the hostile comment was welcomed in Printing House Square and approvingly reproduced. At the same time the forces on the General Council itself making for caution had been strengthened at the 1925 annual election; the untimely death of Mr. Bramley shortly after the Scarborough T.U.C. removed the most influential personality in the fight for unity; and the group of General Council members generally regarded as the Left, whose outstanding representatives were the late A. A. Purcell and Mr. George Hicks, did not seem able to force the pace.

The unmeasured hostility of the Press campaign was enough to show that the international unity movement represented an emphatic Leftward trend. Of the tendencies in the Labour Party during this period the same can hardly be said. There certainly was disillusionment and discontent with the MacDonaldite line; but with many there appeared to be greater eagerness to dissociate themselves from the Communists than to prosecute any determined course against Mr. MacDonald and the Elder Statesmen. Indeed it is scarcely unfair to say that most of those who offered themselves as the spokesmen of the Socialist standpoint against the New Liberalism of Mr. MacDonald condemned themselves to impotence vis-à-vis the Right wing through their fear of seeming to be too far to the Left. There were many voices of opposition and semi-opposition but no united opposition force. The beloved figure of George Lansbury, whose prestige in the movement was then at its height, formed a gathering-point for one group. He started *Lansbury's Labour Weekly* in the spring of 1925 and the paper did valuable general propaganda, stressing the need for unity in action. But an attempt on the part of the Lansbury group to launch a new Socialist programme came to nothing; and the MacDonaldite régime remained unperturbed. Another focal point was provided by the *Sunday Worker*, a Left-wing Sunday newspaper in whose editorial direction Communists participated and whose popularity was such that at the Liverpool Conference of the Labour Party in 1925 a resolution supporting it succeeded in winning 1,143,000 votes against the majority's 2,036,000. This was the highest " rebel " vote recorded at that conference.

By far the largest and most weighty Socialist body, however, was the Independent Labour Party, then in its heyday so far as membership, resources and influence went. Its branches were soon to number more than 1,000 and it counted within its ranks an impressive array of the leading figures both in the trade union and the political movements. The majority of Labour M.P.s, for instance, were members of the I.L.P. Yet it was to this influential organisation that the strictures suggested in the preceding paragraph most particularly applied. Instead of light and leading the I.L.P. only contributed coruscations and confusion, redounding to the advantage of the MacDonaldites. Regarding itself as the " Brain Trust " of the Labour Party, the I.L.P. romped about in a maze of Commissions, Inquiries, Reports and projects of every kind, which all proved still-born—as Mr. John Paton, later general secretary of the Party, has admitted—testimony to the Party's lack of any firm theoretical foundation. The crowning achievement was the Living Wage (or Living Income) policy which formed the starting-point and centre of a campaign to which was given the label " Socialism in our Time." First acclaimed at the 1925 annual conference of the I.L.P., and adopted in its final form the following year, this policy in practice proved itself to be a mass of contradictions.

Briefly, the policy proclaimed the need for a " direct attack on poverty " and proposed that the Labour movement should first make inquiry to determine what constituted a living income (originally it was suggested that this inquiry should be undertaken by the Government). Demand for the standard so set should form the key of Labour policy. But while the demand for a living wage was sometimes presented as equivalent to a demand for Socialism, at other times it appeared as a " policy of directly increasing the purchasing power of the workers as a means of turning the wheels of home industry and bringing an immediate wave of prosperity to the country, in which even the capitalists would have their share," to quote the *New Leader*. The implication that the policy was as much related to capitalist reorganisation as it was to Socialist transformation was heightened by the uncritical extolling of the " high wages " policy of American capitalism (to the great wonderment of thoughtful Americans) and by the advocacy of family allowances, that well-known device to restrain individual wages. " Ford *versus* Marx " was an alternative seriously posed in the I.L.P. in those days, though history in Ford's own country was so soon to come down with such merciless emphasis on Marx's side.

With such a policy as the central feature of its outlook the I.L.P. as a leading Party naturally remained outside the general current of working-class struggle, the activity of its individual members notwithstanding. That was the inevitable accompaniment of a policy based abstractly, in Utopian fashion, on what the workers *ought* to demand (the hereafter-to-be-promulgated living wage) instead of concretely on what the workers were *actually* demanding. It led to dissociation from policies that were really progressive, really responding to the workers' needs, and therefore in fact to association with reactionary policies. Take the vital issue of that time, trade union unity. When *Lansbury's Labour Weekly* in March 1925 featured a bold appeal for national and international unity (" trade union disunity is working-class suicide ") the *New Leader* criticised the appeal, urging instead that the Government should set up a commission to determine a living wage. The *New Leader* had earlier echoed the attacks on the General Council's delegation to Russia, remarking that the delegation was " certainly creating incredible mischief on the Continent."

The historian may fairly say that the I.L.P. in this critical period was the principal means of canalising the wide discontent with MacDonaldism. It provided people with the opportunity to blow off steam while in fact it came down on Mr. MacDonald's side. When the I.L.P. members of Parliament met after the election of 1924 there was a widespread spontaneous feeling that they should retract their support of Mr. MacDonald, and Mr. Lansbury's name was being canvassed as an alternative leader. The question, however, was left open and a " don't-hit-a-man-when-he's-down " speech from Mr. Smillie sufficed to maintain the *status quo*. At the 1925 I.L.P. conference there were criticisms of Mr. MacDonald's leadership of the late Government. A trenchant speech by Mr. Campbell Stephen reduced Mr. MacDonald to livid rage and whispered imprecations; but he need not have worried; the conference passed by a two-thirds majority a resolution endorsing the actions of the Labour Government and including Mr. MacDonald in the I.L.P. delegation to the Labour Party. The same contrast between words and deeds emerged at the Liverpool Conference of the Labour Party, when the Elder Statesmen introduced the resolutions comprising their Liberalised programme. In the *New Leader* Mr. Brailsford had declared editorially that " no process of amendment will ever make this a good programme. It will not inspire the Socialist thinker, nor will it fire the enthusiasm of the simple worker and his wife." But at the conference the I.L.P. delegation actually seconded most of the resolutions, brought forward no major criticisms at all, and in the case of the foreign policy resolution its speaker expressed pride in the fact that Mr. MacDonald was an I.L.P. member.

The conflicting tendencies that have now been described were in a sense overshadowed when the long-threatened coal crisis matured in the summer of 1925. On June 30th the coalowners gave notice to terminate the existing agreement, proposing drastic wage reductions, the abolition of the principle of a minimum wage, and reversion from national to district agreements. These proposals the miners refused to entertain, and placed their case before the General Council of the T.U.C. at a joint meeting on July 10th. That body announced that " they completely endorse the refusal of the Miners' Federation to meet the owners until the proposals have been withdrawn," and further " passed a resolution recording their complete support of the miners, and undertook to co-operate wholeheartedly with them in their resistance to the degradation of the standard of life of their members." A special committee was set up to keep in constant touch with developments.

What was at stake was much more than the future of the coal industry. The issue was plainly stated in an interview between Mr. Baldwin and the miners' representatives on the morning of July 30th, the day before the owners' notices were due to expire. The Prime Minister urged the miners to make a contribution towards " meeting the difficult situation with which the industry is confronted." There ensued this dialogue:

> *Miners:* " But what you propose means a reduction of wages."
>
> *Prime Minister:* " Yes. All the workers in this country have got to face a reduction of wages."
>
> *Miners:* " What do you mean ? "
>
> *Prime Minister:* " I mean all the workers of this country have got to take reductions in wages to help put industry on its feet."[1]

The Government had recently completed the return to the Gold Standard as the central feature of its effort to re-establish the world position of British capitalism. That meant an increased return to the holders of valuable paper; it also meant an increase in the burden of State debt (which now stood to be repaid at 20s. in the £1), and was bound to connote a lower price *and* wage level. In addition the policy of European stabilisation, achieved through the Dawes Plan, had increased foreign competition, especially that of Germany, where extensive rationalisation of industry was being carried through on the double basis of Anglo-American capital investment and the slashing of the German workers' standards (abolition of the eight-hour day and heavy wage reductions). Capital accumulation in Britain was dwindling at a dangerously rapid rate; and, in short, the governing class had to envisage battle along the whole industrial front as the price of its continued rule.

But on the very morning that Mr. Baldwin flung down

[1] *Daily Herald,* July 31st, 1925.

the gauntlet, matters had come to a head on the workers' side. During the previous week the Miners' Federation had had an opportunity to lay their case before the movement at a special Trades Union Congress on unemployment. Presenting a reasoned review of the whole position in the coal industry they concluded by expressing the conviction that assistance for them in their fight "will be readily forthcoming and on this occasion, if a lock-out matures, it will not be left to a section to fight alone, but the struggle will be taken up, and the issue joined, by the whole trade union movement."

They were not mistaken. The Special Committee of the General Council met the Executives of the railway and transport unions and received "very cordial support and the united desire to assist" in operating an embargo on coal transport in the event of a miners' lock-out. Plans were finally drafted by Wednesday, July 29th, and ratified by the Special Committee the following morning, when it met the unions concerned again. At the moment of its utterance the Prime Minister's challenge was bluntly taken up in the "Official Instructions to all Railway and Transport Workers, as agreed unanimously" by their unions "and approved by the General Council of the Trades Union Congress." These were marching orders given by a General Staff to its army:

" Wagons containing coal must not be attached to any train after midnight on Friday, July 31st, and after this time wagons of coal must not be supplied to any industrial or commercial concerns. . . . *Coal Exports*: all tippers and trimmers will cease work at the end of the second shift on July 31st. *Coal Imports*: on no account may import coal be handled from July 31st. . . . All men engaged in delivering coal to commercial and industrial concerns will cease Friday night, July 31st."

These instructions were signed by Mr. George Hicks, as chairman of the Sub-Committee which had drafted them, by the secretaries and presidents of the unions involved, and were counter-signed by Executive members of the unions and by the Special Committee of the General Council. " Unanimous and enthusiastic approval " was accorded them by a special conference of Trade Union Executives which assembled at 3 o'clock on the afternoon of the 30th.

Immediately the Government, which had been absolutely intransigent right up to that moment, was flung into confusion. A special Cabinet meeting was summoned, there were further conversations between the Prime Minister and the representatives of both coalowners and miners; finally, in the early hours of Friday, July 31st, it was announced that the Government would grant a subsidy to the coal industry for nine months to enable a Royal Commission to make a detailed inquiry. The previous Wednesday Mr. Baldwin had stated categorically " that the Government would not grant any subsidy to the industry." Notices were accordingly withdrawn by the owners, and the *Daily Herald*, inspired, put out a bill with two bold words only—RED FRIDAY !

I am sure that those who remember those days will agree that their first reaction was one almost of incredulity. The news seemed too good to be true. As its significance was grasped a mood of real exaltation seized hold of the movement. A circular letter despatched that day to affiliated unions from the General Council, and signed by Chairman A. B. Swales and Assistant Secretary W. M. Citrine (as he then was), spoke truly of the " immense stimulus to every trade unionist," adding that " the manifestation of solidarity which has been exhibited by all sections of the trade union movement is a striking portent for the future and marks an epoch in the history of the movement." At the same time the letter added a warning that " the trade union movement must be alert and vigilant in case the necessity should again arise for it to act in defence of its standards."

It was clear enough that Red Friday was not in any definitive sense a working-class victory, though it " was

regarded by the capitalist Press as a humiliating defeat of
the Government by the organised workers." The diehard
Home Secretary might ask querulously " is England to be
governed by the Cabinet or by a handful of trade union
leaders ? " and be joined by Mr. MacDonald, who complained to the I.L.P. Summer School at Easton Lodge on
August 3rd that " the Government has simply handed over
the appearance, at any rate, of victory to the very forces
that sane, well-considered, thoroughly well-examined
Socialism feels to be probably its greatest enemy." Mr.
A. J. Cook put the whole thing in a nutshell when he said
—" this is the first round. Let us prepare for the final
struggle." And the General Council, preparing its Report
for the Trades Union Congress within a few days of the
crisis, inserted this significant statement :

> " The Special Committee, while gratified at the
> splendid response of the trade union movement to the
> call for assistance, could not escape the feeling that a
> further attempt might be made to enforce wages reduc-
> tions or a lengthening in hours. It felt that its task had
> not been completed, and with the consent of the General
> Council proposed to remain in being, and to apply
> itself to the task of devising ways and means of consolidat-
> ing the resistance of the trade union movement should
> the attack be renewed."

On the Left this warning note was sounded even more
sharply. In its first issue after Red Friday the Communist
Workers' Weekly wrote editorially :

> " What has been achieved is the imposition on the
> capitalist class of an unstable truce, which cannot lead
> to industrial peace but only to renewed class conflict.
> Behind this truce and the industrial peace talk which
> will accompany it, the capitalist class will prepare for a
> crushing attack upon the workers. If the workers are
> doped by the peace talk and do not make effective
> counter-preparations then they are doomed to shattering

defeat. . . . The Government is certain to prepare for a new struggle with the working class under more favourable conditions than this time."

Presiding over a national conference of the Minority Movement at the end of August, Tom Mann asked, " are we prepared to meet the opposing forces when the next round begins ? . . . The miners will require a much more highly disciplined regimentation of the organised forces of the workers when the next battle begins. For this we ought to really prepare, and that without delay."

The justification of these forebodings was cynically provided from the Government side by Mr. Winston Churchill, Chancellor of the Exchequer, in a speech on December 10th. Referring to Red Friday he said that the Government were " impressed with the fact that the country as a whole was not sufficiently informed about the character and immense consequences of such a struggle as that with which it was confronted . . . We therefore decided to postpone the crisis in the hope of averting it, *or, if not of averting it, of coping effectually with it when the time comes* " (my italics).

Meantime a volunteer strike-breaking organisation was set up, at the end of September. This was the Organisation for the Maintenance of Supplies (O.M.S.), directed by personages of impressive standing—ex-Viceroy Lord Hardinge, Lord Jellicoe, General Sir Francis Lloyd, Sir Lynden Macassey, etc. The Home Secretary stated that this body had only been formed after consultation with the Government. He officially welcomed it as an auxiliary to the Government's own plans (" which have long since been made "), telling the public that they " would be performing a patriotic act " by joining it. In addition to acting thus as a semi-official registry office for the mass enrolment of would-be strikebreakers the O.M.S. unostentatiously undertook the technical training of blackleg " shock troops." Big industrialists loaned their private works railways and testing grounds for use, at week-ends and secretly, for the training of locomotive and lorry drivers; and similar arrangements were made for the instruction of volunteers in telephone and telegraph operation.[1] The President and Vice-President of the then existing British Fascist organisation withdrew from it on the grounds that " at the present moment effective assistance to the State can best be given in seconding the efforts of the O.M.S."

During the same period the Government proceeded rapidly with the perfecting of the official war machine. The country was arranged in ten divisions, each under a Minister as Civil Commissioner. A staff of civil servants was appointed for each division, to handle all problems of transport, food, postal services and coal, with a corresponding staff in each local area, where also there was to be " a Chairman selected by the Government to convene and preside over a volunteer service committee for the recruitment of volunteers to assist in maintaining essential national services." These officials were to be armed with the plenary powers conferred on the Government by the Emergency Powers Act; and the authority of the Commissioners was emphasised in the ruling that they would be authorised " to give decisions on behalf of the Government." In this way the Government established from above a system of emergency administration that reliably expressed the will of the central power while enjoying the virtue of decentralisation.

By November the main outlines of the work had been completed, the staff appointments made, and in Circular 636, dated the 20th of that month, the Ministry of Health notified all local authorities of the general nature of the scheme. In succeeding months the finishing touches were put to the arrangements. Divisional conferences in December 1925 and January 1926 went into questions such as the safe conduct of transport, elaborating routes, stressing the need for mobile squads of police to be held ready for instant duty in threatened areas. Further conferences in March overhauled the whole scheme, improving remaining details. All officials concerned were warned to be ready for a final conference on April 27th–28th. By that time it was

[1] Professor W. H. Crook: *The General Strike*, pp. 300–1.

the eve of the crisis; and, although the General Strike had not yet been decided, the Commissioners and their divisional officers were at their headquarters; it was zero hour and everything was ready. The prearranged signal was to be a one-word telegram from Whitehall—" Action." On the night of May 2nd–3rd that telegram was despatched and the machine set in motion.

This cool and calculating preparation by the Government had absolutely no parallel on the side of the Labour movement. The " preparedness " watchword that had been so candidly proclaimed by the leadership immediately after Red Friday proved entirely evanescent. Instead there gained currency what the learned American historian of the General Strike, Professor Wilfrid H. Crook, has called a " studied attitude of unpreparedness," which " had results upon the Labour forces in the actual struggle that were nothing short of disastrous. Even if the experience of the long organisation by the Belgian Labour Party for its general strike in 1913 had not been utilised by the British leaders, common sense should have dictated some modicum of preparation."

That this was not due to any deterioration in the fighting temper of the mass of organised workers, not due to any lack of the will to prepare, was sufficiently shown by the Trades Union Congress at Scarborough. Throughout the Congress debates, the note of militancy, high-pitched and confident, was struck more incisively than ever before; and it met with a resounding response. In his presidential address Mr. A. B. Swales (Engineers) took a strong forward line, and received an ovation. " A militant and progressive policy, consistently and steadily pursued," he averred, " is the only policy that will unify, consolidate and inspire our rank and file." Remarking that " union policy henceforth will be to recover lost ground," he urged that this " renders necessary a greater degree of trade union unity " and that the General Council should be established as " the central controlling and directing body of the British trade union movement " by giving it " full powers to create the necessary machinery to combat every movement by our opponents." " We are entering upon a new phase of development in the upward struggle of our class. All around are signs of an awakening consciousness in the peoples of all countries that the present system of society is condemned."

In this spirit the Congress approached its agenda. By large majorities resolutions were passed declaring that the aim of trade unions must be to struggle " in conjunction with the Party of the workers . . . for the overthrow of capitalism," and pledging Congress " to do all in its power to develop and strengthen workshop organisation "; the General Council's campaign for international trade union unity was unanimously endorsed, as has already been noted; the Dawes Plan was condemned, Harry Pollitt criticising amid cheers the part played by Mr. MacDonald in its enactment; withdrawal of British troops from China was demanded and the General Council instructed to get in touch with the working-class organisations in that country; " complete opposition " to imperialism was expressed, and it was resolved " (1) to support the workers in all parts of the British Empire to organise trade unions and political parties . . . (2) to support the right of all peoples in the British Empire to self-determination, including the right to choose complete separation from the Empire." Opposing this last resolution, Mr. J. H. Thomas asked the Congress not to make itself " ridiculous "; he was over-ruled by 3,082,000 votes to 79,000.

The demonstrative import of the Scarborough Congress was unmistakable. Yet when the cheering had subsided there were to be observed certain facts of a more negative character from the standpoint of preparedness to meet the ending of the nine months' truce. British trade unionism and its leaders had not been magically transformed overnight. Smashing majorities were recorded for resolutions involving no immediate action; on resolutions containing a pledge or an instruction to take specified action majorities dropped at once. A resolution proposing the reaffiliation of the Trades Councils to the T.U.C., thereby reversing the

famous intrigue-induced decision of 1895,[1] was ruled out
of order. On the key issue of the General Council's powers
Congress virtually abdicated by referring the proposals to
the incoming Council itself " to examine the problem in
all its bearings . . . and to report to a Special Conference of
Trade Union Executives." And there was a most significant
alteration in the balance of forces on that incoming
Council, to the disadvantage of the Left. Mr. J. H. Thomas
returned as one of the railwaymen's representatives, after
two years' absence, and Mr. Ernest Bevin was elected to the
Council for the first time.

Scarborough represented the highest expression of the
Leftward move in the trade unions. A month later it was
followed by the Liverpool Conference of the Labour Party,
representing equally the highest expression of the Right-
ward move of Mr. MacDonald and the Elder Statesmen.
Liverpool, in brief, served as an effective counter-demon-
stration to Scarborough. Just as Chairman Swales had set
the militant note that the T.U.C. followed, so Chairman
C. T. Cramp (Railwaymen) set the New Liberal note that
the Labour Party Conference was to follow. Mr. Cramp's
address was detailed and closely argued, not the customary
review of affairs but a considered statement of principle.
" We transcend the conflict of classes," he said, " we ask for
the co-operation of all classes." Making the surprising declaration that the British Labour movement had " always
insisted upon the obligation of Germany to pay reparations," he praised the Dawes Plan and " stabilisation."
Sharply differentiating the Labour Party from revolutionary conceptions, Mr. Cramp struck at the " barren and
destructive policies " of the " tiny minority " of Communists and men of the Left. It was very evident that when
he said " influences have been at work in our movement
which have confused and divided our people " he was not
referring to Mr. MacDonald's equivocal attitude over the
Zinoviev Letter during the 1924 election.

[1] For the expulsion of the Trades Councils in 1895 see the Webbs'
History of Trade Unionism (1920 edition), pp. 562-3.

Three questions dominated at Liverpool—the Communists, the new programme, and the next Labour Government. The Executive recommendations for completing the exclusion of the Communists were that no member of the Communist Party should be eligible as an individual member or be entitled to remain a member, and further that trade unions should appeal to their members to refrain from electing known Communists as their delegates to the Labour Party. Reference back of the first recommendation was lost by 321,000 votes to 2,870,000. Mr. MacDonald employed a quotation from Lenin to imply that Communists set themselves to provoke " heavy civil war " (the quotation in its context plainly says that in the Communist view the working class needs to be ready to face heavy civil war at the hands of the ruling class if its rule is challenged) and was seconded by Mr. Ernest Bevin, who offered no evidence in support of a rhetorical claim that he had endured " crucifixion " in his union at the hands of the Communists when he was bringing about the transport workers' amalgamation in 1921. By a slightly smaller majority the reference back of the second recommendation was also lost (480,000 votes to 2,692,000), though union leaders like Mr. John Bromley accurately predicted that it would lead to a heresy-hunt in the union ranks.

Having thus disposed of the Communists the conference turned to discuss the proposed programme, consisting of a series of resolutions on specific aspects (unemployment, Empire, housing, etc.), prefaced by a general resolution entitled " The Labour Party and the Nation." The title marked the change from 1918. In place of a " new social order " there now appeared what was described as " a co-ordinated policy of National Reconstruction and Reform which seeks, by Parliamentary means and in progressive stages . . . to develop the material and mental resources of the nation." These sentiments inspired the individual resolutions, which shelved the traditional demands for nationalisation; and it was the local Labour Parties that fought, in amendment after amendment, for the reiteration of the old faith. Delegate George Simpson of Wallasey wondered why " they now seemed to be afraid to apply what had been said as a means of remedying their social and economic ills." Delegate Hines of Springburn, unemployed for five years, was scarcely impressed with the proposal that a National Employment and Development Board should be set up " to inquire into the nature of and remedies for unemployment." But every amendment was overwhelmed.

Even more remarkable than this watered-down programme was the attitude Mr. MacDonald adopted to it. It was not really a programme at all, he explained to the conference. It just told the nation the Labour Party's " frame of mind." (" Socialism," he added, " is the idea of the political State acting more and more in co-operation with the industrial State "; an interesting definition, apart from its muddle-headedness, since it makes every modern capitalist politician from Mr. Lloyd George via Mr. Baldwin to Sir Oswald Mosley a Socialist.) In fact its " supreme achievement " would be if it could " convince the nation " that men who believed in it " would never require to be asked what their programme was." Mr. J. H. Thomas intervened to make Mr. MacDonald's meaning unmistakable. He explained that the whole idea of a programme was superfluous. If there were a programme, leaders might find themselves " hampered " by it, and unable therefore to " adapt themselves to the circumstances of the moment." " They asked the delegates to trust them," cried Mr. Thomas, " that was the essence of the resolution." He added that " it was not the Press or the capitalists that defeated them twelve months ago; it was because their own people preferred to listen to others rather than to trust their own leaders "—a remarkable statement whose rich savour will be better appreciated if the reader will turn back to page 97 and refresh his memory on certain facts of the 1924 election.

The whole programme, in short, was a gigantic confidence trick, showing the men of 1931 already well in their stride. It was for this that the militants were excluded, that local Labour organisations were to be disaffiliated, that the Party's Chief Whip, Mr. Ben Spoor, was publicly to advocate a Liberal-Labour alliance. And a suggestive further angle was forthcoming from Mr. MacDonald in the conference debate on the next Labour Government. Mr. Ernest Bevin moved that, in view of the experience of 1924 the Party should not again accept office in a minority. To which Mr. MacDonald, reversing his declarations of two years before, retorted that " he was far more frightened to go in with a majority that had not the team spirit than he was with a minority, because if everybody in the team was going to develop conscientious scruples . . . then he maintained that such a majority was weaker than a minority that had the team spirit." It is only necessary to remember that " team spirit " is a euphemism for political and personal subservience to Mr. MacDonald.

England's rulers were not slow in expressing their satisfaction with the Liverpool Conference. The exclusion of the Communists was hailed by *The Times* as " a great and welcome affirmation " by which " the Labour Party leaves possible the co-operation of all men who are bound together by a common citizenship for the promotion of the national prosperity." It was followed within a fortnight by a Government attack on the Communist apostles of " preparedness," whose headquarters were raided, and twelve of their leaders arrested, tried for sedition and given sentences long enough to keep them out of the way during the vital months up to May 1926. Great indignation was universal throughout the Labour movement, and the Miners' Federation Executive headed the list of protesting organisations; their own members shortly had a taste of terror when some fifty miners were jailed during a fiercely-fought strike in the anthracite district of South Wales.

Meantime the Miners' Federation, disquieted by the lack of practical preparation for May, were pressing ahead with the project of an Industrial Alliance whose initiation has been described in the beginning of this chapter. As finally drafted the Alliance scheme provided for an association of unions in heavy industry and transport for both defensive and offensive industrial purposes. It was aptly described as an attempt to create a " Supreme War Council of Industrial Allies," which would be more homogeneous and effective as a war weapon than the wider and looser T.U.C. General Council, and would at the same time enable the representatives of the allied unions to cast their weight as one in the deliberations of the General Council itself. Paragraph 9 of the Alliance Constitution laid it down that " the conditions of membership of this Alliance shall involve the allied organisations in definitely undertaking, notwithstanding anything in their agreements or constitutions to the contrary, to act as directed by the General Conference of this Alliance."

At a conference of the unions interested on November 5th, 1925, an unexpected blow was struck by the National Union of Railwaymen. The N.U.R. representatives proposed the apparently admirable amendment to the Constitution that a condition of membership of the Alliance should be the preparation of a scheme of fusion between unions catering for the same industry. Everyone knew, however, that this was a wrecking amendment aimed at the Locomotive Engineers and intended to cover the N.U.R.'s own withdrawal from the scheme, of which Mr. Thomas heartily disapproved. The unfortunate effect of this incident was heightened by the more than usually prolonged procedure of ballotting on the proposals in certain other unions. The Alliance, though it eventually secured the support of the Transport Workers, Locomotivemen, Foundry Workers, Iron and Steel Trades, Electrical Trades Union, Engineers and Workers' Union, had had too prolonged a labour and was still-born.

By the turn of the year the enervating atmosphere of unpreparedness stood in sharp contrast to the signs of the coming storm. Apart from the miners, the engineers found themselves faced with a demand for longer hours, the railway companies were talking of wage cuts, the building employers threatened an assault on working conditions. On the Left the alarm was raised with keener insistence than ever. The facts of the industrial crisis, said the Communists in January, "together with the steady, if unobtrusive organisation of the O.M.S., point to a definite determination on the part of the British capitalists to prevent a repetition of Red Friday, to challenge the organised Labour movement and smash it. . . . By this means they hope to achieve the impossible task of stabilising their system, undermined by war, ruin of foreign markets, chaos in production." None the less the Communists expressed their belief that the workers of Britain " can turn their defensive into an offensive, and present a common demand for better conditions which will be the prelude to a complete victory over the capitalists." To this end a programme of action was suggested, including the summoning of a conference of Trade Union Executives to give full powers to the General Council; the completion of the Industrial Alliance; agreement with the Co-operatives; the formation of factory committees in accordance with the Scarborough resolution; organising workers' defence corps and the placing of the workers' case before the armed forces; the formulation of a common wages and hours programme—a £4 minimum for a 44-hour week.

The official leadership, however, was awaiting with bated breath the deliberations of the Royal Commission on the Coal Industry, presided over by Sir Herbert Samuel. A strange, semi-mystical atmosphere seemed to be cast around the Commission, and was reflected in its Report, which was vague in its suggestions of State intervention to secure reorganisation of coal capitalism, but precise in asserting that the miners should accept wage reductions or longer hours. It achieved admirably its main purpose, that of dividing the movement at a critical time; for while so moderate a miners' leader as the late Mr. Vernon Hartshorn instantly said that " a settlement on the basis of the Report is impossible " the Leader of the Labour Party hastened to declare that the Report was " a conspicuous landmark in the history of political thought . . . the stars in their courses are fighting for us."

Before the issue of the Coal Commission's Report the miners' representatives had been in renewed touch with the General Council through the latter's Special Industrial Committee, of which Mr. (now Sir) Arthur Pugh had become chairman and on which Mr. J. H. Thomas now served as a member. After a joint meeting on February 19th, 1926, the Committee issued a statement that " the attitude of the trade union movement was made perfectly clear last July, namely, that it would stand firmly and unitedly against any attempt further to degrade the standard of life in the coalfields. There was to be no reduction in wages, no increase in working hours, and no interference with the principle of national agreements. This is the position of the' trade union movement to-day." On March 10th the Coal Report was made public. Hints and rumours soon came crowding, all suggesting that the General Council had receded from this clear reiteration of support for the miners.

The day before their national delegate conference, which had been called for April 9th, the Miners' Federation again approached the Industrial Committee asking for a declaration of support in the event of the coalowners making any attack on wages, hours or agreements. What they got from the Committee was a statement that it " reconfirms its previous declarations in support of the miners' efforts to obtain an equitable settlement of outstanding difficulties " (a significant change since February 19th), adding that negotiations between the miners and the owners " should be continued without delay, in order to obtain a clear understanding with regard to the Report of the Royal Commission, and to reduce points of difference to the smallest possible dimensions." A covering letter signed by Mr. W. M. Citrine said that " the Committee fully realise the seriousness of the present position, but they are of the opinion that matters have not yet reached the stage when any final declaration of the General Council's policy can be made."

Yet this ominous weakening on the part of the General Council did not deter the miners. Their conference the following day decided to stick by the slogan "not a penny off the pay, not a second on the day," and to adhere to the principle of a national agreement. They decided, in short, to fight. Four days later the Federation met the coalowners, who announced their intention of proceeding to negotiate on a district basis, and shortly thereafter posted lock-out notices. Even the owners' chairman, Mr. Evan Williams, had to admit that the reductions demanded were such that the resultant wage would be "miserable." May 1st loomed ahead as a day of inevitable conflict.

Before they took their momentous decision the miners had had evidence that the mass of trade unionists did not hold the same conciliatory view as the General Council. On March 20th the Minority Movement held a national Conference of Action at which the representation reached a record for any of its gatherings. There were present 883 delegates representing close on 1,000,000 organised workers. The achievement was the more remarkable since the Minority Movement was officially frowned upon. From the chair Tom Mann observed how the Samuel Report "very cunningly continued the policy of splitting the workers." On the motion of rank-and-file miners' leader Arthur Horner a resolution was adopted with acclamation declaring that it was "imperative that all the forces of the working-class movement should be mobilised under one central leadership to repel the attack and to secure the demands of every section of the workers." Each Trades Council, it was urged, should "constitute itself a Council of Action by mobilising all the forces of the working-class movement in its locality," and the General Council should convene a National Congress of Action. Evidently there was not much wrong with the spirit and vision of the rank-and-file of the workers' army; what they needed was generalship and good staff work.

CHAPTER VI

NINE DAYS THAT SHOOK BRITAIN

IT HAS BEEN STATED that the determination of the miners to resist the coalowners' demands, manifested in the second week of April 1926, made a conflict on the appointed day inevitable. Yet at the time the general impression was quite the contrary. There was a vague feeling abroad that somehow or other some sort of settlement would be patched up at the last moment. Not until the last week of April did the atmosphere change; even then it was not until the eleventh hour that there was proclaimed beyond peradventure the certainty of the most gigantic social battle Britain had ever known.

The first result of the coalowners' attempted opening of district negotiations was a hardening of the General Council's attitude. On April 14th the Industrial Committee "reiterated its previous declarations to render the miners the fullest support in resisting the degradation of their standard of life." This lent point to the claim made by Mr. A. J. Cook, in his speeches the following week-end, that the whole trade union movement was definitely pledged to defend the miners and that the coming struggle must involve the entire working class. On the other hand, an important member of the Industrial Committee, Mr. J. H. Thomas, simultaneously stressed that " to talk at this stage as if in a few days all the workers of the country were to be called out was . . . letting loose passions that might be difficult to control. . . . Instead of organising, mobilising, and encouraging the feeling that war was inevitable, let them concentrate on finding a solution honourable and satisfactory to all sides."

An intricate series of negotiations shortly began, involving in various combinations the Industrial Committee, the Government, the miners, and the coalowners. Deadlock succeeded deadlock. On Monday, April 26th, *The Times* reported that the owners had drafted new wage offers, based on a reversion to an eight-hour day, and had proposed to Prime Minister Baldwin that he suggest such a lengthening of hours to the miners. On the very same day the Conservative Party central office circulated a private note to newspaper editors. This document read: " The Government are particularly anxious to draw the attention of the public to the serious economic position of the coal industry as disclosed in the statistical table given in the House of Commons last week, showing the percentage of coal which is raised at a loss. Reference may also usefully be made to the question of hours, upon which it is desirable to concentrate attention rather than upon the reduction of wages." Evidently a very special meaning attached to Mr. Baldwin's rôle as mediator between owners and men.

This underlying unity of the Government and the coalowners was a perfectly natural thing. It connected with the " will to conflict " on the Government's part noted by Professor Laski. In the previous chapter it has been suggested that the ruling class needed to fight a decisive frontal engagement with the forces of Labour in order to carry through the rationalisation and reorganisation of industry that was urgently required if the levels of profit and capital accumulation were to be restored. For this the elaborate preparations of the previous nine months had been made. Now the time was at hand for the launching of the offensive. It was reckoned that the T.U.C. would not do more than stand on the defensive, and stay so; but there was an obvious strategic advantage in getting them to take the first overt steps to war.

Executives of unions affiliated to the T.U.C. were summoned to confer in London on Thursday, April 29th, as a precautionary move. At its meeting the preceding Tuesday the General Council had for the first time, according to

Mr. Ernest Bevin,[1] decided to draft plans for the large-scale action that a breakdown in the coal negotiations might impose. With this in mind Mr. Bevin told the Executives on the Thursday: " You are moving to an extraordinary position. In twenty-four hours from now you may have to cease being separate unions for this purpose. For this purpose you will become one union with no autonomy. The miners will have to throw their lot and cause into the cause of the general movement, and the general movement will have to take the responsibility for seeing it through." Excusing the Council for not producing " some definite plan " there and then, Mr. Bevin emphasised that " we are not going to begin wielding the big stick. We did not start it." At this stage the Conference, it must be admitted, lacked the snap and enthusiasm that marked its predecessor in July 1925. When Mr. W. J. Brown, the Civil Service leader, described the conference atmosphere as " chilly," complained of the " absence of a definite lead," he was an isolated voice and was solemnly reproved by Mr. Thomas.

Undoubtedly it is a good thing to strive for peace; but it is not a good thing to be blind to the approaching reality of battle and all its implications. That was the trouble with the General Council. Equally serious was their equivocal attitude to the miners. They had been fatally bemused by the Samuel Report; and in his opening statement from the chair to the Executives' Conference Mr. Arthur Pugh had urged that " negotiations should have started " with that Report as the basis. In other words the Miners' Federation should accept wage reductions (under the not very comforting guise of " temporary modifications ") on the condition that there was preliminary agreement to adopt " all practicable means " for reorganising the coal industry. Though this was implicit in Mr. Pugh's remarks, he concluded his statement by reading a document embodying the General Council's considered view of the mining situation in which the following passage occurred:

[1] Statement at the post-strike Conference of Executives, January 20th, 1927, according to the official *Report of Proceedings*, p. 10.

" In our view, the wages and working conditions of mine-workers are already so depressed as to render it imperative to seek for remedies other than a further degradation in their standards of life, or the abrogation of the present standard hours." Clearly this kind of contradiction was pregnant with misunderstanding and disaster. It was to lead later to the abandonment of the miners, on the ground that resistance to wage reductions was " a mere slogan " to which the General Council could not " justify their being tied."

No suspicion of such a dénouement entered the minds of the delegates assembled at the Memorial Hall on that April Thursday. They adopted a resolution in general terms endorsing the General Council's efforts to secure a settlement and specially stressing the need to secure a suspension of the lock-out notices in order that negotiations might continue. Mr. A. J. Cook made a speech in the course of which he interpreted the resolution as meaning that the Industrial Committee's original declarations in unqualified support of the miners were confirmed; no exception was taken to this interpretation.

That night, and throughout the following day and night till after 11 o'clock, the Industrial Committee, the miners and the Prime Minister assiduously negotiated in the endeavour to agree a basis for negotiations. Amid the mushroom crop of formulæ that sprang up, two unmistakable sets of facts emerged. One was that the Industrial Committee thought (to judge from subsequent statements by Mr. Thomas) that they had got the miners' leaders to agree to consider wage reductions if the Samuel Report were fully operated, while refusing to commit themselves in advance to wage reductions. The other was that Mr. Baldwin no longer concealed his alliance with the owners; as Professor Laski wrote at the time: " He asked the miners to accept an increase in hours which the Commission itself said had no point; a decrease in wages without any guarantee that the next three or four years would see any benefit to the trade; without even the assurance that the

Eт

timid suggestions of the Commission would be adopted in any thoroughgoing fashion; with the knowledge that this assault on miners' wages would be the beginning of a general attack on the workers' standard of life."

Meantime as Friday wore on the Executives were waiting patiently for news, resuming session and adjourning at regular intervals from 11 a.m. to 11.25 p.m. On each adjournment they received messages from the Industrial Committee indicating the extreme gravity of the situation. They sought to beguile the tedium with community singing; among the items was *Lead, Kindly Light*. Even the weariness of waiting could not offset the growing tension, an electrification of the atmosphere that was fast dispelling the chilliness of the previous day.

When the negotiators finally returned to Farringdon Street they had to report stalemate. The Government would not budge, although the miners' lock-out had taken effect from the end of the last shift on that day. " I suppose," said Mr. Thomas sadly, " my usual critics will say that Thomas was almost grovelling, and it is true. In all my long experience . . . I never begged and pleaded like I begged and pleaded all day to-day, and I pleaded not alone because I believed in the case of the miners, but because in my bones I believed that my duty to the country involved it." The time for grovelling had gone, however. The Government was pushing strongly ahead for war. Anger surged through the conference as the negotiators reported their discovery of the private Conservative message to newspaper editors, referred to above, and as they told of the O.M.S. recruiting posters already on the press. It was likewise learned that a proclamation under the Emergency Powers Act had been issued that day, and all local authorities had been circularised informing them that the measures outlined in Circular 636 were to take effect.

Accordingly each Executive present was handed a memorandum by the General Council which was in fact the General Strike order. The trades to cease work were scheduled as transport (all forms), printing (including the newspaper press), "productive industries" (itemised as iron and steel, metal and heavy chemicals), building (with the exception of housing and hospitals). Unions concerned with electricity and gas supply were recommended to "co-operate with the object of ceasing to supply power." It was directed that the unions should assume responsibility for the continued conduct of health, food and sanitary services. The actual calling out on strike was to be left to the in-dividual unions, although these were asked to "place their powers in the hands of the General Council." Trades Councils were called on to assist in strike organisation. A warning against *agents provocateurs* was inserted. Finally, it was directed by the General Council "that the Executives of the unions concerned shall definitely declare that in the event of any action being taken and trade union agreements being placed in jeopardy, it be definitely agreed that there will be no general resumption of work until those agree-ments are fully recognised."

This plan of campaign the Executives considered before the reassembly of the conference shortly after noon the following day, Saturday, May 1st. Their response was over-whelming. Dramatically the roll was called, union by union; and the "ayes" had it to the tune of 3,653,527 members represented against a mere 49,911 (unions with a membership totalling 319,000 were unable to reply pending further meetings of their governing bodies). Mr. Bevin announced that the trades specified in the memorandum, who were described as the "first grade" or "first line," would cease work as from midnight on Monday, May 3rd. Making a vibrant call to "every man and woman in that grade to fight for the soul of Labour and the salvation of the miners," he cried to the cheering Executives: "We look upon your 'yes' as meaning that you have placed your all upon the altar for this great movement and having placed it there, even if every penny goes, if every asset goes, history will ultimately write up that it was a magnificent generation that was prepared to do it rather than see the miners driven down like slaves."

All was not, however, quite over bar the cheering. Chairman Pugh specifically pointed out that " the scheme requires that the Miners' Federation hand over to the General Council the conduct of this dispute." To this, it was stated, the miners agreed; but around this there were later to be endless and involved recriminations. In the course of his speech thanking the conference Mr. Herbert Smith implied that the Miners' Federation retained the right to state their own case. At this lapse of time the facts can be dispassionately stated: the General Council desired the power to settle on the miners' behalf, even if that involved accepting the wage reduction proposals of the Samuel Report; the miners considered that their only authorisation to the General Council was to act for them on the basis of the declarations of solidarity to resist any reduction whatever in their living standards.

Of this potentially disastrous schism few can have thought in the highly-charged emotional atmosphere of the Memorial Hall that Saturday afternoon. Upstanding, the Executives lustily sang the " Red Flag," and poured out into the sunny streets already humming with excitement. Meantime the greatest May Day demonstration seen since the revolutionary years after the war was gathering in Hyde Park. News that they were going over the top on Monday midnight had aroused the liveliest spirit among the marching columns. In a flash the traditional demonstration assumed the impressive aspect of a *veille d'armes*. Yet there was no solemnity as the red banners flew in the breeze; rather a gaiety, an exaltation. " Shan't see you for the duration ! " grinned an East End busman to his West London opposite number, in my hearing.

While the army was thus marching with quickened step, and giving every sign of superb morale and readiness for the fight, the generals were in conclave with the enemy's Grand General Staff. By the middle afternoon the General Council had notified the Prime Minister that they were now acting on behalf of the miners, and further that they were prepared to maintain food and other services as outlined in their scheme for the strike. By the evening the Industrial Committee was closeted with Mr. Baldwin. Of the complicated comings and goings of that final week-end it is not necessary to speak in detail. Mr. A. J. Cook protested vehemently against the renewed negotiations, claiming that they were being conducted behind the backs of the miners, the Federation Executive having dispersed to their districts to undertake urgent work in connection with the now complete lock-out. Formulæ were being bandied to and fro (and there was much argument later as to who had agreed to what), but the whole thing boiled down to the old point—acceptance of the Samuel Report, implying wage reductions. Eventually the Government and the General Council negotiators seemed to have reached agreement on this, and it remained for the latter to secure endorsement from the Miners' Executive, hastily recalled to London by telegram.

Generals propose, but their armies sometimes dispose. And while in Whitehall events were assuming the shape outlined, an affair of outposts took place that transformed the whole situation. In Carmelite Street the edition of the *Daily Mail* was ready to go to press. A blood-and-thunder leading article proclaimed that the General Strike was " a revolutionary movement intended to inflict suffering upon the great mass of innocent persons in the community. . . . It must be dealt with by every resource at the disposal of the community." " For King and Country " blared the headline. Set, made up, moulded, plates cast and on the grey lines of rotaries—the paper had gone through its usual routine. But down in the vast machine-room angry men in blue overalls read that leading article as they glanced through trial copies. They gathered together and talked it over. The Natsopa Chapel met and after a brief discussion told the management that they could have their newspaper if the leader was deleted, but not otherwise. Other Chapels in machine-room, foundry, packing department, backed them. There was no *Daily Mail* that night. Perhaps no other single act of the whole General Strike evoked such universal delight throughout the whole working-class movement.

Immediately it heard this news the Government acted. The General Council negotiators were called out of their conference with the miners, handed a document treating the *Daily Mail* skirmish as an " overt act " of war, and refusing to continue negotiations unless the General Strike was unconditionally called off. This ultimatum flung the General Council into consternation, and a letter to the Prime Minister repudiated the action of the *Daily Mail* men. When the negotiators returned to Downing Street bearing this missive they were coolly told by an attendant that Mr. Baldwin had gone to bed and given to understand that their continued presence was entirely superfluous. And so at last, as Mr. Kingsley Martin put it, " the T.U.C. stood as a combatant in a war which had been forced upon it and which it feared to win." With such a background there was indeed ironic pathos in the *Daily Herald's* leading article of Monday, May 3rd: " TRUST YOUR LEADERS: Never was this more necessary than it is now. It is indispensable to success. Heed none who speak ill of those in command, who even ' hint a doubt or hesitate dislike '—whether they are open enemies or professing friends."

The point that the General Council were forced by circumstances to embark on a struggle with which they were fundamentally out of sympathy has been made so often that it is apt to obscure one more positive angle on their attitude. That was the fear of the movement sweeping beyond their control, developing in a revolutionary sense. Here, perhaps, is one of the most significant keys to their action alike in the calling of the strike and in the hasty capitulation. Writing subsequently in his union journal, *The Record*, Mr. Ernest Bevin said: " It must not be forgotten that apart from the rights and wrongs of the calling of a General Strike, there would in any case, with the miners' lock-out, have been widespread unofficial fighting in all parts of the country, which would have produced anarchy in the movement." And on May 13th, the day after the call-off, Mr. Thomas told the House of Commons:

" What I dreaded about this strike more than anything else was this: If by any chance it should have got out of the hands of those who would be able to exercise some control, every sane man knows what would have happened. I thank God it never did. That is why I believe that the decision yesterday was such a big decision, and that is why that danger, that fear, was always in our minds, because we wanted at least, even in this struggle, to direct a disciplined army."

Still franker was Mr. Charles Dukes, of the General and Municipal Workers, who claimed that " every day that the strike proceeded the control and the authority of that dispute was passing out of the hands of responsible Executives into the hands of men who had no authority, no control, and was [sic] wrecking the movement from one end to the other."[1] And the following dialogue took place between one of the most eminent officers of the General Council and a Continental inquirer:

Q. " Was the strike called off because, as some said, it was breaking down ? "
A. " No."
Q. " Was there any sign at all of it breaking down ? "
A. " Oh, no. The strike was at its highest point, absolutely its highest point."
Q. " And yet it was called off although there was no sign of it breaking down ? "
A. " Well, you see, there were some people on the General Council who thought it was going *too* far."[2]

Thus from the start a whole gulf was cleaved between the attitude and aims of the strike leaders and of the millions

[1] January 1927 Conference of Executives, *Report*, p. 58.
[2] This private conversation was reported to me at the time by the foreign inquirer, a prominent Dutch trade unionist; and I transcribe the text here given from the note I then took.

of strikers themselves. I suppose it is difficult now to re-
capture the apocalyptic atmosphere which prevailed in
every working-class area, the rousing enthusiasm and
dogged determination which in those days of wonder was
the mark of every working man and woman. I well remember turning out of my Fleet Street office a few minutes
after midnight on Monday, May 3rd, and meeting the
builders on the night-shift constructing the new *Daily Mail*
building in Tudor Street, who had just struck. One burly
labourer said to his mate, in the loud and clear tone of one
finally disposing of a matter: " Well, Bill, they can 'ave
my —— shovel ! "

Next day everyone knew how complete was the stoppage.
" We have from all over the country," said the T.U.C.
communiqué, " reports that have surpassed all our expect-
ations. Not only the railwaymen and transport men, but
all other trades came out in a manner we did not expect
immediately. The difficulty of the General Council has
been to keep men in what we might call the second line
of defence rather than call them out." That afternoon,
armed with my union card, I took a motor-bicycle trip
along the East India Dock Road. The street swarmed with
striking dockers. I have seen mass pickets enough; but
this was a mass turn-out of the local population. Along
came a solitary lorry. It was brought to a standstill by a
human barrier, scores upon scores deep, which lapped
over the whole roadway. Out the driver was hauled and
then one, two, three—strong arms and shoulders went to
work, the lorry swayed and swayed and with a crash went
over on its side. The street was littered with offending
vehicles to which like justice had been meted out. All over
London, in those early days of the strike, blackleg transport, whether lorry, bus or tram, was being similarly dealt
with.

It was a strange situation. A vast army had entered
battle with incomparable *élan*; but at its head stood generals
anxious above all to avoid decisive actions, fearful of victory,
concerned to bring the war to an end on any terms. It

was opposed by forces far smaller, though enjoying the advantages of superior organisation and long preparation in advance; and the leaders of this army were anxious to achieve a decision, were determined that it should be a victorious one, and had no qualms about the means they employed to gain the desired end. The Baldwin Government, in short, showed its teeth from the start. It realised that ruthlessly directed propaganda was vital for shaking the morale of its opponents; accordingly it took over the radio and, gravely hampered by the stoppage of the Press, commandeered the plant of the *Morning Post* to produce its own propaganda-sheet, the notorious *British Gazette*, with Mr. Churchill as super-editor. It treated the strike as an attack on the Constitution, as a struggle for power potentially raising the issue of civil war—" threatening the basis of ordered Government and going nearer to proclaiming civil war than we have been for centuries past," said Mr. Baldwin.

Upon which the Government proceeded to lay themselves out as civil war-mongers in the biggest possible way. The army and navy were employed to the full. London in particular had never before seen such a mobilisation of military force against the civil population, the troops all in battle order, armoured cars in great number. The *British Gazette*, referred to the strikers as " the enemy " and on Friday, May 7th, the following Government announcement was broadcast: " All ranks of the Armed Forces of the Crown are hereby notified that any action which they may find it necessary to take in an honest endeavour to aid the Civil Power will receive, both now and afterwards, the full support of His Majesty's Government." Next day two battalions of Guards, with attendant cavalry and armoured cars, were occupying London's docks, guarding 500 strike-breakers and providing convoy for a hundred lorry-loads of flour through the centre of the metropolis. The convoy troops had been ordered to " get through at any cost."

Simultaneously the police forces were extended by the large-scale enrolment of special constables. When these proved insufficient a new force was raised as a kind of police " Black-and-Tans "; this was entitled the Civil Constabulary Reserve, a full-time paid body consisting of ex-soldiers " who can be vouched for," to serve in plain clothes but wearing steel helmets and armed with truncheons. Baton charges sought to break up the mass pickets. The tale of arrests mounted into the hundreds. In the " state of emergency " any form of strike activity could be, and was, construed as an illegal act. Jail sentences rained down. A bare recital of the cases within its knowledge —and the list was certainly far from complete—filled two-and-a-half solid columns of the *Sunday Worker* in that newspaper's first post-strike issue. Any kind of appeal to the troops was anathema. A youngster who called out " Don't shoot the Workers ! " received three months' hard labour to enable him to meditate upon his rash words. Production, distribution, or even being in possession, of literature " calculated to cause disaffection "— the official term for the duplicated strike bulletins which were produced in every locality—was worth anything from three weeks to three months.

There was no hesitancy about the way in which the Government set about shaking the morale of its opponents. It followed up its initial branding of the strike as an attack on the Constitution by publicising to the limit the declaration of Sir John Simon and the *obiter dictum* of Mr. Justice Astbury pronouncing the General Strike illegal. Special stress was laid on Sir John's warning that every leader and promoter of the strike was " liable in damages to the uttermost farthing of his personal possessions." No doubt this served to make the General Council's flesh creep; but it was laughably bad law, as the bulk of legal opinion hastened to point out; the fact that the Government had later to introduce legislation declaring General Strikes illegal confirmed this view, which was unanswerably expounded by Mr. A. L. Goodhart, the eminent editor of the *Law Quarterly Review*.

Daily the Government's tone became more menacing.

" His Majesty's Government will not flinch from this issue, and will use all the resources at their disposal and whatever measures may be necessary " proclaimed the *British Gazette*. " An organised attempt is being made to starve the people and to wreck the State," ran an official communiqué dated May 7th, " and the legal and constitutional aspects are entering upon a new phase." Non-Governmental expressions of opinion in favour of the Government were played up in order to give the impression that Mr. Baldwin stood at the head of a solid bourgeois front. Thus the *British Gazette* gave great prominence to statements by Liberal oligarchs like Lords Oxford and Grey. It (and the radio) equally suppressed any reference to mediatory appeals, of which the principal was that made by the Archbishop of Canterbury " after full conference with the leaders of the Christian Churches in England," proposing a sort of simultaneous " cease fire," the strike to be called off, the miners' lock-out notices to be withdrawn and the Government to renew the coal subsidy for a definite period to enable a settlement to be concluded.

The Government had good reason to maintain this diehard line. Its position was in many respects far from strong and any weakness might have had serious consequences from its point of view. The Archbishop's appeal was paralleled by similar appeals from public bodies like the Newcastle City Council (where there was a Conservative majority). *The Times* began to reflect a semi-critical attitude on the part of influential governing-class circles that assumed a certain sharpness when the Government commandeered part of its newsprint stocks in common with those at the disposal of the General Council. Outraged, the authorities at Printing House Square addressed a personal appeal to Mr. Baldwin, who handed it to Mr. Churchill to reply. The bellicose Chancellor's answer was significant. " I do not at all agree with your idea," he wrote, " that the T.U.C. have as much right as the Government to publish their side of the case and exhort their followers to combined action," for there were masses of people who

" feel quite detached from the conflict; they are waiting, as if they were spectators at a football match, to see whether the Government or the trades union is the stronger."[1]

In this private pronouncement for the enlightenment of a deviating brother, Mr. Churchill at once showed the acuteness of his political perception and condensed the Government's strategy into a single sentence. It was to convince the " spectators " that the Government was the stronger that the greatest concentration of military force, and the main strike-breaking efforts, were made in the centre of the stage, London. Despite this sound strategy, however, as the strike proceeded the opinion of many " spectators " was hardening against the Government; such was my own firm impression at the time.

Unfortunately the General Council did not have Mr. Churchill's clarity of perception. To them the problem was not the strategic one of showing the " spectators " that they were stronger than the Government. It was the apologetic one of expounding their case in accents meek and mild, of conducting a war as if it were a peace conference. There was a wide difference between the conduct of publicity in, say, the railway strike of 1919[2] when the initiative never left the hands of the strikers, when the Government attacks were answered by counter-attacks and all efforts deliberately and successfully concentrated on the task of breaking up the Government morale, and the conduct of publicity in the General Strike. But for the strange formalism which impartially closed down the Labour and Socialist Press with the capitalist Press the Government would not have been able to take the initiative with its strike sheet. Only when the Government put out the *British Gazette* did the General Council issue the *British Worker*. Welcome though that was, and gallant though its fight to continue publication—it was born in a police raid and performed the most astonishing feats

---

[1] Quoted in *Strike Nights in Printing House Square*, p. 34 (privately printed account of *The Times* during the strike).
[2] See pp. 28-9 above.

in its machine-room when its own newsprint stocks were commandeered by the Government—it was held rigidly to the General Council's strangely nerveless line of propaganda by a specially appointed censorship committee.

In 1919 it had been shown how propaganda could triumph if it carried the war into the enemy's camp; but the *British Worker* remained throughout on the defensive. To the Government's reiteration of the constitutional issue, in other words treating the strike as a political struggle, the General Council could only " emphasise the fact that this is an industrial dispute." " The General Strike is not a ' menace to Parliament,' no attack is being made on constitutional Government. We beg Mr. Baldwin to believe that," wrote the *British Worker* editorially. Had not Mr. Thomas said in the House of Commons on May 3rd, " I have never disguised that in a challenge to the Constitution, God help us unless the Constitution won " ? Apart from this fundamental issue, moreover, there was constant evidence of the General Council's anxiously restraining hand at work. In its very first issue the *British Worker* prominently displayed an injunction to strikers to stay at home and/or organise games. The Council's organ likewise refrained from reporting many of the early arrests and prison sentences, in order, it was claimed, not to embitter the conflict.

From the standpoint of organisation the strike suffered from the lack of preparation and from the manner of its calling. Last-minute improvisation naturally had its effect in the vital matter of communications, though the crowds of volunteer despatch-riders and car-drivers performed prodigies of endurance and never failed to get through. Illustrative of the unprepared state of the General Council's headquarters is the fact that not until the second day were five sub-committees set up to deal with various aspects of guidance of the strike, this task clearly being beyond the existing Strike Organisation Committee, despite the energy of its chairman, Mr. Bevin. The greatest confusion in the line of battle arose, however, from two sets of circumstances.

First of these was the calling out of the men by their individual unions, to which attention has been directed above. When it is realised that the membership of no less than eighty-two unions was wholly or partly on strike it is easy to conceive the difficulties that arose. Old craft sentiments and prejudices, the whole tradition of sectionalism, of loyalty above all to one's own union and to the behests of one's own officials and Executive, cut across the lines of general solidarity. Union strike committees overlapped with Trades Councils in some cases. The printing trades were particularly sticky, requiring much coaxing and lengthy negotiation in several instances before they would undertake provincial editions of the General Council's own organ.

Confusion was made worse confounded by the attempt, under these conditions, to operate the initial decision, unexceptionable in principle, that food and health services should be continued. When the Government rejected the General Council's offer to run food trains, this question resolved itself into one of the issue of permits for the road transport of food. Headquarters tried to systematise the business by instructing the localities that the only authority to issue permits was the Joint Transport Committee, to consist of delegates from the transport and railway unions. In very many cases, however, this authority was assumed by the local Trades Council or Council of Action, special powers being delegated to the individual union secretaries most concerned. Endless stories are told of the chaos that ensued. Obviously the difficulty of determining what transport should and should not be permitted was in practice insuperable. When to this was added the grave abuse of permits by concerns who sought to use them as a cover for transporting anything from boot-polish to blacklegs (" people are often found masquerading as loaves of bread," reported one local strike bulletin), it was not surprising that there was a general close-down on the issue of permits.

Another source of difficulty was the dividing of the

workers' forces into two " lines," of which the second, embracing principally the engineers and shipyard workers, was held in reserve. Mr. Bevin, whose plan this was, appears to have considered that the military analogy of maintaining an effective reserve was more apposite than the analogy of concentration of forces. It will be recalled that the official General Council statement on the first day recorded the general difficulty in holding in the men in the second line. Certainly the general effect of the plan was that in important engineering and shipbuilding centres like Coventry and the Clyde the strike was much more limited in its effect; the railwaymen and others who were out felt themselves somewhat isolated. In any event the delay of a week before the second line received their battle orders (they responded with magnificent eagerness, even though in some poorly-organised shops in backward areas the union men were walking out to certain destruction) seems inexplicable even if the soundness of Mr. Bevin's theory be assumed. Nor has it ever been explained why they were called out at all, since that very night the General Council had already decided to abandon the strike. Additionally, there does not appear to have been adequate consideration of the importance, as shock troops, of the workers engaged in electricity supply (the General Council desired to close down power but to maintain light) and of the Post Office staffs. It was currently reported that the operators in the Central Telegraph Office, nerve-centre of the country's telegraphic system, were seething with unrest and even talking of spontaneous strike action.

To gloss over the defects that have now been touched on would be historical dishonesty. None the less the immense and inspiring thing about the General Strike, as the reader will already have gathered, was its amazing completeness, its unprecedented solidarity. Is it not an astonishing reflection that in London, centre of the most splendidly equipped newspaper printing plants in the world, the mighty British Government could not get one single linotype operator to set up its propaganda sheet ? The *British Gazette* would not have seen the light of day had it not been for the beneficent Lord Beaverbrook, who loaned one of his mechanical superintendents, Mr. Long, himself a former operator, to act as the Government sheet's sole typesetter.

On the railways the stoppage was the completest known, and remained so. The propaganda emitted by the Government stood in the sharpest contrast with the facts set down in the confidential daily reports of the Ministry of Transport.[1] In these official surveys it was recorded that 99 per cent of the employees of the London Underground railways ceased work. The strike's stranglehold on the trunk lines was exemplified by the figures of freight movements. The number of goods trains run on the L.M.S. was less than 1 per cent of normal on May 5th, and only 3 per cent on May 11th; on the Great Western the figure on May 11th had not risen to more than 8·4 per cent of normal; while the L.N.E.R. had only reached 2·2 per cent of normal even by May 11th. According to the railway companies' own memoranda, issued after the strike, the walk-out of the locomotive-men, for example, was so complete that on the L.M.S. only 1·5 per cent sought to blackleg, on the L.N.E.R. a mere fraction of 1 per cent.

All the evidence, official and otherwise, leads to the conclusion that any suggestion of an appreciable weakening towards the end of the strike can be dismissed as mythical. There are always casualties in war, and there were returns to work in certain industries and certain parts of the country. The important fact is that the casualty rate was so low as to be negligible, and was more than offset by new sections entering the strike. Even in its issue of May 12th, the last day of the strike, the *British Gazette* had to admit that " there is as yet little sign of a general collapse of the strike," while in its issue of the preceding evening the *British Worker* declared prominently—" the number of strikers has not diminished; it is increasing. There are more workers out to-day than there have been at any moment since the strike began."

[1] Quoted by Professor W. H. Crook: *The General Strike*, pp. 390–6.

Keener international solidarity had been evoked by the strike than by any other movement of the working class since the war, save only the Russian Revolution. This solidarity grew daily in practical effectiveness as the strike proceeded and, in the opinion of continental trade unionists, could have been indefinitely expanded given the proper approach from Britain.[1] The International Transport Workers' Federation worked day and night to rally seamen, dockers, railmen, to place an embargo on " black " cargoes consigned to Britain. Their efforts met with substantial success. From the trade union centres of France, Holland, Germany, the United States, Canada and elsewhere news of support and solidarity action poured in. In Paris printers struck when asked to print extra editions of the *Continental Daily Mail* destined for London. The All-Russian Central Council of Trade Unions was one of the first in the field, issuing the appropriate solidarity orders to workers in Soviet ports and crews of Soviet vessels trading to Britain; it also offered a contribution of 2,000,000 roubles to the strike funds which the General Council, fearful of the stigma of " Moscow gold," hastened to decline.

" It was a wonderful achievement, a wonderful accomplishment that proved conclusively that the Labour movement has the men and women that are capable in an emergency of providing the means of carrying on the country." Those words of the late A. J. Cook, written immediately after the strike, sum up the story of the Nine Days in the far-flung battle-line itself. Here it is clearly impossible to present even a summary picture of a struggle which involved every town in the country. One natural result of the Government's deliberate concentration of its strike-breaking efforts in the capital was that the provincial industrial centres gave the impression that the strike was more solid than in London; or, it would be more accurate to say, that the close-down was more complete. This was

[1] Interview with Mr. P. J. Schmidt, of the Netherlands Federation of Trade Unions, in the *Sunday Worker*, June 6th, 1926.

overwhelmingly true of the great coal and heavy industry regions like South Wales, Yorkshire and the Midlands, the North-East Coast and Scotland. There, in factory town and mining district, in railway centre and port, the strike from start to finish was solid and immovable as a rock. It was also marked in the case of cities like Birmingham, where working-class organisation had traditionally been over-shadowed by the strength and cunning of the other side.

The forms of strike organisation locally showed great variation, from the simple union strike committee to the elaborate Council of Action, covering all the unions and other working-class organisations in the area and duly departmentalised in a series of sub-committees. In many cases the local Trades Councils carried on without a change. Sometimes the executive power was placed in the hands of *ad hoc* bodies called Central Strike Committees or Joint Strike Committees. Northumberland and Durham set up a General Council to co-ordinate activity throughout the whole of that great industrial region. Generally speaking the initiative and vigour of these local strike centres con-trasted with the formalism at headquarters, where the term Council of Action was " not recognised " (even the term General Strike was soon to be changed to the supposedly less subversive " National " Strike). It was with justice that a middle-class observer later wrote that " the Councils gave striking testimony to the latent capacity of the British working classes for spontaneous self-organisation."[1] Heroism and humour, always closely linked in the spirit of British working men, showed up strongly in the daily activity of the militants who led the Councils and the millions who followed their lead. Coolness and courage on the picket-line, unflagging energy in taking duty for twenty and more hours at a stretch, an exhilaration that overcame all obstacles—of this everyone who was in the line during those immortal days can give examples enough and to spare.

Many of the duplicated strike news bulletins whose

Robert M. Rayner: *The Story of Trade Unionism*, p. 257.

production was a feature of the local Councils' work were remarkable for their snap and satire, expressed in roughly-drawn cartoons, in verse, and in pointed paragraphs. Headed " To Heaven by L.M.S.," the Bristol bulletin had the following ditty:

> *Early in the morning, per broadcast from London,*
> *See the little puff-puffs all in a row,*
> *D'Arcy on the engine, pulled a little lever,*
> *Expansion of the boiler—UP WE GO !*

Paisley was positively elegant in the construction of this " Railway Triolet " :

> *There's a train comin' in*
> *At the station, my boys;*
> *Tho' there's only the yin*
> *There's a train coming in.*
> *O ! the noise and the din,*
> *O ! the din and the noise;*
> *There's a train comin' in*
> *At the station, my boys.*

Not for the rank and file the fears that were reputed to affect some of their leaders. " Sir John Simon says," jeered the Kensington bulletin after that legal luminary's pronouncement, " the General Strike is illegal under an Act passed by William the Conqueror in 1066. All strikers are liable to be interned in Wormwood Scrubs. The three million strikers are advised to keep in hiding, preferably in the park behind Bangor Street, where they will not be discovered." Preston's *Strike News* ironically inquired " if, after the blackleg Amateur Signalman at Ribble Sidings had failed after trying for forty-five minutes to get an engine into the Sidings and out again, the engine went to the shed disgusted ? " The St. Pancras bulletin cracked— " Notices posted on Cemetery Walls at Highgate and Finchley calling for Volunteers. We suggest that it should be picketed by Underground men."

The authors of the contemporary *Workers' History of the*

Great Strike[1] summed up that " by the second week the strike organisation, in nearly all the towns of which we have information, was in full working order and the workers were reaching out to fresh development. They were, as numerous reports put it, 'just beginning,' and the full force of their attack was only commencing to be felt. Mass pickets, defence corps, propaganda, commissariat, federation over wider areas—all these were just coming into play."

This sense of the strike sweeping onward to new heights was also an indication that it was, despite the attitude of the General Council, assuming a definite political character. Nothing could be more natural; for through realising their power in the strike workers began to realise their power in society, began to see that they were in fact engaged in no ordinary industrial struggle, but in what must become a struggle for power between their organised forces and the organised forces of the governing class. A report from the Dartford Divisional Labour Party recorded that " after the third day of the strike if you spoke about the coalowners the audience would listen with a polite indifference, but if you attacked the Government, or even mentioned the word, you had the audience with you and that with cheers and wild enthusiasm. The issue was the T.U.C. and the Government—the miners and the owners were secondary to this issue." And this point was essentially conceded by the leaders, though not till after the strike. Speaking in June the late Mr. C. T. Cramp, general secretary of the National Union of Railwaymen, said " Let us not trifle with the facts. Although denials were made to the charge that this was a struggle against the Government, it obviously was such a struggle. A moment's reflection is sufficient to reveal this."[2]

On the second day of the strike the Communists issued a manifesto in which they referred to its " political meaning," saying that it " is not only a magnificent act of brotherly

---

[1] Ellen Wilkinson, M.P., J. F. Horrabin, R. W. Postgate.
[2] *Railway Review*, June 18th, 1926.

support to the miners, it is an act of self-defence on the
part of the working class who, with their families, constitute
the majority of the people." " Simply to beat off the
employers' present offensive means that they will return to
the attack later on," the manifesto added, and since " the
Government in this struggle has dropped the pretence of
being above all classes . . . If the strike ends, though it be
with the defeat of the coalowners, but with the Government's power unshaken, the capitalists will still have hopes
of renewing their attack." Warning was therefore uttered
" against the attempt being made to limit the struggle to
its previous character of self-defence against the capitalist
offensive. Once the battle has been joined, the only way to
victory is to push ahead and hit hard. And the way to hit
the capitalist hardest is for the Councils of Action to throw
out the clear watchwords—Not a Penny off the Pay ! Not
a Second on the Day ! Nationalise the Mines without
Compensation, under Workers' Control ! Formation of a
Labour Government ! "

Sufficient backing was provided for this interpretation
by the progressive emergence of the local strike bodies, the
Councils, as alternative authorities to the Governmental
authorities. Here were the elements of a Dual Government
—the organisations of the working class facing the existing
State machinery. Take the matter of permits. Apart from
the difficulties that arose in the allocation of permits, to
which reference has already been made, it was clear that
the issuing of these documents rested on the assumption
that the unions and/or the Councils of Action had powers
to do, or allow to be done, certain public things that would
ordinarily be regarded as exclusively within the province
of the constituted authorities, national and local. In the
great majority of cases these powers thus tacitly assumed
by the strike organs were effective powers; that is to say,
without a permit in due and proper form, persons were
prevented by the *force majeure* of mass picketing from freely
transporting goods from place to place. Of the plain class
issue implicit here the local strike organisers were sensible.

An Ashton sheet-metal worker, member of his local Permit Committee, wrote pungently in his union journal:

"Employers of labour were coming, cap in hand, begging for permission to do certain things, or, to be more correct, to allow their workers to return to perform certain customary operations. . . . Most of them turned empty away after a most humiliating experience, for one and all were put through a stern questioning, just to make them realise that we and not they were the salt of the earth. I thought of the many occasions when I had been turned empty away from the door of some workshop in a weary struggle to get the means to purchase the essentials of life for self and dependants. . . ."

The same sense of power was imported by the simple sight of cars and vans bearing the black on yellow labels "BY PERMISSION OF THE T.U.C."

Mass picketing showed the workers' power in its most spectacular form. Typical was the following B.B.C. news item—"Middlesbrough: at 9 p.m. Thursday night, a train at a main line crossing in the middle of the town was stopped by a crowd who invaded the station and blocked the line with heavy wagons." In and around mining areas, where the miners had no need to picket their blackleg-proof pits, mass picketing was overwhelming. Roads were absolutely impassable for any transport lacking a permit. At Longcroft, near Edinburgh, the strike committee reported that the picket was so effective that the football park was jammed full with impounded vehicles of all descriptions. At Falkirk the driver of a blackleg newspaper van stated that he was formally arrested by the picket and taken up an alley where other suspect drivers were also "under arrest" prior to being turned back. Another driver was stopped and forced to turn back outside Fauldhouse by a picket of 300 miners. Traffic circulation on the great north-south arteries running through Durham and Northumberland was completely stopped by the implacable tourniquet of the miners' mass picketing; and it may be noted here that in Newcastle the Government's Commissioner was forced to go to the Joint Strike Committee with a suggestion for dual control of food services in view of the breakdown of the efforts of the O.M.S.

Naturally the authorities did not take mass picketing lying down. In the Doncaster area, for instance, a mass picket of 1,000 miners was repeatedly charged by the police and broken up, 80 arrests being made. Incidents of this kind pointed to the need for some effective defence corps. Methil, the strike centre for the East Fife coalfield, has always been cited as the outstanding example. There the Council of Action had established a Workers' Defence Corps in the early days of the strike, enrolling 150 men; the Corps remained more or less a formality until a police v. picket battle at a level-crossing roused the neighbourhood. The Corps was enlarged to 700 men, organised in companies each under the command of an ex-N.C.O., an ex-sergeant-major being appointed as Corps commander. Armed with pick-shafts, the companies patrolled the district in column of fours. There was no further police interference with pickets.

I knew Methil and the local personalities very well. The organisation and inspiration of the Council of Action there was first-class (it ran a courier service for information and propaganda covering the whole area, with the aid of three motor cars, 100 motor-cycles and push-bikes galore), not unconnected with the fact that a little group of very able, energetic and respected Communists had long stood at the head of the local movement. The strike sent their numbers sky-rocketing up, incidentally, from a dozen to 400 ! When I spent some time there immediately after the strike it did not seem strange to hear men saying that, when the call-off came, they themselves had been thinking—" Well, in another day or two we'd better walk into power. . . ." That may have been a naïve sentiment; but it reflected the sense of strength that prevailed in these solid industrial areas.

To leave this cursory survey of the battle-line for an examination of the state of headquarters is like leaving the wind on the heath for the clammy pall of a thick fog. As the strike grew stronger the leaders more rapidly neared the point of cracking-up. After all, before the war began, Mr. Thomas had described it as " the greatest calamity for this country." Mr. MacDonald, leader of the Labour Party, had told the House of Commons on May 3rd that " with the discussion of General Strikes and Bolshevism and all that kind of thing I have nothing to do at all "; later he averred that " I don't like General Strikes . . . I am terribly cold-blooded about the matter." Addressing an enormous strike demonstration at Hammersmith on Sunday, May 9th, Mr. Thomas said bluntly, " I have never favoured the principle of a General Strike "—a sentiment which the *British Gazette* gladly seized on for prominent display. Mr. Thomas—the first half of whose speech was listened to in dead silence by a vast audience that later rose and sang the " Red Flag " at a tempo and with a fire that I have never heard before or since—devoted himself to rebuking " those who, on whichever side they may be, are talking of a fight to a finish." He spoke of the leaders' responsibility to " accept the first moment for an honourable settlement " and declared that " even now I am not one that will shut the door."

His hearers did not know it; but Mr. Thomas was not speaking without his book. The day before, Sir Herbert Samuel, chairman of the Coal Commission, had returned post-haste from a holiday in Italy and had met the General Council's Industrial Committee; a second meeting quickly followed and Sir Herbert drafted a statement which the Industrial Committee discussed with the Miners' Executive on Sunday, May 9th, the latter eventually rejecting it. In a broadcast on that Saturday Mr. Baldwin had proclaimed that he was " a man of peace " (on condition that the strike was unconditionally called off) and had asked " cannot you trust me to ensure a square deal, to secure even justice between man and man ? "

It was curious that on Friday, May 7th, the *British Worker* had featured a denial on behalf of the General Council, that any " official or unofficial overtures have been made to the Government by any individual or group of individuals, either with or without the sanction of the General Council." There was " no truth in the assertion " that Mr. Ramsay MacDonald, Mr. Herbert Smith, Mr. A. J. Cook, or other union leaders had been so engaged. On the other hand the New York *World* carried a cabled despatch from its well-informed London correspondent, under date May 8th, relating how Mr. MacDonald had given reporters in the House of Commons " an interview wherein he stated he was keeping in continual touch with the Government side, and was hourly in conference regarding settlement of the strike." This report, the correspondent added, caused " immediate and profound consternation " in the censorship committee of the *British Worker* when it reached them, and they forbade its publication.

Be this incident as it may, the fact remains that from Saturday, May 8th, onwards, the General Council's attention was wholly concentrated on negotiations that had as their aim the ending of the strike. As the talks proceeded it became evident that the conclusion of the strike, irrespective of the terms obtainable, had become an end in itself. " It seemed," wrote Mr. A. J. Cook, " that the only desire of some leaders was to call off the General Strike at any cost, without any guarantees for the workers, miners or others." The mystic aura that had surrounded the Coal Commission enveloped the distinguished figure of Sir Herbert Samuel and served as a substitute for guarantees.

Sir Herbert himself was in a peculiar position. He repeatedly made it clear to the General Council negotiators that " I have been acting entirely on my own initiative, have received no authority from the Government, and can give no assurances on their behalf." Yet in a letter to Sir Herbert Samuel, dated May 8th, and not published until the strike was over, the

Minister of Labour (Sir Arthur Steel-Maitland), declared that the Government " hold that the General Strike is unconstitutional and illegal. They are bound to take steps to make its repetition impossible. It is, therefore, plain that they cannot enter upon any negotiations unless the strike is so unreservedly concluded that there is not even an implication of such a bargain upon their side as would embarrass them in any legislation which they may conceive to be proper in the light of recent events." It was in the light of this exposition of the Government's attitude and intentions, with which he did not record disagreement, that Sir Herbert entered on his negotiations with the General Council.

The Government's point was unmistakable. They were out for victory, for the unconditional surrender of the T.U.C. and for a subsequent disarming of the unions. They wanted a Versailles peace, in short, and they were committing themselves to nothing, to no suggestion of terms, assurances, bargains.

Tuesday, May 11th, saw the negotiations reach their climax. Sir Herbert had drafted a Memorandum which re-hashed the Coal Commission's proposals, including the implication of wage reductions if reorganisation of the industry were operated. It was the story of May 2nd all over again. The prolonged talks had merely sought, as Mr. Herbert Smith contemptuously put it, " to provide a new suit of clothes for the same body." That Tuesday evening the Miners' Executive, who had been unrepresented in the last critical stages of negotiation, were summoned to meet the General Council. Chairman Pugh informed them that the Council had unanimously endorsed the Samuel Memorandum, considering that it constituted a fair basis for negotiating a settlement in the mining industry, and that the General Strike would accordingly be terminated. He added that the Council had guarantees satisfying them that the Government would accept the Memorandum and urged the miners to accept it too. The ensuing scene was vividly pictured by Mr. A. J. Cook:

" Mr. Pugh was continually pressed and questioned by Mr. Herbert Smith, myself, and my colleagues as to what the guarantees mentioned were, and who had given them. We got no answer. But J. H. Thomas said to me personally, when I asked him whether the Government would accept the Samuel proposals and what were his guarantees: ' You may not trust my word, but will you not accept the word of a British gentleman who has been Governor of Palestine ? '

" Our President, myself, and my colleagues put several other questions; asking what was the position of other workers in regard to the unanimous decision arrived at that we should all return to work together, to protect one another from victimisation, and to secure a return by all workers on the same conditions as when they left. We were informed that ' that was all right.' "[1]

Profoundly suspicious of the whole business, the Miners' Executive retired for a separate meeting, at the conclusion of which they adopted a resolution stating that " at best, the proposals imply a reduction of the wages rates of a large number of mineworkers, which is contrary to the repeated declarations of the Miners' Federation, and which they believe their fellow trade unionists are assisting them to resist. They regret, therefore, whilst having regard to the grave issues involved, that they must reject the proposals. Moreover, if such proposals are submitted as a means to call off the General Strike such a step must be taken on the sole responsibility of the General Council."

The General Council had in fact anticipated being able to call off the strike that night, and with that in view had arranged an interview with the Prime Minister. This had to be postponed to the next day in view of the miners' opposition, which was maintained when a General Council deputation visited them in the forenoon of Wednesday, May 12th. The Miners' Executive then resolved " that

[1] A. J. Cook: *The Nine Days*, p. 20.

having heard the report of the representatives of the T.U.C. we reaffirm our resolution of May 11th, and express our profound admiration of the wonderful demonstration of loyalty as displayed by all workers who promptly withdrew their labour in support of the miners' standards, and undertake to report fully to a conference to be convened as early as practicable." A quarter of an hour after that resolution had been handed to their deputation the General Council was in attendance on Mr. Baldwin at Downing Street.

Historic surrenders have often been affairs of dignity and noble bearing in adversity; but there was nothing of Lee at Appomattox Court House about the General Council that May noontide. Humiliation must surely attend the generals of an unconquered army who capitulate, not even on terms, but without condition or reserve; and humiliation was not lacking here. The Council were kept waiting on the mat until Mr. Baldwin had assured himself, through the intermediary of an official, that they had in fact come to announce their surrender. They were then admitted to the presence, finding the Prime Minister accompanied by most of the members of the Cabinet.

Chairman Pugh announced, after a somewhat involved preamble, that the " General Strike is to be terminated forthwith in order that negotiations may proceed." It was at once evident that the General Council had had no sort of assurances or guarantees of any kind whatsoever; and that for his part Mr. Baldwin was pledging himself to nothing. Anxiety contrasting strangely with the assurances given to the miners the previous night was marked in the speeches of Mr. Thomas and Mr. Bevin. The former begged the Prime Minister to " assist us by asking employers and all others to make the position as easy and smooth as possible, because the one thing we must not have is guerilla warfare." Mr. Bevin persisted doggedly in the endeavour to extract a pledge from Mr. Baldwin that " ready facilities for reinstatement " would be requested by the Government, and further that the miners' lock-out would be raised

so that there could be " free and unfettered negotiations."
Mr. Baldwin point-blank refused to make any definite
statement at all, not even as to the date on which he would
answer these questions, brusquely dismissing the General
Council with the words: " Now, Mr. Pugh, we have both
of us got a great deal to do and a great deal of anxious and
difficult work, and I think that the sooner you get to your
work and the sooner I get to mine the better."

Dismissed thus empty-handed it was not surprising that
" Mr. J. H. Thomas came out with the look of a man both
bewildered and depressed," as the *Manchester Guardian*
correspondent wrote, or that the other members of the
General Council " too all seemed very depressed, and
obviously in no mood for saying anything." Their bewilder-
ment was nothing to that of the millions of front-line
fighters, upon whom the news of the call-off, flashed all
over the country by 1.30 p.m., descended like a thunder-
clap. Uncertainty and suspicion alternated with wild
hopes that so sudden and unexpected a cessation of
hostilities *must* mean a great victory. The result was
unutterable chaos.

That afternoon and evening the *British Worker* ran three
editions which successively showed the evolution of the
General Council's presentation of its case. The first edition,
announcing the termination of the strike, headlined
" General Council Satisfied that Miners Will Now Get
a Fair Deal "; at the same time its inside pages, prepared
before the call-off, reported the entry of the engineers into
the fight as if the strike were still on. Without comment
the text of the Samuel Memorandum and of the correspondence between the General Council and Sir Herbert
Samuel was printed. The Council's final letter to Sir
Herbert, dated May 12th, informed him that " they are
taking the necessary measures to terminate the General
Strike, relying upon the public assurances of the Prime
Minister as to the steps that would follow. They assume
that during the resumed negotiations the subsidy will be
renewed and that the lock-out notices to the miners will

be immediately withdrawn." After the interview with the Prime Minister it must have been painfully evident that that assumption had absolutely no basis whatever; but not a word of the detailed exchanges between the General Council and Mr. Baldwin that day appeared in the *British Worker*. At the same time there was no hint that the Miners' Federation were not an assenting party to the whole proceedings.

On the last point the second edition went a step further and by an astonishing manipulation of the Miners' Executive resolution of that morning, quoted in full above, contrived to convey the impression that the miners were in agreement with the General Council. A full-page streamer heading read " Miners' Thanks to Their Allies " and the story opened: " The miners have expressed to the T.U.C. their ' profound admiration of the wonderful demonstration of loyalty as displayed by all workers,' " etc. The key sentence " *we reaffirm our resolution of May 11th*," or any reference to that unequivocal rejection of the General Council's surrender plans, was suppressed. Mr. Cook issued a Press statement on the afternoon of May 12th that the Miners' Federation were " no party in any shape or form " to the call-off of the strike; that statement is not to be found in the *British Worker*.

The third, and final, edition featured a manifesto by the General Council repeating that they had " obtained assurances that a settlement of the mining problem can be secured " and had accordingly decided " to terminate the general stoppage in order that negotiations could be resumed to secure a settlement in the coal-mining industry, free and unfettered from either strike or lock-out." " The Unions that have maintained so resolutely and unitedly their generous and ungrudging support of the miners," the manifesto concluded, " can be satisfied that an honourable understanding has been reached."

Comment on the misleading nature of these communications can be left to the reader. How some unions were deluded may be seen from the circular letter addressed by the Railway Clerks' Association to its branches on May 12th. Signed " Yours in the Victory " by General Secretary A. G. Walkden, this letter ran in part: " I am very glad to say that the efforts of the T.U.C. General Council during the stoppage have resulted in ensuring for the miners the inauguration of the large measures of reorganisation which have long been overdue in their industry, and the adoption of reforms which will bring for them a brighter and better future," while they " also brought about an undertaking for the withdrawal of the lock-out notices and the continuance of the subsidy for such reasonable period as may be required for completing the negotiations." Mr. Walkden added that " it was part of the understanding on which the General Strike was concluded that there should be no victimisation on either side." At no single point did this letter bear any sort of relation to the facts; and since Mr. Walkden, an upright and able man of exceptionally high repute as a union administrator, was at the same time a member of the General Council, this really fantastic document may serve as a final example of the abyss of self-deception into which the Council had plunged.

As that chaotic Wednesday wore on there was a general hardening in the strikers' attitude. Rage mingled with dismay and a new determination, typified by the report from Stourbridge: " The men were like rock. The first man to bring the news was the sub-editor of the *County Express*, and after giving the news he asked what we were going to do about it. The answer was *Double the Pickets*." The Stourbridge men had sound instincts. For, as usual, Mr. Baldwin's peace talk was a smoke-screen. In the House of Commons on Wednesday afternoon he proclaimed that " we should resume our work in a spirit of co-operation, putting behind us all malice and vindictiveness." That same afternoon a Government statement was issued commencing: " His Majesty's Government have no power to compel employers to take back every man who has been on strike, nor have they entered into any obligation of any kind on this matter." Next morning the *British Gazette*

carried that statement under the significant headline
" Reinstatement : No Obligations Incurred."

It was enough. On the railways and docks, in passenger
transport and printing, the employers took the Government's tip. Men returning for work on the Wednesday
night and Thursday morning found themselves faced with
a frontal attack. Railwaymen all over the country were
presented with a document for individual signature.
" Peace—with a Thick Stick " ran the headline of the
Scottish Worker's front-page lead in its issue of May 14th,
and its story opened: " From all over Scotland and England come reports that the employers are determined if
possible to impose non-unionism, reduced wages or servile
conditions upon the workers." The employers, in fact,
thought that the surrender of the leaders meant the collapse of the rank-and-file, and were proceeding on the
principle that the best time to kick a man hard is when he
is down. American observers saw the thing clearly. The
New York *Herald-Tribune* headlined " British Employers
War on Unions." " The strike is over but the lock-out has
begun . . . it is now the turn of the employers to strike,"
cabled the correspondent of the *New York Times.*

Where now was the boast of Mr. J. H. Thomas, made at
the Tuesday discussions with the miners, that " I have
seen to it that the members of the railways will be pro-
tected " ? His colleague, the late C. T. Cramp, admitted
that after the call-off the railwaymen " found themselves
left in the air. They had to fight for their own hand, and
for their very existence."[1] And how they fought ! " When
the leaders fail, the workers must take things into their own
hands " ran the conclusion of a Communist appeal on
the Wednesday. That is what happened on the Thursday;
the mighty rally of the ranks all over the country, making
the strike tie-up more acute than ever, was in many ways
the most amazing thing of the whole conflict. Overnight
the dogged good-humour of the Nine Days had changed
into bitter anger. Peremptory telegrams poured in on the

[1] *Railway Review*, July 9th, 1926.

General Council demanding that the General Strike be officially resumed. The Council replied by a statement, issued on the Thursday evening, in which it said: " The General Strike is ended. It has not failed. It has made possible the resumption of negotiations in the coal industry, and the continuance, during negotiations, of the financial assistance given by the Government " (a repetition of the misleading statements of the previous day that now had not the least shred of justification). " Your union will protect you," the statement went on, " and will insist that all agreements previously in force shall be maintained intact."

That final clause was a mockery. The spontaneous rally had winded the Government and the employers. In the House of Commons Mr. Baldwin, alarmed, said that " if this situation is allowed to last . . . you do run a risk of anarchy. . . . Let us get the workers calm as soon as we can." The *Daily Mail*, from howling " Dissolve the T.U.C." and " Revolution Routed," turned to proclaim " No Reprisals ! " But the unions negotiated new agreements which abrogated not a few long-standing conditions, admitted that they did a " wrongful act " in striking, and opened the door to much victimisation. On the railways, for instance, where union leaders hailed the settlement as " satisfactory," conditions were such that in October Mr. J. H. Thomas stated that the N.U.R. " had 45,000 men out who had not gone back to work since May 1st, and 200,000 who were working three days a week."

Two things remain to be said. One refers to the revelation of the peaceful, democratic and constitutional outlook so characteristic of the British governing class that was afforded after the strike had ended. There was, for instance, the affair in Poplar on the night of Wednesday, May 12th. According to the *Westminster Gazette* of May 14th, and the detailed cabled despatch in the New York *Evening Post* of the same date, a peaceful meeting of dockers was in progress outside the Town Hall, when a lorry filled with police drove up and went straight through the crowd, injuring several. The lorry then stopped, the police

FT

dismounted, doubled back and charged the crowd twice with batons. Thirty-five people were treated at local hospitals, mainly for head injuries. When Father Jack Groser, the Vicar, " upholding a crucifix approached the police and tried to explain that the meeting was peaceful, he was struck down." Immediately after, a tender with a score of police drew up outside the nearby strike head-quarters of the Poplar branch of the N.U.R. Entering the building with batons drawn, they " started batoning right and left without any explanation." The Mayor of the borough, Mr. Hammond, a railwayman, was present. He was clubbed over the head.

Another not untypical example of many hundreds of like cases may be quoted from the report of proceedings at the Gateshead County Police Court given in a local Durham newspaper, the *Blaydon Courier* of May 22nd, 1926. A forty-year old miner named Edward Wilson, member of the Labour Party, was charged under the Emergency Regulations with " doing a certain act which was likely to cause disaffection among the civil population." He was said to have distributed copies of the *Northern Light*, the bulletin of the Chopwell Council of Action. The police prosecutor declared that those associated with the Council " were a menace to the neighbourhood and would have to be dealt with, and now that they had got them in their hands he was going to ask the Court to stamp them out." The newspaper report of the unanimous verdict of the Bench is as follows :

" ' We cannot have Chopwell and the neighbourhood governed by a set of men like you. The inhabitants of Chopwell have to live under the laws passed by Parliament and approved of by the King. They are not to be governed by a set of laws which you and your colleagues and hooligans of your description choose to draw up. . . . The manner in which Chopwell has been governed for some time past now is a scandal, and this Bench is determined, if it comes to us, that that state of affairs shall be put an end to. . . . We don't want you, or anybody else like you. You are just a danger to the community, and the sooner you make up your minds to reform, or get away, the better for all concerned.'

" The accused was sentenced to prison for three months with hard labour, the chairman adding that if he had had his own way he would have sent him to prison for three months and fined him £100."

And at the same time, while teaching the workers much about their enemies, the strike taught them much about themselves. Once more it was seen how unity and fighting spirit could bring advances on every front; it was noteworthy that immediately before the strike the Labour candidate had won a by-election in East Ham North with the highest Labour vote ever recorded there, and that after the strike the Labour candidate walked away with the North Hammersmith seat, increasing his vote by over 2,000 on a record total poll.

Last comment of all may be taken from a national Labour Party organ, the *Labour Woman*, which carried a powerful frontispiece in its issue of June 1926—captioned " There *shall* be a Next Time ! "—and wrote editorially: " the most important thing is that the people themselves now know and feel their own power. Genuine class-consciousness was born in the ten days of the strike and the three days which followed its cessation. . . . The General Strike has made a united working class."

CHAPTER VII

"NEVER AGAIN!"

Scarcely had the seismic shocks of the General Strike
died away when the late Mr. C. T. Cramp publicly cried
" Never Again ! " The cry was heartfelt, no one could
doubt; nor was there any uncertainty that it represented
the profoundest sentiments of the general run of the movement's leaders. In those days of May they had gazed too
closely at what Mr. Arthur Henderson subsequently
called the " terrible prospect " of a collapse of the present
social and political order. They were filled, not with
exaltation but alarm at the thought that " genuine class-
consciousness was born " out of the General Strike, that
" a united working class " had arisen.

Because the change was so clearly marked, the break
with the past so decisive, the General Strike stands out
as the principal turning-point in the whole historical
period that forms the subject of the present book. Perhaps
the inner nature of this change is most easily made plain
by considering the definition of the " object and purpose
of the workers " and their movement laid down by the
Webbs in the concluding paragraphs of the final (1920)
edition of the *History of Trade Unionism*. The intellectual
inspirers of our Labour leaders there stated that that
object was " no mere increase of wages or reduction of
hours. It comprises nothing less than a reconstruction
of society, by the elimination, from the nation's industries
and services, of the Capitalist Profit-maker, and the consequent shrinking up of the class of functionless persons who
live merely by owning. Profit-making as a pursuit, with its
sanctification of the motive of pecuniary self-interest, is

the demon that has to be exorcised." Remarking that " in the painful ' Pilgrim's Progress ' of democracy the workers will be perpetually tempted into by-paths that lead only to the Slough of Despond," they warned against " the temptation of particular trade unions . . . to enter into alliances with Associations of Capitalist Employers." While " co-partnership " with individual capitalists had been seen through :

> " The ' co-partnership ' of trade unions with Associ-
> ations of Capitalists—whether as a development of
> ' Whitley Councils ' or otherwise—which far-sighted
> capitalists will presently offer in specious forms (with a
> view, particularly, to Protective Customs Tariffs and
> other devices for maintaining unnecessarily high prices,
> or to governmental favours and remissions of taxation)
> is, we fear, hankered after by some trade union leaders,
> and might be made seductive to particular grades or
> sections of workers. Any such policy, however plausible,
> would in our judgment be disastrous undermining of
> the solidarity of the whole working class, and a formidable
> obstacle to any genuine Democratic Control of Industry,
> as well as to any general progress in personal freedom
> and in the more equal sharing of the National Product."

It will be seen that those words might well have been written with a prophetic eye on the years that this chapter has to discuss. For what now began was a general retreat of the leadership of the British Labour movement from the aim of a " reconstruction of society by the elimination of the Capitalist Profit-maker " to the aim of just such a " co-partnership " with that same Capitalist Profit-maker as the Webbs had criticised. Peace in industry and coalition in politics were henceforth to figure, explicitly or implicitly, as the objective set before the movement by its directors; and at the end of the road, as the Webbs accurately foretold, there lay nothing but the Slough of Despond.

This retrograde movement by the leaders corresponded

with the requirements of the ruling class. It has been noted that a decisive victory over the working class as a whole was an essential for our rulers if they were to operate the measures of rationalisation and capitalist reorganisation that their difficult economic position imposed. In the General Strike surrender they believed that they had won such a victory; but it was a victory that needed consolidation. For one thing, the miners remained in the field. Their resistance had at all costs to be crushed. Thereafter it would be necessary to keep the workers disarmed and divided if rationalisation, necessarily involving increased unemployment and worsened conditions, was to be put through on any scale. Hence the importance to the governing class of alliance with the leaders of the Labour Party and above all of the trade unions.

The prolonged and stubborn resistance of the miners cut sharply across the schemes of the union leaders as much as it did those of the Government and the coalowners. Mr. Arthur Horner, now president of the South Wales Miners' Federation, wrote bitterly from his post in the front line of that grim and heroic struggle—"when the General Council betrayed the miners, its members had perforce to prevent the miners from winning in order to secure justification in the eyes of their own men. There being no neutrality in the class struggle, the traitors were bound to turn assassins of their previous allies in their own defence. Having made prophecies of a miners' defeat, they must now assist events to prove that they were right." What were the facts behind that hard saying? They lay in the official blanketing of the widespread demands for the most effective forms of solidarity with the miners—a levy on all working trade unionists and an embargo on the importation of coal from abroad.

The Communists and Minority Movement supporters were from the start the most active and determined sponsors of the levy and the embargo; and wherever trade unionists had the opportunity to express their views through official channels they showed themselves wholeheartedly in favour of such action. This was seen in unanimous emergency resolutions of official conferences of Trades Councils, in London and Lancashire for example, called on the eve of the 1926 Trades Union Congress at Bournemouth. It was witnessed by ballots of the Amalgamated Society of Woodworkers and the Union of Postal Workers. And when the pressure grew so strong that a conference of Trade Union Executives was called, which decided on the compromise of a voluntary levy, that levy raised over £43,000 in eight weeks; the miners' fund formally opened by the General Council at an earlier stage only raised £9,525 in nineteen weeks.

On the embargo it is instructive to consider the following exchange at the Bournemouth Trades Union Congress between a delegate and Chairman Pugh:

A. G. Tomkins (Furnishing Trades): " What steps has the General Council taken to get the International Federation of Trade Unions to hold an inquiry into the possibility of preventing black coal coming into Britain ?"
Pugh: " That does not arise in this part of the Report."
Tomkins: " On what part does it arise ? "
Pugh: " I am afraid I cannot tell you."

At the Margate Conference of the Labour Party a month later rather more stage-management was required. I recollect the occasion very well. Harry Pollitt and Arthur Horner had roused the conference with powerful speeches urging the reference back of the Executive's resolution on the mining crisis, which was silent on the levy and embargo. Horner, incidentally, won the most crashing applause of any speaker in the whole conference. Then came moving and militant words from a Yorkshire miner's wife. Delegates were clamouring for the vote, moving that the question be put. The chairman, however, called on Messrs. Thomas, Tillett and MacDonald to save the resolution; this they did by drowning the levy and embargo in a cold douche of despair.

Heightening the gloomy contrast of official passivity

stood the sterling work of the Women's Committee for the Relief of Miners' Wives and Children, headed by the genial Chief Woman Officer of the Labour Party, the late Dr. Marion Phillips. The miners' lamp emblem of the Committee became a popular symbol of solidarity with the miners; while the fact that it was able to raise voluntarily the immense sum of £313,000—though even this paled beside the £1,000,000 produced by the Soviet trade unionists' levy—indicated the response that was there for the organising.

Of the epic fight of the miners to the last ditch in December it is impossible to speak in detail. In passing it may be recalled that Mr. G. A. Spencer, whom we have met as a strong anti-Communist speaker and supporter of the Executive at earlier Labour Party Conferences, emerged as the organiser of the " Non-Political " Miners' Union which engineered the serious breakaways in the Midlands. As a whole the army of the coalfields followed the militant lead, repeatedly rejected all compromise proposals (like the Bishops' Memorandum in the summer), showed its unbroken spirit by the adoption in October of the South Wales resolution for intensifying the fight by withdrawing all safety men, etc., and even at the very end rejected surrender by 480,000 votes to 313,000.

As to Mr. Baldwin and his Government, they showed neither scruple nor restraint in their efforts to break the strike to the greater profit of the coalowners. The Seven-Hour Act of 1919 was repealed. Pickets and other active fighters in the coalfields were arrested and jailed by hundreds under the Emergency Regulations, which were kept in force. Pressure was brought to bear upon local authorities to withhold relief and to suspend services like free milk for babies and free meals for necessitous school children. In face of these acts of his Government, Mr. Baldwin sent a letter to the United States, on the eve of the arrival there in August of a miners' delegation on a collecting campaign, stating that there was no want in the British coalfields. In this mean effort he was seconded by

The Times and the National Society for the Prevention of Cruelty to Children, which issued a report on the position in the coalfields, claiming that there was no urgent need among miners' children. An N.S.P.C.C. headquarters official, asked by a journalist whether the possible effect of the report would not be to check financial assistance for the miners both at home and from abroad, replied shortly, " It is intended to."[1]

The problems raised by the continuance of the miners' struggle could not be dissociated from the problems left by the General Strike. Upon the General Council there reposed the obligation to report to its constituents at the earliest possible moment. A bewildered movement was anxious, and had the right, to thrash this matter out and fix responsibilities. Weeks passed. The General Council remained silent and no Conference of Executives was called. It was said that the Council was unwilling to prejudice any possible settlement of the miners' lock-out. Under pressure from affiliated unions, however, it was eventually decided to summon the Conference for June 25th, 1926, whether the lock-out were over or not. The General Council completed its report on June 16th. Suddenly, three days before the Conference was due to meet, it was announced that an agreement had been signed between the General Council and the Miners' Executive postponing the Conference till after the conclusion of the miners' lock-out. It was stated that this step was taken in order that nothing should accrue to the detriment of the miners, and on the same grounds it was laid down that mutual criticism should cease, Mr. A. J. Cook undertaking " for the duration " to cease publishing his sensational pamphlet *The Nine Days*, which with its deadly indictment of the Council was proving a best-seller throughout the movement.

This procedure was constitutionally of doubtful propriety. The General Council was responsible to all the unions which had mandated it to lead them in the General Strike, and could not evade that responsibility by separate

[1] Marion Phillips: *Women and the Miners' Lockout*, pp. 60-2.

agreement with one particular union. It was no less evident that the argument from the angle of the miners' interests was specious. Frank and searching discussion and settlement of the issues that had convulsed the whole movement would strengthen that movement and the miners in their fight. To burke discussion would—and did—have precisely the opposite effect. In no way, as the facts already adduced will have suggested, did the Council demonstrate any more effective solidarity with the miners because of the June Pact.

Unfortunately the affair had a still more disingenuous aspect. The miners' leaders, with naïve trustfulness, stilled their criticisms of the General Council. But the General Council's criticisms of the miners were not stilled. A member of the Council, Mr. John Bromley, the Locomotivemen's general secretary, published in the July issue of his union journal—which must have gone to press just about the time of the June Pact—the greater part of the General Council's report. The attacks on the Miners' Federation and its leaders with which this document was filled, earned it immediate and immense Press publicity; appropriate passages were displayed on bills in the Midland coalfields in the owners' all-too-successful efforts to break the fight there. In the report the General Council no longer advanced the Samuel Memorandum, as they did on May 12th, as their main reason for the calling-off of the strike. " The strike was terminated," they concluded, " for one sufficient reason only, namely, that in view of the attitude of the Miners' Federation its continuance would have rendered its purpose futile." That attitude was, of course, the steady refusal to agree to lower wages or longer hours, which the report elsewhere characterised as " being tied to a mere slogan," or " a policy of mere negation."

The Bromley publication could be considered as a flagrant—even if unintentional—breach of the June Pact, or at least as rendering the Pact null and void. Perhaps the General Council's attitude can be deduced from the fact that Mr. Bromley himself was its chosen spokesman at the

Bournemouth Congress on the official mining resolution. That choice resulted in a scene without precedent in the history of the T.U.C. The storm broke directly the speaker was announced. Rising as one man the miners' delegation, shouting with rage, voiced the hot anger that was generally felt. All over the hall delegates rose with them. The uproar was tremendous. Closing their ranks, the miners' delegates kicked chairs round them, barricade fashion, in the expectation of a free fight. Then came the suspension of the sitting for an hour, the miners' delegation meeting, and the imposition of Mr. Bromley as a matter of discipline.

Symptomatic though the Bromley episode was, there was more importance in the use of the June Pact to burke all discussion of the General Strike at Bournemouth. Chairman Pugh, amid protests from delegates of by no means militant temper, ruled that the Congress—the supreme authority of the trade union movement, and the body that elected the General Council—could not discuss the Strike and the General Council's conduct of it. Arguing that this could only be done by the Conference of Executives, he thereby placed an appointed over a democratically elected body, and refused to allow the movement itself to decide whether it should or should not maintain silence on the current issue which was of paramount importance. Unquestionably the temper of the Congress was such that this ruling would have been decisively rejected, if it had not been for one thing. That was the intervention of Mr. A. J. Cook. Appealing to the June Pact—whose signing he later said he personally regretted—Mr. Cook supported Mr. Pugh's ruling. At that time Mr. Cook's prestige throughout the movement was immense. He had the Bournemouth Congress at his feet. A few frank words from him, and the General Council would surely have been over-ruled.

Like the T.U.C., the Labour Party Conference at Margate in October 1926 produced its crop of official hits at the miners. In a presidential speech so wretched that it cost him his seat on the Party Executive in the subsequent elections, the late Mr. Robert Williams sneered at the miners, who " may be likened to the sightless Samson feeling for a grip of the pillars of the Temple, the crashing of which may engulf this thing we call British civilisation. . . . This despairing policy may be magnificent, but it is not war." At the same time he struck the note of impotence, of surrender, of the acceptance of capitalism world-without-end-amen, which was henceforth to be a prime feature of Labour leadership. " Let us seek industrial peace through methods of conciliation," he cried. " We cannot subvert or overthrow, we must supersede capitalism," though " whether Socialism will come in our time . . . is a matter for conjecture." In an article appropriately featured in Lord Rothermere's *Answers* he had earlier written: " The General Strike failed because the resources of the country were—and are—stronger than the resources of the trade unions," adding that " our unions can do good work by discrediting the theory " that every employer " is an ' enemy of the working classes.' "

It was becoming difficult to distinguish authoritative expressions of trade union opinion from orthodox capitalist statements. At Bournemouth Mr. Pugh had laid stress on the need for a " scientific wage policy," in contrast to Mr. Swales' militant words from the chair at Scarborough the year before. He claimed that the unions were an " institution " of capitalist society, " as much a part of the life of the community as the Law Courts or Parliament itself." This claim tallied with the assertion of Mr. Baldwin on May 13th that " there can be no greater disaster than that there should be anarchy in the trade union world. It would be impossible in our highly-organised and highly-developed system of industry to carry on unless you had organisations which could speak for and bind the parties on both sides." More directly, if more crudely, the sentiment behind this kind of talk was voiced by Mr. W. L. Hutcheson, fraternal delegate from the American Federation of Labour to the Bournemouth Congress. He affirmed that " we must always have what you might term the capitalist." Symbolically enough the second A.F. of L. delegate never appeared at

Bournemouth; he was a reactionary union leader named Farrington who had just at that time, in circumstances which made a great stir in the States, openly gone on the pay-roll of one of the biggest coal corporations in Pennsylvania.

Given this attitude on the part of the most responsible leaders the Government had little to fear in pressing ahead with their attack. Conciliation, as always, only served to encourage the aggressor. Both on the home and international fronts the battle was joined. In China all the forces at the disposal of British imperialism, from gunboats to graft, were employed in the effort to stem and break up the victorious advance of the national revolution that was arousing from their slumber of centuries hundreds of millions of mankind. Those who have a common enemy are potential allies; and it required no deep political perception to sense the community of interest between yellow factory-hands and farmers fighting Mr. Baldwin and his class on the Yangtse, and white miners fighting Mr. Baldwin and his class in Yorkshire. Yet it was left to the Communists to take the initiative in proposing the establishment of " Hands off China " committees, as they were foremost in the work of founding, early in 1927, the League Against Imperialism. These moves were cold-shouldered by the official leadership, though the readiness of the movement was indicated by the fact that seventy " Hands off China " committees were nevertheless set up in various parts of the country and did good work.

Anglo-Soviet relations assumed special importance with the determination of the Government to force a breach, which duly followed the provocation of the Arcos raid. Protests apart, there was no strong reaction on the part of the movement's leaders here. After the General Strike the Anglo-Russian Joint Advisory Council had virtually been allowed to lapse so far as the General Council was concerned. Despite the strongest pressure from the Soviet trade unionists only one meeting of the Council had taken place, at the end of July 1926. The Home Office had stepped in to ban the attendance of Soviet fraternal delegates at the Bournemouth T.U.C., and the highly critical message which was telegraphed in Tomsky's name to the Congress aroused only hostility. Even the Arcos raid and the breach of diplomatic relations failed to deflect the General Council from its evident intention to end an association that had become distasteful. It only remained for the formal declaration of a break with the Soviet trade unions, of the ending of the Joint Advisory Council, to be put through the Edinburgh T.U.C. in September 1927.

On the home front the forces of reaction were able to secure the support of leading Labour representatives in what might have been thought an unlikely field. That was in the attack on the conditions of the unemployed mapped out by the committee of inquiry presided over by Lord Blanesburgh. The Blanesburgh Report proposed serious cuts in unemployment insurance benefit, extension of the notorious " not genuinely seeking work " clause and consequential modifications, for the worse, of many items in the system of unemployment relief. Working-class anger over this Report had to reckon with the fact, of which many were incredulous, that among the signatories were the three Labour members of the committee—Miss Margaret Bondfield, Mr. Frank Hodges (ex-secretary of the Miners' Federation), and Mr. A. E. Holmes (of the Printing and Kindred Trades Federation). Though it can scarcely be supposed that these recommendations commanded the assent of the movement's leadership as a whole, it was noteworthy that far from any general repudiation of the signatories there was rather a tacit effort to shield them from the storm of criticism that sprang up. At the same time the General Council of the T.U.C. terminated the fruitful co-operation that had existed between it and the organised unemployed in the shape of the Joint Advisory Council with the National Unemployed Workers' Movement.

All this augured ill for the resistance that was soon needed against the Government's central and most deadly attack—the tabling of the Bill that was to be rushed into law, with the revival of the " guillotine " and the mobilising of the inflated "Zinoviev Letter" Tory majority, as the Trade Disputes and Trade Unions Act, 1927, commonly called the "Blacklegs' Charter." It was a year to the very day (April 29th) that the Conference of Trade Union Executives again met—to face the fact that, as Chairman George Hicks put it, "the trade union movement is in the greatest danger . . . we must not hesitate to use any weapon in Labour's armoury to safeguard the integrity of our movement." Secretary Citrine justly said that "not since the repeal of the Combination Laws has the Labour movement been faced with such a serious menace." The accuracy of that view has long been a matter of history; authoritative opinion is summed up in Professor Wilfrid H. Crook's statement that "even as amended the Act stands to-day as the most reactionary sample of British Labour legislation placed on the statute book since the evil Combination Laws of 1799–1800."

The whole movement was united in opposition to such a measure. In its vague and clumsy drafting, roundly condemned by lawyers of the eminence of Lord Reading, and in the sponsoring of it by important capitalist groupings like the Association of British Chambers of Commerce and the National Union of Manufacturers, by great industrialists like Mr. Dudley Docker of the Vickers combine, the Bill exhibited its punitive purpose. How was it possible adequately to characterise the class cynicism of the intentional omission of any reference to lock-outs in a Bill which set out to penalise certain kinds of strikes ?

Even with such preposterous anomalies removed on Labour insistence during the debates in the Commons, the whole temper and aim of the Bill survived unaltered in the Act. Not only were general strikes henceforth declared illegal; the ban fell upon all sympathetic strikes or strikes which could be construed as likely to "coerce the Government" either directly or indirectly. For the better protection and encouragement of blacklegs it was prescribed that they could, if trade unionists and expelled for their actions, claim damages from the union; at the same time mass picketing was forbidden and even the "peaceful persuasion" of ordinary picketing, legal for a couple of generations, virtually abolished by a blanket definition of "intimidation." Civil servants were forbidden to join any unions other than those catering exclusively for State employees, which must have no political objects and must cease affiliation with the T.U.C. or the Labour Party. Employees of any local or public authority were rendered liable to criminal prosecution for breach of contract of their employment; while such authorities were forbidden to require trade union membership as a condition of employment or even as a condition to require of their contractors. Most unscrupulous of all, the Act sought to hamstring the Labour Party financially by a radical change in the right to maintain a political fund as enjoyed by the unions under the Trade Union Act of 1913. Instead of the levy for such a fund being applicable to all union members except those who specifically claimed exemption (" contracting-out "), in future it was only to apply to those members who specifically " contracted-in." Finally, there was an extraordinary definition of a strike as, among other things, " a refusal under a common understanding of any number of persons who are, *or have been*," employed in any trade or industry, " to continue to work *or to accept employment*." This could clearly be operated to apply the penalities of the Act to unemployed men who refused to backleg in an illegal strike ; here was industrial serfdom with a vengeance.

Evidently a Government that was prepared to stand by a measure of this kind could only be stopped by decisive action. What action was to be taken in opposition to the Bill ? Seven years before, the Webbs had soberly summed up the possibilities of a General Strike in this country; such a strike would be most likely, they concluded, " if any Act were passed depriving the trade unions of the rights and liberties now conceded to them," and " it would be supported not only by the wage-earning class as a whole, but also by a large section of the middle class." " That is one reason," they added, " why, short of madness, no such act would be committed by the Government or by Parliament. If any such act were perpetrated, it would probably involve a revolution, not in the British, but in the continental sense." The Baldwin Government, however, were not mad. They justly reckoned that 1926 had effectively inoculated the leaders against the General Strike virus. A platform campaign and demonstrations, they insolently announced, would not deter them in the least; but it was to such a campaign that opposition was limited.

It would, however, be unfair to the General Council and to the union leaders by and large to overlook the justification they had for their limited opposition to the Trade Union Bill. After all, they were now looking to industrial peace and collaboration in capitalist revival as the main line of their policy. So they could hardly object in practice to some of the provisos of the Bill, in which the governing class from its point of view was endeavouring to ensure peace in industry (by the one-sided disarmament of the workers, of course). Be that as it may, the fact remains that little over a month after the passage of the Bill into law the leaders took the initiative in offering to co-operate with the employers " in a common endeavour to improve the efficiency of industry and to raise the workers' standard of life." The words are those of Mr. George Hicks, noted as one of the pre-General Strike " Lefts " on the General Council, in his presidential address to the Edinburgh T.U.C. in September 1927. Not till late in November was this " surprisingly magnanimous " offer (as Professor Crook rather acidly calls it) taken up. A group of twenty leading industrialists, headed by the late Lord Melchett (then Sir Alfred Mond), founder of the mammoth Imperial Chemical Industries combine, wrote to the General Council intimating their willingness to discuss general questions of " industrial reorganisation and industrial relations." The first joint meeting took place on January 12th, 1928, in the sedate surroundings of Burlington House. Mondism was born.

That initial letter of the Mond group of employers was significant in its emphasis. The view was stressed that

" industrial reconstruction can be undertaken only in conjunction with, and with the co-operation of, those entitled
and empowered to speak for organised labour." It was
added that " the prosperity of industry can, in our view, be
fully attained only by full and frank recognition of facts as
they exist, and an equally full and frank determination to
increase the competitive power of British industries in the
world's markets." In short, effort must be directed to securing capitalist revival and prosperity in which some of the
workers might, or might not, be able to obtain a minor share.

In adhering to this viewpoint the General Council were
following the lead of MacDonald and Snowden. The former
had recently condemned the " Samson policy " of struggle,
claiming that even if the balcony with the Philistines fell
" it will be shored up; it will be rebuilt; the workers will be
weaker than ever," while arguing on the other hand that
" a defeat that retains the potentiality of prosperity is a
victory." The latter publicly asserted as early as April 1926
that, given intelligent exploitation by " wideawake capitalists " of the " new age of electricity and chemistry " which
the world was said to be entering, " then the capitalist
system will be given a new and long and more powerful
lease of life."

Reporting to the Swansea Congress in 1928 the General
Council outlined three possible policies for trade unionism.
The policy of consistent working-class struggle it dismissed as " futile, certain to fail, and sure to lead to bloodshed and misery." The conventional trade union policy of
letting the employers run industry while the unions fought
for their members' interests alone was also dismissed as
" inconsistent with the modern demand for a completely
altered status of the workers in industry." Number three
(approved) was " for the trade union movement to say
boldly that not only is it concerned with the prosperity of
industry, but that it is going to have a voice in the way
industry is carried on . . . the unions can use their power to
promote and guide the scientific reorganisation of industry."

From the very first meeting with Mond root and branch

opposition to the whole idea of such conversations had been forcibly expressed by one member of the General Council, Mr. A. J. Cook, who would not budge from a plain working-class line despite Secretary Citrine's hint that " Mr. Cook's action is now a matter for the General Council itself to consider," or amiable references by another of his Council colleagues to " criminal idiocy . . . a mendacious charlatan." The more formal view that the employers' group represented no official authority, and that talks with them might compromise established union principles, was voiced in particular by the leaders of the Amalgamated Engineering Union. When the Swansea T.U.C. discussed the situation in detail even Mr. George Hicks, initiator of the talks, was found to have been converted to the opposition. But an A.E.U. motion for the suspension of the conversations pending a reference back to the affiliated unions was defeated by 2,920,000 votes to 768,000 at that Congress and the General Council's policy endorsed; the minority, it will be observed, was not unsubstantial.

At the opening of the Mond talks it was said that they were purely for purposes of investigation, were " exploratory." The General Council asserted that they entered these discussions " without surrendering principles which they held to be fundamental." When the first Joint Report was agreed by both sides on July 4th, 1928, however, it appeared to embody a conception of trade unionism that surrendered a good deal. The Report declared that the " tendency " to rationalisation and trustification " should be welcomed and encouraged." It then proposed the establishment of a National Industrial Council, composed on the one hand of the General Council of the T.U.C. and on the other hand of an equal number of employers, nominated by the National Confederation of Employers' Organisations and the Federation of British Industries. Through a Joint Standing Committee this body was to operate a system of compulsory conciliation; that is to say the right to strike was to be waived in the event of an employer applying for a case to be heard before a joint conciliation board. " Such a partnership," *The Times* approvingly commented, " will also tend to ease the adjustments of wages and other conditions of employment which must constantly be required as the conditions of industry change." The whole implication was that the Report envisaged trade unionism, not as an instrument in the workers' hands, but as an auxiliary organ of capitalist industry.

Taken in conjunction with these proposals the section of the Report dealing with trade union recognition assumed an ominous aspect. Under this section the employers conceded, in return for the General Council's agreement to work for " the most effective co-operation " in industry, recognition of those unions only that were " recognised by the General Council of the Trades Union Congress as *bona fide* trade unions." They engaged to encourage their workers to be members of such " *bona fide* trade unions," and to guarantee against victimisation those engaged in " legitimate trade union activities." What in effect this meant was the universalising of the ingenious system of disguised company unionism devised by Mr. Havelock Wilson to the greater profit of the shipowners and the easier exploitation of the seamen. Immediately after the Edinburgh Congress an astute and experienced leader, Mr. Emanuel Shinwell, M.P., had noted:

> " We have seen how in the Mercantile Marine membership of a certain trade union has become obligatory, the employers actually collecting subscriptions for the union. The corollary is, of course, acquiescence, and the adoption of stern measures against men who kick over the traces. It is a blunt bargain. The trade union keeps the men in order; the employer in return agrees to employ union men only. Scores of prominent men in the trade union movement have stated quite openly that no fault is to be found with the system, and indeed regretted it could not be applied to their industry."

Such a " blunt bargain " was implicit in the Mond Report's conceding of union recognition. Surely a union leadership that was ready to co-operate in " easing adjustments of wages," in supporting rationalisation, in banning strikes, could provide all the tangible advantages of company unionism with none of its expense ? As for the guarantee against victimisation that might easily turn into a guarantee *of* victimisation; for " *legitimate* trade union activities " presumbly meant those permitted by law (as " declared and amended " by the Blacklegs' Charter), and endorsed by the General Council. A militant trade unionist victimised by the employers might therefore expect to be regarded as outside the scope of the Mond Report (militant activities not being " legitimate ") ; alternatively he might be expelled from the union because of his militant opposition to the leaders' policy, and thereupon dismissed by the employers as not being a member of a *bona fide* trade union. It was significant that at the initial meeting with Mond a member of the General Council was reported to have said : " There is another school of thought abroad that fights against co-operation. We [i.e. union leaders and employers] must fight together against this school."[1]

It was soon made clear that the policy of industrial peace meant war within the trade unions. There was a substantial body of trade union opinion that did not believe in the line that found expression in Mondism; and it was inevitable, as the quotation above indicates, that the leadership should fight against those forces of militant opposition in the unions that more and more were gathering round the banner of the Minority Movement. Already at the Bournemouth T.U.C. the strong sentiment in favour of the militant line was made plain. Although the Baldwin Government conveniently held in jail the Minority Movement's leader, Harry Pollitt, the group of delegates who adhered to that movement's viewpoint made their mark on the Congress. They were the principal advocates of the resolution on industrial unionism and amalgamation which was adopted by 2,164,000 votes to 1,658,000. On other resolutions they sponsored, they scored substantial minority

[1] Quoted in *The Labour Monthly*, vol. x, No. 2 (1928), p. 81.

votes—848,000 votes on a resolution to grant full powers to the General Council and 738,000 in opposition to the General Council's appeal to Trades Councils not to affiliate to the Minority Movement. While, on the latter vote, the majority carried the day with a total of 2,710,000 it was noteworthy that there were 1,000,000 abstentions.

It was at this Bournemouth Congress, and in the debate on the right of Trades Councils to affiliate to the Minority Movement, that the General Council's spokesman, Mr. A. Conley of the Garment Workers, made a statement that requires no comment. According to the *Daily Herald* report he said: " If the Council had agreed to this affiliation, within a short time the Minority Movement would become the majority." One can only assume that the fear so candidly expressed of the minority rapidly becoming the majority if it were given a clear run was also responsible for the steps that were soon taken to bar from office (even when democratically elected), and finally to expel from the unions, the most prominent fighters for a militant policy. The powerful National Union of General and Municipal Workers had the distinction of entering on this disruptive career at an early stage. One of the leading officials of that Union, Mr. W. Sherwood, frankly described the process in his speech as British fraternal delegate to the Convention of the American Federation of Labour at Los Angeles in 1927.

Mr. Sherwood said: " Branches of our organisation in London, over 15,000 strong, refused to comply with the instructions of our General Council. Well, Mr. President, we simply smashed the branches. . . . We had on our General Council two men who represented great areas in our country, but they were going to Minority meetings, and we said: ' Sign a declaration or get out.' Well, they had to get out." To which President Green, no doubt speaking out of the richness of the A.F. of L.'s experience in maintaining the rule of the officialdom by gangster methods, replied: " We were made happy when we listened to those words. We felt that our own position had been thoroughly vindicated, that the traditional course of the American Federation of Labour had found additional approval from our older brothers across the sea."[1]

By the spring of 1928 the example of the General Workers had been followed in varying degrees by the Railwaymen, Transport Workers, Shop Assistants, Natsopa, Electrical Trades, Boot and Shoe Operatives, Bakers and Painters. Several of these unions by rule disfranchised Communists or Minority Movement members from holding any office. The leading case was that of the Boilermakers, whose executive stepped in to ban the nomination of " any known Communist " as delegate to the T.U.C. or the Labour Party Conference; this was directed against Harry Pollitt, who for six years in succession had been elected top of the poll for these positions.

Most striking of all was the case of the Scottish Miners' Union, which deserves description in some detail. This body was a federation of the six county miners' unions in Scotland, of which the two largest were those of Lanarkshire and Fife. In these two counties Communist miners and their supporters had won much influence during the lock-out and immediately thereafter had gained numerous successes in the unions; in Fife they had led the campaign to heal a union split dating from 1921. William Allan, a Communist, was elected general secretary in Lanarkshire and the executive board in Fife found itself with a decisive phalanx of Communist and militant delegates. The annual conference of the Scottish Union, which had not been held since 1925 owing to the lock-out, was eventually notified for December 1927, and in accordance with rule the county unions were desired to send in their nominations for official positions and at the same time to appoint their representatives on the Scottish executive.

Fife and Lanarkshire thereupon proceeded to take branch or ballot votes. The other counties contented themselves with a vote of their executive boards or else by leaving it to the officials. Out of 92 branches in the Lanarkshire Union, 81 voted, the returns being the highest since 1923

[1] Quoted in *The Labour Monthly*, vol. x, No. 4 (1928), p. 203.

(in 1925 when the sitting representatives and officials were returned, only 58 branches voted out of 113). The result of the vote was that the Communist-supported candidates secured nomination for the posts of president, vice-president and secretary and for six out of the eleven Lanarkshire seats on the Scottish executive. In Fife 49 branches voted out of 54. Two successive branch votes were taken and on each vote the Communist candidates for the official posts named came out on top, the second branch vote giving them in each case even more decisive majorities. For Fife's five representatives on the Scottish executive no less than three successive individual ballots of the members were taken. Out of 12,500 union members well over 11,000, or more than 90 per cent, registered their votes—probably a record for any union election. With each ballot the votes of the Communist and Minority Movement candidates steadily increased until finally they swept the board. Appeals by the defeated officials to defer the declaration of the third ballot were referred to the branches who by the impressive majority of 45 branches against 6 demanded the declaration and acceptance of the ballot.

There could hardly be any question that the democracy of the Scottish coalfields had expressed its desire for a change in its leaders. Since Fife and Lanarkshire together commanded a majority of the whole Scottish Union, all that remained was for the formal changeover to take place at the annual conference. A remarkable Press campaign then began in Scotland, headed by the *Evening Times* of Glasgow (whose proprietors had gone rigidly non-union after the General Strike), which shortly made the inspired pronouncement that a plan had been formed to " dish the Reds." The plan was Napoleonic in its simplicity; for the defeated officials just decided that they would postpone the annual conference at which their own democratically decided defeat would take effect.

Nominally the postponement was said to be for three months, and the excuse the heavy arrears of affiliation fees accumulated by all the counties. Branch votes in Fife and

Lanarkshire repudiated this procedure and mandated the representatives of these counties on the executive to vote against further postponement. Upon this the officials took the further step of not summoning any meeting of the Scottish executive. When that body was finally called together, under great pressure from the counties, on April 5th, 1928, the Fife and Lanarkshire representatives ignored their county mandates; the executive decided in favour of further delay, agreed to issue a manifesto to the members and to remit the whole matter to the Miners' Federation of Great Britain.

The manifesto was an interesting document. Arrears no longer figured as the " paramount reason " for the conference's postponement. The defeated officials now directed their full attack against the Communists and the Minority Movement, who, it was stated, " are members of our unions mainly for the purpose of furthering . . . the subversion of constitutional trade unionism and of Labour Party principles." The Communists were accused of acting " at the behest of an alien body, whose decisions are an outrage on every principle of democracy." The impartial observer might feel disposed to say that those who drafted that sentence had very little to learn in the matter of outraging democracy. Indeed, when the facts set forth above are considered, the whole of the manifesto assumes an air of absurd paradox. " We refuse," it went on, " to take our instructions from this or any other outside body " (was not the point rather that these worthy persons refused to take their instructions from the members who paid them ?). " Communism," they said, " seeks to displace constitutional trade unionism by unconstitutional means " (an odd description of branch and ballot votes conducted according to rule and custom). In conclusion, they applied to themselves the curious description, for defeated candidates in an election, of " the leaders you have chosen and tested and found not wanting." " We ask you to do your part," the manifesto fulminated, " in purging your organisation of this evil, disruptive influence." The authors of the manifesto were not referring to themselves.

Up to this time the " evil, disruptive influence " of the militants in Fife and Lanarkshire had been shown in a marked improvement in the position of the miners' organisation in those two counties. In Fife the members were gaining new heart from a 100 per cent recruiting campaign carried out along lines proposed and pressed through by the Communists, led by the two Communists who had been elected miners' agents for the county. In Lanarkshire the branches had adopted the militants' proposals for union reconstruction, including such sinister points as the periodical election of agents, the use of the ballot vote for all elections to official positions, reductions in official salaries and so forth. Dues from branches in Lanarkshire rose from £548 in July, 1927, to £1,157 in November. The Communist county officials and executive members had taken office in August.

On the other hand the confusion into which the " old gang " flung the Scottish coalfields by their action, soon had its effect. As the fight inside the unions proceeded, it had a dispiriting effect on the union members and made the unorganised men feel that it was a squabble between rival groups for place and power. Membership began to decline alarmingly. In Fife the late Mr. William Adamson, when voted out of his position as general secretary, proceeded to form a new breakaway union of his own, thus emulating the egregious Spencer. Eventually the militants had no alternative but to form their own organisation to try and save something for trade unionism in the Scottish coalfields. Accordingly the United Mineworkers of Scotland was established, its principal strength being in Fife.

Not till March 1929 did the M.F.G.B. Executive issue a final decision on the position in Scotland. But there had already been sufficient signs that the national leaders shared the sentiments of their defeated Scottish colleagues. At the Llandudno conference of the Miners' Federation in August 1928, President Herbert Smith had indulged in a little " propaganda of the deed," when he physically assaulted Arthur Horner, an executive member, arising out of an incident connected with the Scottish issue. At the Swansea T.U.C. in the same year, Mr. Smith had announced his readiness to "dissect the movement to the very ground" if this were required in the furtherance of the official policy. The final M.F.G.B. statement added to a general condemnation of the Communists a pledge to help "the *bona fide* Scottish Miners' Federation" in "carrying out the principles of the Miners' Federation, the T.U.C. and the British Labour Party." It appeared, therefore, that the right of franchise in the unions, if it may be put that way, was to depend on the acceptance of the Liberal policy with which Mr. MacDonald and the Elder Statesmen had been successfully saddling the Labour Party.

The progress of Mondism and its accompanying subversion of democracy in the unions was reflected in a significant shrinkage in union membership. Between 1926 and 1928 Trades Union Congress affiliations declined by half a million. During the latter year union membership receded by 16 per cent on the railways, by 15 per cent in iron and steel, by 14 per cent in mining. The example of the miners suggested the inaccuracy of the conventional argument that a policy of fight drove members way. In 1926–27 the miners' unions lost 72,000 members, it is true; but in 1927–28, when peace at any price was the watchword, they lost 160,000.

No surprise can be felt at this process of decline when it is realised that working-class conditions were deteriorating and that the union leadership proved itself incapable of staying this deterioration; indeed the whole Mondist outlook was one that predisposed to an acceptance of worsened standards in the higher interests of industrial "efficiency." The railways were a good example. Between 1925 and 1927 there was a decline of 3 per cent in the number of railwaymen employed; but freight carried did not decline; on the contrary it increased by 3 per cent, while engine-miles run rose by no less than 29 per cent. At the annual general meeting of the National Union of Railwaymen in April 1928 Mr. J. H. Thomas said, "Do not let us waste our time talking about capitalism, a new social order and a change of system," while the late Mr. C. T. Cramp opined that " there were some people who still believe in a senile theory of Socialism which says that the issue lies between the employers and the workers. It did not." On the same day that those remarks were uttered the railway companies made public their demands for new wage cuts, Sir Felix Pole of the Great Western announcing that " employees must be prepared to recognise economic conditions which compel retrenchment." Shortly afterwards the union leaders agreed to a cut of $2\frac{1}{2}$ per cent—6d. in the £—and the *Daily Herald* headlined the news " Railwaymen's Concessions to Help Companies," while the *Observer* quaintly described the agreement as " Mutual Gains."

Coming on top of their defeat in 1926 Mondism brought nothing to the miners but deepening misery. A year after the first Mond meeting there were 220,000 fewer miners at work than there were in 1925, but the aggregate output was no less. On the average production had been sweated up to 3 cwts. per man-shift more than before the lock-out. Production costs per ton in 1928 were 3s. 7d. less than in 1925; of this 3s. 3d. was accounted for by reduction in wages cost. The average wage was no more than 30 per cent over the 1914 level, while the official cost-of-living index stood at 67 per cent. In Durham and South Wales the owners made further concerted attacks on wages, an award in the latter coalfield reducing the subsistence wage to 7s. $10\frac{1}{2}$d. a shift. Short time increased. With the longer working day the accident rate rose and the country was shocked by a terrible disaster at Cwm in Monmouthshire early in 1927. In face of this situation the attitude of the miners' leaders was summed up by Mr. William Straker of Northumberland, who said in August 1927: " I am not without hope that before this year is out we will have got back some of our markets." Reality was not kind to these Micawberish hopes; by the end of the following year the coal industry had touched new depths, output being 3,000,000 tons less than in 1925 when the industry was

" heading for irretrievable disaster." So alarming had the impoverishment in the mining areas become that *The Times* in April 1928 featured a series of sensational articles portraying the " bitterness and despair " in South Wales. A Lord Mayor's Fund was started, and the following winter a big charity-mongering Press campaign opened, the *Morning Post* candidly explaining that this was dictated " not only by benevolence but by self-interest."

During 1927–29 it could be said that throughout industry conditions were harsher than for a generation. In engineering reports from all the principal centres spoke of excessive overtime, increase in piece work, breaking of previous prices, victimisation of trade unionists. " Even the inadequate agreements we have with the employers are being observed more in the breach than in practice," wrote the *Foundry Workers' Journal* in October 1928. In the boot and shoe trade, which had for long prided itself on its unbroken peace, factories were closing down wholesale and the union president apostrophised the employers : " Gentlemen, with so much tranquillity in the industry, how comes it that the operatives are not kept better employed ? "

At the same time capital was strengthening its position. Profits were already on the upgrade in 1927, the returns of the *Economist* showing an average dividend of 10·8 per cent on ordinary shares. The list of representative securities published by the *Bankers' Magazine* showed a 4 per cent rise in value on the year, amounting to an aggregate increase of £269,000,000. Income tax returns showed that the number of super-tax payers (those with incomes exceeding £2,000 a year) was a record.

While all this was taking place the position in the Labour Party continued to be one of a determined effort on the part of Mr. MacDonald and his fellow leaders to enforce their Liberal policy at the expense of the party's unity. The Liverpool decisions against the Communists were carried out without flinching. At the Margate Conference of the party in 1926 it was reported that thirteen constituency and local parties had been disaffiliated for persistently refusing to expel Communists. In these cases new local parties, loyal to the Liverpool line, were gradually established. Yet both at Margate and at Blackpool, the scene of the 1927 conference, it was noticeable that the platform had to employ all the known arts of steam-rollering to get its way. The technique at times was distinctly slim; for example, at Blackpool the general desire for a critical discussion of the part played by Labour representatives on the Blanesburgh Committee on unemployment was side-tracked by the curious announcement that the acceptance of the references to unemployment in the Executive Report covered this point. All the same, the MacDonaldites had to fight hard to defeat the opposition. No less than twenty-eight different organisations put down resolutions for the Margate Conference calling for the Liverpool decisions to be rescinded. A national Left Wing Movement was established in the course of 1926 and was shortly able to report that forty-eight Labour Parties had endorsed its programme.

At the Blackpool Conference the question of a new detailed programme for the Party was already on the order of the day. It was at that Conference that Mr. MacDonald accurately summed up the coming programme by saying airily that it would, of course, always keep Socialism " in the background." It did. It was the political counterpart of Mondism. The new programme itself, entitled *Labour and the Nation* (the 1925 omission of the " New Social Order " was permanent, it seemed), was endorsed at the Birmingham Conference in 1928. The traditional slogan of nationalisation became a back number, its place being taken by " public corporations." Mr. Snowden said: " We are going to get our Socialism largely in that way, through a public corporation controlled in the interests of the public by the best experts and business men." Gone was any thought of that " elimination of the capitalist profit-maker " of which the Webbs had spoken. Responsible City opinion greeted the proposals as they applied to the Bank of England, for instance, as " little more than a pious aspiration " (*Economist*), or as " a modest document " (*Financial Times*).

Capitalists could hardly feel alarmed when the Labour Party told them that they " will be well advised to begin by setting their own house in order—to modernise their organisation, improve their technique, eliminate waste and apply intelligently the resources which science has revealed." It was hard to see the dividing line between this programme and the programme of the Liberal Yellow Book with its endorsement of the " public concern " as the future type of industrial organisation.

A sympathetic continental observer, Herr Egon Wertheimer, then the London correspondent of the Berlin *Vorwärts*, expressed his surprise at the programme's failure to analyse the existing economic and political situation of Britain. He noted its " weakness and lack of accentuation as against the 1918 programme," observing that it was " amazing how many times it falls back on the expedient of a Royal Commission." On foreign policy he drily remarked that the " elimination of every class interest from its international policy has enabled the Labour Party . . . to describe its programme as the only true national programme in foreign politics."

For Socialists those were difficult years. The Independent Labour Party still stood out as the largest Socialist body, and began to reflect, albeit uncertainly and unclearly, the Left moods that prevailed among the rank and file. Yet the " Socialism in our Time " policy, continuing the Living Wage propaganda, was a highly contradictory line, expressing the internal crisis that was taking shape in the I.L.P. as well as the growing tension in its relations with the Labour Party. To our age, inured to world crisis, it seems strange to recall the I.L.P. propaganda of ten years ago, with its talk of the need for " an assault upon poverty " as a necessary prelude to Socialism, with its prescription of State fixing of wages and prices as the means whereby the working class could march to Socialism " not through starvation but through an era of prosperity." While the old leaders were abandoning the Party that had made them—Snowden resigned at this time and MacDonald was soon to follow—

the I.L.P. leadership never presented itself as an alternative to MacDonald and MacDonaldism. On the contrary it continued to treat that sinister figure with strangely exaggerated politeness and respect. It did, however, present itself as an alternative to Communism. The *Socialist Review* wrote in February 1928 that the function of the I.L.P. was " to attract the really important and aggressive working-class forces which are growing up and which at the moment are hesitating painfully as to whether or not they must enter the Communist Party." Inspired by similar conceptions of some " middle course " for Socialists was the 1928 manifesto issued by Mr. James Maxton, the I.L.P. chairman, and Mr. A. J. Cook, announcing a nation-wide campaign. Uncertainty in the minds of the two protagonists as to what they were really at led to the speedy fade-out of the campaign, which the late John Wheatley had been prepared to back heavily and from which he had expected much.

What of the Communist Party ? The General Strike and its aftermath undoubtedly afforded large-scale confirmation of the justness of the Party's predictions and current policy. But in fact the Communists of Britain failed fully to seize the opportunity so offered them to win really unshakable authority among the decisive sections of the working class. Certainly their influence increased greatly. By the autumn of 1926 the Party membership, always small, had doubled, rising from 5,000 to over 10,000. The circulation of the Communist Press mounted rapidly. Still there was failure to consolidate and extend this big spontaneous movement towards the Communist Party by giving it consciousness and understanding. Members flooded in; and then they steadily trickled out. Among the majority of those who were then the principal Party leaders, men who had come over from the previously existing Socialist groupings and bore strong marks of sectarian dogmatism in their outlook, there seemed a strange hesitancy in appreciating the need for the Party now to assert its full independence and to change its tactics and approach accordingly. Of course the circumstances were far from easy. Victimisation and prolonged unemployment wrought havoc in the ranks of the Party and its nearest supporters. Theoretical understanding remained at a low level.

It soon became evident that the Communists had to face up to a key issue here. And so from the end of 1927 there was waged for two years the keenest battle of ideas the Party had so far known around the question of its " new line." This line sought to prescribe a new independence for the Communist Party both in political and economic struggles. It was widely misinterpreted as meaning simply a new phase in election policy, enjoining opposition to the Labour Party in that field. It also, not unnaturally, opened the door wide to " ultra-Left " tendencies which turned independence into isolation. The main thing was that it represented a necessary break with the past. As such it was stubbornly resisted by the dominant section of the Party leadership, who showed themselves more and more averse to any suggestions involving departure from existing traditions and methods; they had, for instance, persistently shelved the question of the establishment of a daily newspaper, which had been commended to them as a matter of urgency since the ending of the General Strike. Thoroughgoing changes in the leadership were obviously necessary if the Party were not to stagnate. These, however, were not finally achieved till the Party's Congress held at Leeds in December 1929.

By the opening months of 1929 one thing stood out sharply. The tide of revolt was once more rising. Throughout 1928 there had been a series of keenly-fought local strikes in mining, cotton, and wool textiles. With the new year these struggles assumed added importance. National attention was centred on disputes like the ten weeks' strike of the girls at the Rego clothing factory in London for union recognition, which was victorious although it did not receive the endorsement of the union executive; on the strike of 8,000 men at the Austin motor works against piece work changes and regrading, the significant thing being

GT

that three-quarters of these workers were unorganised; on
the fifteen weeks' strike of 3,000 miners at Dawdon Colliery,
Durham, against a wage cut of 3*s*. a shift; on the London
busmen's drive for an improved agreement. In the Nottinghamshire coalfield the General Council of the T.U.C.
intervened to take a ballot of the men for or against the
Spencer union; by an overwhelming majority Spencerism
was rejected. Symptomatic of sharpened struggle was the
police attitude. A demonstration of strikers at Nine Mile
Point Colliery, Monmouthshire, was met with a police
charge in which women and children were batoned in a
way that was subsequently described at the Standing Joint
Authority of the County Council as " the most callous,
brutal, and vicious that could be made " and was alleged,
according to the *Daily Herald* report, to have been
" prearranged."

On every side new keenness was returning to the movement from the revived enthusiasm and activity of the
workers themselves. The hour of reckoning for the Baldwin
Government was approaching. Not least in significance for
the immediate future was the national Hunger March on
London organised by the National Unemployed Workers'
Movement in February–March 1929. Despite official frowns
the March infused a spirit of unity everywhere that turned
it into something more like a victory procession. The
demonstration of welcome from the workers of the capital
was the biggest thing since 1926; and the Government,
which had been threatening to operate plans for transitional
benefit which would have struck 200,000 off the unemployment register, had to capitulate. Up to this revival in the
movement the Labour Party had been slumping badly. In
1927, for instance, by-election results showed votes drop-
ping below the 1924 level, while in the municipal elections
the Labour vote, greater than Liberal and Tory combined
in 1926, fell by 9 per cent, the Tory vote increasing by
28 per cent, so that the Labour vote was not even equal to
the Tory figure alone. Now there were signs of change.

CHAPTER VIII

THE SECOND LABOUR
GOVERNMENT

"LABOUR WON THE ELECTION—or would it be more correct to say that the Conservatives lost it?" That comment[1] on the General Election of 1929 contains an important truth. Mr. MacDonald himself during the campaign stuck firmly to the view he had expressed years before that he preferred to be in a minority, provided that that minority was composed of his unquestioning supporters, rather than in a majority which might inconveniently insist on things being done. Mr. Strachey, noting how " in 1929 a clear majority was perilously near," says, " I recollect the great anxiety which Mr. MacDonald showed just before election day. He kept reassuring himself by saying he was sure the Liberals would do well. He remarked several times that it would be much better not to have a majority than to be at the mercy of those Labour supporters whom he described as ' some of our easey-oozey asses.' "

The Labour Party won 127 new seats and returned 289 strong. The Conservatives lost 141 seats and were reduced to 260. The Liberals gained 12 seats and returned with 58. It was in mining areas like South Wales and provincial urban areas like Manchester that the Labour increases were most decisive. In London, on the other hand, the Labour Party did not register an increase proportionately as great as the decline of the Conservatives. Including Northern Ireland the aggregate Conservative vote was still the highest at 8,664,000; excluding the Irish figures it was

[1] Egon Wertheimer: *Portrait of the Labour Party* (2nd edition), p. xxv.

a few score thousand below Labour's aggregate of 8,362,000. Incidentally, there were a large number of three-cornered contests and these helped the Labour Party to score. The Communist Party, pursuing its new independent line, put forward twenty-five candidates but except in West Fife and Rhondda East their votes were tiny and the aggregate Communist poll totalled 50,000.

Few Governments had fallen into more acute popular disfavour than had the Baldwin Government by the summer of 1929. Correspondingly high hopes were entertained by the millions whose votes made a second Labour Government possible. Those hopes were early condemned to disappointment. Dr. Hugh Dalton, the present chairman of the Labour Party, has written:

> " From their first day in office some Ministers were in full retreat from their election pledges. The first King's Speech chilled the Parliamentary Labour Party. When all allowance is made . . . the second Labour Government missed great opportunities on the home front. Looking back, it is easy to put most of the blame for what was done, or not done, on the three men who occupied key positions in the Cabinet in relation to home policy, and who crossed over when the crisis came. . . . But all of us, I feel, must take some share of the responsibility. . . . We should have kicked up more row, been less loyal to leaders and more loyal to principles."

That is a plain summing-up of the case written some years afterwards. The tragedy was that the fatal " loyalty " of which Dr. Dalton speaks was as widespread as it was blind. Even level-headed and able men like Mr. Herbert Morrison were afflicted with the disease. In his presidential address to the Labour Party Conference at Brighton in 1929, Mr. Morrison declared that Mr. MacDonald's personality was " a real factor for success," hailing him as " political leader of the nation " and saying that " he will live in history, not only as the first Labour Prime Minister, but as a statesman and servant of the people of the first order." When the Clyde M.P.s sought in concert to follow a critical line in the House, 66 of their fellow back-benchers, also members of the I.L.P., met together and made a formal repudiation of the Clyde men, declaring their unswerving loyalty to Mr. MacDonald. This was at the end of 1929.

Unemployment and the treatment of the unemployed was a main issue. In an interview on the eve of the Government's formation, Mr. MacDonald had said: " In our first session we shall deal with unemployment and will bring relief and hope to the workers of this land." There was, it is true, some administrative easing of the conditions of benefit payment, and the period of transitional payment was extended. Yet by the autumn of 1929, cases of disallowance of benefit by insurance officers exceeded 308,000 as compared with under 219,000 during the same period of the previous year. The new Minister of Labour, Miss Margaret Bondfield, and her Parliamentary Secretary refused to receive a deputation of unemployed representatives. When the deputation, nevertheless, managed to find their way into the Ministry on July 23rd, they were ejected by a large force of police.

The imposition of test and task work as a condition for the receipt of Poor Law Relief, long a detested thing, which many Labour local authorities had refused to operate, was maintained. Indeed, the Ministry of Health, now headed by Mr. Arthur Greenwood, called to order Boards of Guardians which were not imposing any task on relief recipients. Many Boards in mining areas had accumulated large debts for relief granted during the lock-outs of 1921 and 1926, which it was virtually impossible for them to recover from the underpaid and under-employed miners. The Guardians of Swansea, Whitehaven, Mansfield, for example, accordingly applied to the Ministry for permission to cancel their relief debts. Permission was refused and they were informed that they would be surcharged if they liqui-dated the debt. The Pontefract (Yorkshire) Guardians were refused an extension of the time allowed them for the repay-ment of the remaining £16,000 of a loan advanced by the

Ministry in 1926, of which £164,000 had already been repaid. When the deputation from the Pontefract Guardians, which had waited on the Minister and had received his refusal for any extension, reported back, its chairman told his colleagues that " Mr. Arthur Greenwood was as inaccessible as, and no more sympathetic than, his predecessor, Mr. Neville Chamberlain." That such a comparison could be made within the first few months of the Labour Government was scarcely of good augury.

With the onset of the world economic crisis, heralded by the Wall Street crash of October 1929, the unemployment problem dominated all others. Blind beforehand to the likelihood of crisis (it was in September 1929 that Chairman Ben Tillett told the Belfast T.U.C. to regard America's " ever-expanding prosperity "), the Labour Party leaders in office seemed to grow more helpless as the crisis sharpened and unemployment figures mounted. Mr. J. H. Thomas, specially appointed Minister for Unemployment, rapidly earned his title in a sense other than that intended. In 1929 he had announced that by the following February the figures would be much better. February 1930 came and the figures were much worse. Mr. Thomas made a much publicised trip to Canada and returned empty-handed. In the summer of 1930 the man who was supposed to be the wizard work-provider was telling the Oxford Union that " it is true that certain schemes of rationalisation, which I am encouraging because they are in the interests of the country, must have the effect of adding to the number of unemployed." Clearly Mr. Thomas was rapidly advancing along the path which was to bring him to the point where he could wittily announce, " I broke all records in the number of unemployed."

By the end of 1930 the unemployment figures had passed the 2,300,000 mark; and in face of what Mr. G. D. H. Cole has called the Government's " plainly demonstrated incapacity " (he notes that " it was not even prepared to go as far as its Liberal supporters would have allowed it to go in promoting a programme of economic reconstruction and development ") there were increasing signs of discontent and division not only throughout the Labour movement, but within the Government itself. At the Brighton Conference of the Labour Party in 1929, a keenly critical debate had taken place on the treatment of the unemployed, and a motion to refer back a paragraph in the Parliamentary report stating that the Ministry of Labour had not yet had an opportunity to deal with unemployed grievances was only lost by the extremely narrow margin of 1,100,000 votes to 1,270,000. Next year at the Llandudno Conference of the Party Sir Oswald Mosley, who had resigned his ministerial post as Mr. Thomas's lieutenant following the Government's rejection of his celebrated Memorandum, obtained 1,046,000 votes for a motion to circulate his Memorandum to the Party; the vote against him was 1,251,000.

In December 1930 the Government appointed a Royal Commission on Unemployment under the chairmanship of Judge Holman Gregory, upon which there sat two Labour representatives. The following summer an interim report was called for; and it was on the basis of this report that the Government drafted the Anomalies Bill. Passed into law in August 1931 this measure was to redound very heavily to the Labour Party's discredit, particularly in Lancashire. The new discrimination that it introduced against unemployed married women struck the cotton towns hard. Over a year afterwards, when I was investigating the situation in Lancashire, I was struck by the number of cases of hardship that had resulted from the operation of the Anomalies Act, and by the rankling bitterness that this had understandably induced.[1] In addition the Act hit at the benefit conditions hitherto enjoyed by casual and seasonal workers.

" The Labour Party holds," the election programme had run, " that to attempt to cheapen production by attacking the standard of life of the workers of the nation is not only socially disastrous, but highly injurious to the economic prosperity of the whole community." Yet every major

[1] See my *Condition of the Working Class in Britain*, pp. 59–60, 68–9.

point in the record of the second MacDonald Government was a pioneering of " social disaster," so defined. It will not seem surprising to those who have followed in previous chapters the story of MacDonaldism's development.

The whole outlook of the Cabinet was hidebound; the limits of orthodox capitalist precept and practice were their limits. When Mr. Clynes, for instance, said: " There are people in the Labour movement who say that reorganisation or rationalisation are of no use to the workers. My answer is that unless we equal our competitors in every point of efficiency we shall be committing industrial suicide "—there could be no question that his views marched with those of the City. It was with the Government's foreknowledge and approval that the Bank of England took the lead in establishing (in April 1930) the Bankers' Industrial Development Company, for the financing of rationalisation. The previous month Governor Montagu Norman had referred to the desirability of the Bank gaining financial " hegemony " in this country; and Mr. Thomas gave glowing advance publicity to the scheme. Sometimes the gulf which had been cleaved between the Government's leading figures and the movement had consequences almost grotesque. Dr. Dalton has recorded how Snowden " reached his climax of detachment from Labour opinion in reappointing to the Public Works Loans Board the aged and egregious Lord Hunsdon who, in a well-remembered speech had compared British miners, on strike against wage reductions, with Germans in wartime, equally ' enemies of this country,' who, he urged, should be starved into surrender."

Cotton provided a touchstone of the intentions of the Government while it was still young. Some time previously the master spinners had demanded a general 12½ per cent cut in wages (the first general cut to be demanded since 1922), and the operatives had returned an all but unanimous vote for resistance. At the end of July 1929 a general lock-out began on the spinning side of the industry. The Government shortly appointed a board of arbitration, presided over by Mr. Justice Rigby Swift, who had sentenced the twelve Communists in 1925, and including Sir Arthur Balfour, an influential financier, Sir Archibald Ross, President of the Engineering Employers' Federation, with Mr. Walkden and Mr. Cramp from the railway unions as the trade union representatives. On August 20th the board opened its sittings and two days later announced a unanimous award of a 6¼ per cent wage cut, " having decided that the employers' case for a reduction had been made out." Anger swept Lancashire, the columns of the *Cotton Factory Times* teeming with reports from the local cotton unions stigmatising the award as " a disgrace " (Great Harwood), and expressing the operatives' " deep resentment " (Burnley).

After the spinners the weavers. In the summer of 1930 the manufacturers began to press for the abandonment of the traditional four-looms per weaver in favour of six or eight. The " more-looms " question rapidly became a burning issue. At length strike action was taken in Burnley, where the system had been operated " experimentally " at certain mills, in the early days of January 1931. The Burnley employers replied with a local lock-out, taking effect from January 10th. A week later the lock-out became general throughout the weaving side of the industry. Seeking powers for their Central Committee to continue negotiations on the " more-looms " system, the leaders of the Weavers' Amalgamation balloted their membership; but though the ballot paper was confusingly worded the mandate they received was unmistakable. There were 91,000 votes against the continuance of negotiations to 45,000 votes favouring that course.

Nevertheless, the leaders of the Amalgamation ignored this vote and proceeded to London to negotiate with the Master Manufacturers and the Government; the latter had proposed that more-looms working should be agreed to as an experiment. So strongly did the weavers feel about these developments that there was wide support for a delegation of local officials and committee men which came up to London on February 2nd. One of the principal figures in the delegation, Mr. Zeph Hutchinson, secretary of the Bacup Weavers' Association, declared that " Lancashire weavers were having to fight, not merely the employers, but their own Central Committee and the Labour Government itself." It was the solidarity of the weavers and certainly not the attitude of the Government (Mr. MacDonald refused permission for time being given in the Commons to discuss a motion on the cotton situation) that caused the Master Manufacturers to capitulate on February 13th and withdraw their demand for more-looms working.

In the other great branch of textiles, wool, the Government showed up no better. There the employers had demanded heavy wage cuts in the autumn of 1929. These demands were rejected on a ballot vote of the woollen unions by the impressive majority of no less than 80 per cent of those voting. Next spring, when the employers were still pressing their demands, the Government set up a Court of Inquiry under Lord Macmillan, who eventually awarded reductions averaging $9\frac{1}{2}$ per cent, and as one of the reasons for so doing referred to the social services as " lightening the burden on wages "; which sounded as if it might create a most sinister precedent. The operatives would have nothing of this award, rejecting it by a 7 to 2 vote. A general lock-out therefore began in the West Riding, and the *Manchester Guardian* noted that the " solidarity and grim determination to resist wage cuts at all costs was remarkable." Pointing out that the demands of the employers would reduce certain classes of workers in the woollen industry far below Trade Board rates, the General Council of the T.U.C. opened a solidarity fund.

For more than two months the fight continued. Heavy police reinforcements were drafted into the West Riding and there were baton charges in Bradford and elsewhere which evoked strong protests, from Mr. Kirkwood for instance, in the House of Commons. The union leadership had, however, no desire to intensify the struggle. Proposals

by the militants for the establishment of mill strike committees came to nothing. Although at the end of May further
union ballots showed majorities for continuing the dispute,
the National Association of Unions in the Textile Trade
decided at a conference on June 4th to abandon any central direction of the struggle and to leave the individual
unions to negotiate separately what settlements they
might.

During 1929 and 1930 the guerilla warfare of pit and
local strikes in the mining industry considerably extended.
Some strikes, such as that at the Binley Colliery in Warwick-
shire and that against non-unionism in the Garw district
of South Wales, attracted much more than local attention.
The elephantine mobilisation of police to protect the
handful of blacklegs in the Garw certainly did not make
a favourable impression in the coalfields. The biggest
question, of course, was the 7-hour day and the miners
had set all their hopes on the election pledge that " the
disastrous Act by which the Tory Government added an
hour to the working day must be at once repealed." It
was not repealed (" they must face facts " said Snowden).
Only after great and continuous pressure had been brought
to bear was a 7½-hour day conceded, hedged round with
complicated qualifications permitting " spread-over " of
hours and accompanied by an Act designed to encourage
amalgamations and marketing schemes.

Mr. A. J. Cook put the position mildly when he said
early in 1931 that " the general feeling was that the Government had not done all it could to protect the miners."
The spread-over proviso irritated the men. It led to a
strike in Scotland in December 1930 and to a lock-out in
South Wales in January 1931 ; as a result of the latter the
owners in that coalfield agreed to abandon it, though,
on the other hand, the miners conceded that wages questions
should be settled locally without any reference to the
National Wages Board which the Government's legislation
proposed. The following March an arbitration award
reduced the South Wales men's minimum percentage on

basis rate from 28 to 20 and made various cuts in the subsistence wage. At the same time the Miners' Federation
in conference decided by a large majority to set a term
to the working of any spread-over.

Workers in many other industries found themselves
exposed to the full blast of the crisis-urged attack of the
employers; nor were they to get any protection from the
MacDonald Government. Engineers, agricultural workers,
dyers, potters, among others, were all facing demands for
wage cuts by the early spring of 1931. The railwaymen were
saddled with a new award by the Railway Wages Board;
overtime rates were reduced and an hour's spread-over
conceded to the companies, and all earnings over 40s.
a week subject to an additional 2½ per cent cut. Against
this there was a good deal of sporadic " working to rule "
and one or two brief strikes in local depots and yards.
Dockers were confronted with demands which not only
involved cuts amounting in several cases to between 3s.
and 4s. a day, but which, in Mr. Bevin's words, " tore up
by the roots the whole of the conditions fixed by the Shaw
Award of 1920."

In 1923 Mr. MacDonald himself had said that a Labour
Government " that did not please its people with its work
had better remain in opposition." There was ample evidence of the displeasure of the great body of " its people "
—the trade union movement—with the second MacDonald
Government. Prominent trade union leaders more and
more found it impossible to abstain from public criticism.
At the Labour Party Conference of 1929 Mr. Ernest Bevin,
for instance, justly took Snowden to task for his defence
of the Bank of England's increasing of the Bank rate. At
the same Conference, incidentally, plain speaking by one
of Mr. Bevin's colleagues in the Transport and General
Workers' Union gave the lead for the decisive rejection
of the Executive's proposal to open the Party ranks still
more to bourgeois infiltration by the institution of a new
category of National Associate Members who would require
to be members of no Party organisation or affiliated body.

The long promised repeal of the Trade Union Act of 1927 was in this connection an issue of prime importance. "Among the first tasks of the Labour Party," it was written in *Labour and the Nation*, "will be the repeal of the cynical measures of class legislation by which the Conservatives have sought to cripple the strength of trade unionism both on the industrial and the political field." It was soon seen that the Government was in no greater hurry to honour this pledge than any of its others. Government circles began to put it about that the Act could not be repealed as a whole since it codified previous trade union law and if thus repealed would leave the unions without any declared legal status. The late Mr. C. T. Cramp got this view accepted by the 1929 Annual General Meeting of the National Union of Railwaymen, which passed a resolution hoping that the Government would repeal the "obnoxious clauses" of the 1927 Act. When the Government at length introduced its new Trade Union Bill doubts were expressed in many quarters as to the extent that the Bill really repealed the 1927 Act. The Attorney-General said "this Bill legalises nothing which was illegal in 1926." Mr. Thomas assured the House of Commons that "you are not asked to legalise a General Strike." Meantime the feeling of the movement had been made plain at the Labour Party Conference in 1930, where on the motion of Mr. Bevin it was unanimously resolved that the 1927 Act should be repealed, the mover declaring that "the unions wanted without any equivocation at all the complete restoration of the pre-1927 position." In March 1931 the Government withdrew its Bill, the Attorney-General announcing that a simple one-clause Bill repealing the 1927 Act would be submitted. After that, the matter dropped.

Looking back it appears that the union leaders had made it hard for themselves to pursue any really effective opposition to the MacDonald Government's capitalist policy by their own continued and tenacious support of Mondism. This was the case at the Belfast T.U.C. in 1929. A resolution demanding the cessation of the relations with the organised employers, moved by the Furnishing Trades, and seconded by the Engineers, was decisively rejected, Mr. Bevin announcing that he " objected to the inferiority complex." Of a piece with this was the adoption by the same Congress of the General Council's report on " disruption," despite the voices raised against it, notably by some of the younger miners' delegates. There were also prominent personalities in the trade union movement who appeared to function as Mr. MacDonald's mouthpieces. In a remarkable presidential address to the Nottingham T.U.C. of 1930, Mr. John Beard dismissed " Socialism in our time " with a sneer; asserted that " expediency must be our guide "; boldly announced that " the figure of 2,000,000 unemployed does not appal me."

The initial hopes of the pioneers of Mondism had, it is true, not been fully realised. Both the Federation of British Industries and the National Confederation of Employers' Organisations had rejected the proposed National Industrial Council. During 1929, however, these two bodies conferred with the General Council of the T.U.C. and a Joint Committee was set up to examine the best methods of co-operation. So far as the enunciation of policy was concerned both sides had clearly much in common. The General Council and the F.B.I. prepared a joint memorandum for the Imperial Conference of 1930. This document urged the need for an Empire economic bloc and suggested the need for tariffs. Submitted to the Nottingham T.U.C. this memorandum was only endorsed in the face of a respectable minority, the voting figures being 1,878,000 to 1,401,000. In the course of the debate Mr. Bevin attacked what he called Soviet " dumping " (" stuff on which practically no wages even have been paid in its manufacture "), declared that Russian trade " is very often only 10 per cent orders and 90 per cent propaganda," and averred that the Soviet Union was an " Empire " whose " attitude to subject races is very much the same " as that of other Empires.

Early in 1931 the character of the General Council's new associates was rather startlingly illuminated by a statement issued on behalf of the National Confederation in which that body demanded that Unemployment Insurance Benefit be reduced by one-third, that the benefit fund be placed on a strict insurance basis, that all State and Municipal wages be reduced, social services limited and the operation of Trade Boards curtailed. A little later on, in its evidence to the Royal Commission on Unemployment Insurance, the National Confederation went further: it declared that unemployment insurance was " insidiously sapping the whole social and financial stability of the country " since it was preventing " unemployment from acting as a corrective factor in the adjustment of wage levels."

If the industrial policy pursued by the trade union leaders hampered them politically in rallying a solid and positive opposition to the catastrophic line pursued by the MacDonald Government, there were as yet no signs that the forces of the Left were able to assume this rôle. At by-elections and in the Municipal Elections of 1930 there were ominous signs of breakers ahead in a falling Labour vote (it was noteworthy that Labour's municipal slump was most marked in the cotton areas), yet despite valiant pioneering efforts there was no corresponding gain by the Left. When a by-election took place in such a typical West Riding constituency as Shipley, immediately after the woollen strike of 1930, the most serious thing about it was certainly the fact that the Labour vote in a long-held Labour seat slumped so badly that the Conservative candidate won. At the same time, considering the intense activity that had been displayed in the area during the strike by the Communists and their supporters, the fact that the Communist candidate only polled 700 votes was a sign that the Communist Party was still substantially isolated from the decisive mass of the workers.

Some initial success was scored by a campaign which the Minority Movement launched for a Workers' Charter. The

proposal was for a simple programme embodying demands
for increased Unemployment Benefit, extended social
services, a 7-hour day and a national minimum wage of
£3 a week, reductions of rents and the building of a million
houses by the State, etc. A pamphlet by Harry Pollitt, out-
lining these aims, rapidly sold over 100,000 copies. In April
1931, the First National Charter Convention met in
London; it was attended by 788 delegates from 316
organisations, rather more than one-quarter of the delegates coming from the provinces. Much enthusiasm was
shown and a vigorous campaign pursued. Yet there remained the problem of an insufficiently firm and extensive
basis among the organised workers. At the Convention, for
example, little more than one-sixth of the delegates were
representative trade unionists—146 delegates from 68
trade union branches. The problem of combining militant
vision and inspiration with the organised strength of the
existing movement had not yet been solved. Some idea of
the potential response may perhaps be deduced from a
conference that was organised by the Manchester Trades
Council in May of the same year. This was attended by
over 2,000 delegates who resolved to demand a 40-hour
week and to resist determinedly all cuts in wages and attacks on social services.

The experience of the MacDonald Government had
brought the crisis in the relations of the I.L.P. and the
Labour Party to its final stage. An I.L.P. amendment criticising the Government's " timidity and vacillation in refusing to apply Socialist remedies " was heavily defeated—
by 1,803,000 votes to 334,000—at the Labour Party
Conference in 1930. Disaffiliation from the Labour Party
was discussed at the I.L.P.'s annual conference at Easter
1931, but was rejected by 173 votes to 37. Negotiations proceeded between the two parties on the question of discipline; the right of I.L.P. members of Parliament to speak
in opposition to the Labour Government proved the
principal bone of contention. The Labour Party leadership wanted to ban such opposition absolutely. At the

Party Conference of 1931, meeting at Scarborough, Mr. Henderson expounded the Executive's objection to what he called the "organised conscience" of bodies like the I.L.P. At that Conference new standing orders, tightening up Party discipline in the sense indicated, were adopted by 2,117,000 votes to 193,000.

Symptomatic of new trends in the movement were developments in the newspaper field. On January 1st, 1930, the Communists launched their first daily newspaper, the *Daily Worker*, which from primitive beginnings and in face of grave obstacles, such as a boycott imposed by the wholesale newsagents, was to become within the next half dozen years by far the most influential voice of the militant Left. In March appeared the first issue of the new *Daily Herald* as the product of Odhams Press, the millionaire newspaper trust, to which it had been made over by the Trades Union Congress and the Labour Party. By the terms of the arrangement with Odhams, political control of the *Daily Herald* was to be retained by the T.U.C. and the Labour Party jointly, though Odhams were to hold 51 per cent of the controlling shares. The *Herald* blossomed out as a magnificent technical production, competing successfully with the largest national newspapers, gaining a mass circulation and a huge advertisement revenue. The old editorial staff of the paper was gradually disposed of and replaced by editorial executives drawn mainly from the Beaverbrook and Rothermere Press. Very different was the acquisition by the Co-operative Movement from the late Lord Dalziel, a hard-bitten trafficker in newspapers, of the semi-derelict *Reynolds News*. For the first time the Co-operatives had entered the national newspaper market and proved themselves able to maintain and improve the position of the property, eventually transforming it into the front-rank national Sunday newspaper that it is to-day, without having recourse to outside capitalist aid.

It is time to resume the story of the second Labour Government's final stage. As 1931 advanced it was obvious that the profound crisis of capitalism in this country was approaching the acute stage of financial crisis. Of the attitude of the governing class itself there could be no doubt. They desired that the full burden of the crisis should be borne by the working class and the lower middle class. At the end of January an " economy " movement was started by influential politicians and business men at a meeting at the Cannon Street Hotel; it was presided over by Mr. E. C. Grenfell, the Tory financier, who was one of the M.P.s for the City, and was addressed by Sir Robert Horne, Lord Grey, and other personalities of like calibre. To the considerable astonishment and alarm of the Labour movement, the aims of the promoters of this Tory ramp were implicitly endorsed by the Chancellor of the Exchequer. Speaking in the House of Commons on February 11th Mr. Snowden announced that the position of the national finances was so grave that to balance the Budget would require drastic and disagreeable measures, including " sacrifices from all." In protest against the character of this statement twenty-three Labour M.P.s went into the division lobby against the Government.

The Government appointed a committee on national expenditure, headed by Sir George May, of the Prudential, which presently reported that the Budget deficit for 1932–33 was likely to be £120,000,000. The Committee suggested ways in which just on £100,000,000 of this deficit could be made good by economies; of their proposed economies over £66,000,000 was to be obtained at the expense of the unemployed. A Cabinet Committee, consisting of MacDonald, Snowden, Henderson, William Graham and J. H. Thomas, was appointed to go into the whole question of the economies that could be enforced. Subsequent recriminations suggested that there was very little disagreement in this Committee. Division eventually occurred when the necessity of a 10 per cent cut in unemployment benefit was pressed. By this time the financial crisis had become exceedingly grave—France and the United States granted credits amounting to £50,000,000 on August 1st—but even on August 21st when the General Council of the T.U.C.

met the Cabinet Committee they were told by Snowden " that the Government were making no proposal for a cut in the amount of benefit." Yet such a proposal was in fact made, the Cabinet split on Sunday, August 23rd, and the next day Mr. MacDonald, accompanied by Snowden, Thomas and Lord Sankey, had combined with the Tories and Liberals to form the first " National " Government.[1]

Stunned by the desertion of its best-known leaders, the movement as a whole, from top to bottom, stood wonderfully firm; though unfortunately, as Mr. G. D. H. Cole has said, " the break with MacDonaldism was far more instinctive than rational." There was no desire among the leaders to probe seriously and thoughtfully into the reasons for the Labour Government's collapse. Mr. Arthur Greenwood was later to urge that " there is little to be gained by holding coroners' inquests on the corpse of the Labour Government." When the Labour Party Conference met at Scarborough in 1931, the natural agitation of the rank and file was expressed in the motion, proposed and seconded by delegates from constituency parties, for the reference back of the section of the Executive's report dealing with the circumstances that led up to the Government's crash. Answering queries as to whether the Executive had no alternative proposals to put before the Cabinet and complaints of the lack of contact and confidence between the Executive and the membership on the one hand and between the Parliamentary Party and the Cabinet on the other, Mr. Henderson opined that it would take too long to go into the matter and that the conference had better get on with the consideration of the future instead of going into the past.

It did not appear that Mr. Henderson, for one, was opposed in principle to the kind of coalition which Mr. MacDonald had formed. He had told the Trades Union Congress at Bristol in September that he " would have

---

[1] The reader who desires a more detailed analysis of the 1931 collapse and the reasons for it should turn to John Strachey: *The Coming Struggle for Power*, ch. xvii, " Mr. MacDonald and the 1931 Crisis in Britain."

preferred that the idea of a National Government had been seriously considered and approached in a proper way, and that the Labour movement should have been consulted, preferably at a specially convened Labour Conference." Referring to the increasing power of the vested interests of finance he added that " if they could formulate the right policy in that matter he believed there were a great number of manufacturing concerns in this country which would support them." Mr. Henderson's statement did not evoke any critical reaction from the Congress which had once more endorsed the policy of Mondism by large majorities, in spite of the criticisms voiced by delegates from the Loco-motive-men and Patternmakers; the latter, Mr. Ellis Smith (who is now M.P. for Stoke) pointedly asked how Congress " could condemn MacDonald, Snowden and Thomas for collaborating with opposed political parties when the General Council did the same thing in the in-dustrial field."

The General Election of 1931 was fought in an artificially produced atmosphere of panic. While the Labour Party were able to retain the respectable total of 6,648,000 votes, they lost no fewer than 213 seats and returned to Parlia-ment only 52 strong. The Conservatives soared to over 11,800,000 votes, gaining 208 seats and returning to Parliament 471 strong. The Communists had increased their total poll from 50,000 to 75,000 but still made no serious impression outside the coalfields of Fife and South Wales, not yet returning a single member. It is hardly necessary to spend time controverting the view that Labour's electoral defeat of 1931 was due to the fickleness or ignorance of the electorate. For the remarkable thing was that so many Labour supporters stood firm, taking into account the fact that—to quote Mr. Cole again—" the Labour Party had not only been stripped of its most picturesque figures, who chiefly stood for it in the minds of the less political electors, but was also manifestly without a policy for dealing with the crisis. Taken by surprise, as it ought never to have been, it repudiated Mr. MacDonald's policy without presenting any considered and workable alternative of its own. Nor could it have presented one to any purpose; for it was led by men who had acquiesced in the policy of the late Government, to which Mr. Mac-Donald's proposals for dealing with the crisis were the logical sequel."

The only true " workable alternative " was the policy of consistent working-class struggle. Such a policy, soberly thought out and propounded with fire and conviction by a united movement, would surely have served as an effective antidote to the demoralisation spread by the MacDonaldite defection. But the adoption of such an alternative policy implied just that " rational " (that is, conscious, reasoned) break with MacDonaldism which was lacking.

CHAPTER IX

A SOLDIERS' WAR

THE AUTUMN OF 1931 was marked by a sharpening
of social conflict recalling in its acuteness the tension of a
dozen years before. Through the National Government the
ruling class sought to save its rent, interest and profit from
the raging storm of crisis at the expense of the whole
working population. And the people fought back, unrest
rising headily, not only throughout the working class, but
among the professional workers and the lower middle
class, even among the armed forces of the State. Around
the régime there now hung all the atmosphere of emergency. Traditional constitutional forms were infringed in
the enforcement of the 10 per cent cuts at the expense of
the unemployed and of all public employees, of the sweeping " economies " in social services and local government
expenditure, in the imposition of tariffs and the hasty
departure from the gold standard. Coupled with this
practical revelation of the growing instability of capitalism
it was evident that the fall of the Labour Government
meant much more than the end of a ministry. The whole
system and outlook of MacDonaldism, whose rise to
dominance we have sketched, had come to its logical
conclusion; and so a whole stage in the development of the
Labour movement had come to an end.

What was the next stage to be ? Of the will to resist among
the working class there was soon plenty of evidence; but the
war that was waged during the period now opening was
essentially a soldiers' war, a spontaneous popular upsurge
which lacked authoritative generalship, though the small
but energetic forces of the men of the Left served to provide

effective partisan or guerilla leaders. In this war against the cuts a leading part was naturally played by the now nearly 3,000,000 strong army of the unemployed, whose discontent additionally centred on the Means Test for transitional benefit which the National Government had introduced. It is worth recalling that over a million registered unemployed were immediately affected by this inquisition, with its complex questionnaire, designed to drag out every detail of a worker's individual and family position. Through the agency of the Means Test the unemployed were deprived of nearly £30,000,000 a year. The number of cases disallowed benefit soon totalled hundreds of thousands. In its first year of operation 50 per cent of all those coming within its scope were only granted benefit at rates below the standard benefit rate or else were refused benefit entirely. The numbers on Poor Relief rose rapidly. Impoverishment and want spread apace. The Socialist Medical Association reported that Unemployment Benefit and Poor Relief " are entirely insufficient to keep their recipients in physiological health." The Public Health Committee of Deptford stated, on the ·basis of a special inquiry, that " it is clear that in the case of families in receipt of Public Assistance the amount of relief afforded cannot assure the recipients the minimum varied diet recommended by the Ministry of Health in their publications relating to nutrition and diet in Poor Law homes."

The war against the cuts can be divided into two major campaigns. First came the general movement of the unemployed, together with the civil servants, teachers, and other public employees, which occupied the period from the beginning of September 1931, to the General Election at the end of October. Then the operation of the Means Test, which began on November 12th, was the starting point for a wide and vehement protest movement of the unemployed, commencing locally, but soon becoming national in scope, and rising to its greatest height in the autumn and winter of 1932. From the beginning the meetings and demonstrations that were held all over the country, in an endless succession, were at once larger in numbers and marked by a more determined and militant spirit than had been known in this country since the great days of the Council of Action or the General Strike. While there was a new ruthlessness in the employment of force by the police to disperse demonstrations, more striking still in law-abiding England was the way in which workers fought back at the police with their fists or with stones, sticks, railing bars—any weapons that were at hand.

September opened with a march of unemployed Welsh miners, organised by the National Unemployed Workers' Movement, to the Trades Union Congress at Bristol. The marchers desired to present the case of the unemployed to the Congress, and ask for the support of trade unionists in their battle against the cuts. Secretary Citrine ruled other-wise; the leaders of the march were Communists. On their arrival in Bristol, on the evening of September 7th, the marchers and a welcoming demonstration were met with police baton charges. A strong police cordon surrounded the Congress Hall, and when a deputation from the marchers secured· admission to the outer lobby they were forcibly expelled by police and stewards. Meantime the metropolis had its first skirmish in a demonstration of un-employed to Parliament Square—within the forbidden limit of one mile of the House during its sessions—in the evening of September 8th. Many M.P.s witnessed the scene and Mr. J. J. McShane, the Labour Member for Walsall, among others, subsequently pronounced severe strictures in the House on the action of the police. This he described as an " extraordinary and most provocative display of force . . . although there had been no attempt at violence by the crowd." Mr. McShane told how he saw numbers of demonstrators bleeding from the bludgeoning they had received. There were eighteen arrests.

Events now followed at a great pace. London witnessed the remarkable spectacle of teachers taking to the streets *en masse* and marching with banners blazoned with slogans ·of protest, to hold great meetings in Westminster and a demonstration in Trafalgar Square. Civil servants were also on the move, their protest campaign culminating in a packed Albert Hall meeting in October. Most remarkable was the demonstration to Hyde Park on October 11th, when the men and women of Whitehall joined with the teachers, postal workers and the unemployed in a great turn-out a hundred thousand strong.

Protests came with unpleasant determination from quarters that were as unexpected as they were disagreeable for the governing class. Representatives of the police, assembled in a special meeting of their Federation at Scotland Yard, had taken a strong line. But the most severe blow was that delivered by the Navy. On September 12th the First Lord of the Admiralty had announced the cuts which were to apply to all officers and ratings. The celebrated " equality of sacrifice " was seen in such facts as the common application to Lieut.-Commanders and able bodied seamen of a cut of 1*s.* a day; but whereas, after the cut, the officer was left with £1 6*s.* 8*d.*, the skilled rating was left with 3*s.* Three days after the announcement the Atlantic Fleet, preparing at Invergordon to leave for autumn exercises, refused to sail. The world was staggered by the news of the biggest movement of revolt in the British Navy since 1797. Prepared by protest meetings ashore at which representatives from each ship reported on the feelings of the men and at which the " Red Flag " was sung, the mutiny began at 6 a.m. on Tuesday, October 15th, when the ship's company of *Rodney* collectively refused duty. They mustered and gave three cheers, the signal for the rest of the Fleet to follow suit. A manifesto, drafted by the men on *Norfolk*, and circulated to the Fleet by picket boat, said: " It is evident to all concerned that these cuts are the forerunner of tragedy, poverty, and immorality amongst the families of the men on the lower deck. The men are quite willing to accept a cut which they, the men, think within reason, and unless this is done we must remain as one unit refusing to serve under the new rates of pay." They did " remain as one unit." The officers were helpless and every ship was under the complete control of the lower deck. By Wednesday evening the Admiralty capitulated. An inquiry was set up and the pay cuts revised on a per-centage basis, which meant a substantial victory for the men. A month later twenty-four ratings, who were con-sidered to have been leading spirits in the mutiny, were discharged—" services no longer required."

Invergordon had filled the authorities with alarm; and in the endeavour to deal with what they conceived to be the source of infection, they were prepared to set their own legality at nought. Characteristic was the police raid on the *Daily Worker* offices and printing plant on September 25th. Not only did the Special Branch carry out a ransack-ing search without the formality of a search warrant (in-cluding the search of personal belongings of members of the staff), but they also instituted a thoroughly Tsarist pre-liminary censorship of the paper which was not allowed to go to press until Special Branch officers had read the proofs and ordered a number of deletions to be made. For the first time in English history a newspaper appeared, just as if it were in Poland or some Central European backwoods State, with blank spaces in its columns—censored by the police.

Turning now to the unemployed, the story of the weeks from the end of September to the end of October reads like a series of war communiqués. From Scotland's industrial centres, from Manchester and the cotton towns of Lan-cashire, from Cardiff and the Welsh mining valleys, from Midland cities like Nottingham and Derby, reports flowed in telling of mass demonstrations, of marches to the Town Hall or the Public Assistance Committee, telling of repeated clashes with the police, of baton charges that became regular street battles. In London demonstrations in White-hall and through the West End on September 29th and October 6th, to County Hall on October 16th, were accom-panied by running fights between demonstrators and police. Glasgow proved a significant gauge of the rising temper of the unemployed. There a demonstration of 20,000 on

September 23rd clashed with the police; next day a second demonstration was called and 50,000 turned out, among them a defence corps 500 strong, carrying heavy sticks; this time no clash with the police was reported. On October 1st an unemployed demonstration of similar magnitude rallied at Glasgow Green. What took place is described by Wal Hannington, the leader of the National Unemployed Workers' Movement, as follows:

" The police tried to ban the demonstration, and as the ranks were being formed for a march through the city mounted and foot police charged into the multitude of unarmed workers. The workers, however, fought back ferociously; iron railings around the Green were torn up and used as weapons. The fighting spirit of the Glasgow workers had been stirred by the unprovoked attack, and they fought their way out of the Green on to the main roads; the battle, which had started at the Green, rapidly extended throughout the centre of the city. For hours it raged, shop windows were smashed and extensive damage was done, and not until after midnight did the struggle come to an end."

That this fight had had a deep effect in arousing the Glasgow workers was witnessed at a further demonstration four days later when the turnout totalled a hundred thousand; and the city on the Clyde reached the climax on October 9th, the day following the cuts in unemployed benefit, when 150,000 workers paraded through the centre of the city in the evening in the most impressive demonstration witnessed anywhere in the country during this period.

Manchester told a similar tale. Forty thousand unemployed had marched to the Public Assistance Committee of the cotton capital on September 29th. On October 7th double the number rallied for a march to the City Council and soon found themselves involved in a pitched battle with the police. To quote Hannington again: " It was one of the fiercest fights that had ever been seen in Lancashire. Fire hoses poured tons of water into the crowd in an effort to disperse them. Mounted police repeatedly charged with their sword batons, clubbing down old and young. The resistance of the unemployed was such that the fighting lasted almost three hours. Several mounted police officers were dragged from their horses and received punishment from the demonstrators."

After the General Election, as has already been noted, the campaign entered into its second phase, that of an almost exclusively unemployed movement against the Means Test. Though many employed workers naturally participated in the larger demonstrations, their organisations did not mobilise them to unite as a body with their unemployed brethren. Instances like the call of the anthracite district of the South Wales Miners' Federation for a one-day strike of protest against the Means Test were isolated. It seemed that the General Council of the T.U.C. was more concerned to deflect the unemployed themselves away from the fighting leadership afforded by the National Unemployed Workers' Movement; for it was in January 1932 that the General Council recommended Trades Councils to form local unemployed associations under their own auspices, laying stress on the recreational and social functions of such associations. It was, however, noteworthy that Bristol, whose local unemployed association had served to inspire the General Council, came to the fore as the scene of particularly tenacious demonstrations by the un-employed and exceptionally fierce battles with the police.

From November 1931 to February 1932 the story of the autumn was largely repeated, with the difference that while the demonstrations were not of the same order of magnitude, they spread to a large number of towns which had not previously been affected. The unemployed were now on the move on the North-East coast, in Yorkshire, on Merseyside. The Potteries were put on the map by a march of the unemployed from each of the Five Towns to besiege the City Hall at Stoke. In a number of areas the Public Assistance Committees were constrained to modify the operation of the Means Test; in Bootle a spirited demonstration at the end of December secured a grant of extra winter relief.

With the approach of spring the movement began to climb to new heights. In Birmingham over 40,000 signatures were collected in a very short space of time to a petition calling for the abolition of the Means Test, which was presented to the Lord Mayor. Tyneside came to the fore on March 14th with a record demonstration on Newcastle Town Moor; there were 100,000 present. National direction was given to the agitation by plans, initiated by the National Unemployed Workers' Movement, for a nation-wide protest against the Means Test. A widely attended conference at the end of May endorsed these plans, which included the collection of signatures to a petition urging (1) the abolition of the Means Test; (2) the repeal of the Anomalies Act; (3) the restoration of the 10 per cent cut in unemployment benefit; (4) the restoration of the cuts in social services. Climaxing the campaign was to be a national Hunger March on London in the autumn. Throughout the summer the campaign was carried on. Battles in Bristol culminated in June in an affair described as follows by the local *Evening Post*:

" The demonstrators assembled at night on the Welsh Back, and, following a meeting, singing the ' Red Flag ' and the ' International,' moved in procession, banners flying, up Bridge Street into Castle Street. They were escorted by three or four policemen, but there was no hint of trouble till the crowd was half way down Castle Street. . . . Suddenly there emerged from side-streets and shop doorways a strong body of police reinforcements with batons drawn. They set about clearing the streets. Men fell right and left under their charge, and women who had got mixed up in the crowd were knocked down by the demonstrators in the wild rush to escape. . . . Then came a troop of mounted police charging through Castle Street from the Old Market Street end, scattering the last of the demonstrators. In a few minutes the streets were clear, save for the men who lay with cracked heads, groaning on the pavements and in shop doorways, where they had staggered for refuge."

Growing response in the unions to the demands of the unemployed, as voiced in this campaign, found its reflection at the Trades Union Congress, meeting at Newcastle in September 1932. Following the example of previous years a regional march of unemployed to the Congress was organised. The official ruling that a deputation from the marchers should not be admitted was only upheld after a keen debate by 1,577,000 votes to 963,000 (and protests by miners' delegates next day suggested that the casting of the big Miners' Federation vote with the majority did not represent the unanimous viewpoint of the coalfields). In the debate Sir Ben Turner pleaded that the marchers should be heard, Mr. Collick (Locomotive-men) said, " I would like a gesture to be made in this matter showing that Congress is going to get back to that real working-class spirit that was its foundation," Mr. Brown (Patternmakers) urged Congress to " allow them to come and state their case and show them by the way they listened to them that we are with them heart and soul," Mr. Rowlands (Painters) declared that " the display of force outside this Congress hall to-day is a disgrace to the whole trade union movement . . . it is not a credit to the trade union movement to see the number of police and ' Cossacks ' parading the streets outside." Secretary Citrine intervened to point his accusing finger at Wal Hannington; he declared that the National Unemployed Workers' Movement was " a subsidiary of the Communist Party," aiming " to hold up the General Council to ridicule and contumely." He was followed by Mr. Dawson (Textile Workers) who said that he was not a member of the Communist Party, but " a loyal officer of the trade union movement who has stood four-square on all occasions with the movement." Mr. Dawson's view was that the Congress ought not to " waste our time as to who is behind this unemployed organisation." " Do not," he urged, " be sidetracked by Mr. Citrine's reference to Mr. Hannington. What he has said may be correct. I do not challenge it at all, but as men and women facing this problem, we ought to be able to co-operate with either angels from heaven or fiends from hell."

Hardly had the delegates to Congress returned to their homes when the storm broke in Birkenhead. After the Public Assistance Committee there had received a deputation from the unemployed and had agreed to telegraph the Government demanding the abolition of the Means Test, a demonstration which had peacefully accompanied the deputation came into collision with the police as it marched away. A number of arrests were made. Two days later a second demonstration to the P.A.C. was suddenly charged by police and this led to the assembly of a large demonstration of protest that night. Again the police sought to disperse the demonstrators by a sudden baton charge. The demonstrators rallied and hurled the police back. That night and the three following days and nights fighting went on intermittently throughout the working-class streets of the Merseyside city. A report in *The Times* said:

" During what amounted to a series of pitched battles between the mob and the police nine officers and seven other persons were taken to hospital. . . . The police tried to break up the mob, but were met with a rain of bottles, stones, lumps of lead, hammer-heads, and other missiles. . . . Wherever the police were seen sweeping up a street the rioters disappeared into houses, from the windows of which women threw all kinds of missiles. . . . In one street the manhole cover of a sewer was lifted and a wire rope was stretched across the street. A number of police fell over this. . . . One of the motor omnibuses conveying police reinforcements had all its windows broken."

Reinforced from other towns the police carried out a series of night raids in the working-class areas of Birkenhead which were described at the time as a " reign of terror." Lorryloads of police halted late at night in front of tenement buildings, broke in and made arrests, using their batons indiscriminately. This began on the night of September 16th, was repeated the following night and reached its climax on the night of Sunday, September 18th. So great was the scandal that the International Labour Defence conducted a special inquiry; from evidence given by witnesses at that inquiry the following statement by Mrs. Davin, wife of an ex-Serviceman, invalided out of the Army, deserves quotation:

" But the worst night of all was Sunday night, about 1.30, September 18th. We were fast asleep in bed at Morpeth Buildings, having had no sleep the two previous nights and my husband was very poorly. My old mother, 68 and paralysed, could not sleep, she was so terrified. I have five children, a daughter 19, one 15, a son 17, one of 12, and one 6. Suddenly my old mother screeched, she is unable to speak. We were all wakened at the sound of heavy motor vehicles, which turned out to be Black Marias. Lights in the houses were lit, windows opened to see what was going on. Policemen bawled out ' Lights out ! ' and ' Pull up those —— windows.'

" Hordes of police came rushing up the stairs, doors commenced to be smashed in, the screams of women and children were terrible. We could hear the thuds of the blows from the batons. Presently our doors were bashed by heavy instruments. My husband got out of bed without waiting to put his trousers on, and unlocked the door. As he did so, 12 police rushed into the room, knocking him to the floor, his poor head being split open, kicking him as he lay. We were all in our night-clothes. The language of the police was terrible. I tried to prevent them hitting my husband. They then commenced to baton me all over the arms and body. As they hit me and my Jim, the children and I were screaming, and the police shouted ' Shut up, you parish-fed bastards ! ' "

When Mr. Davin was taken to hospital he was found to have six open head wounds, one over the eye, and body injuries. He was one of over a hundred hospital cases. There had been forty-five arrests during these proceedings including Joe Rawlings, the local unemployed leader, and the whole committee of the local branch of the N.U.W.M. Rawlings and Leo McGree, Liverpool unemployed leader who had crossed the river to assist in the demonstration, both received sentences of two years' imprisonment. But the militancy of the Merseyside men had had its effect. The Public Assistance Committee raised the scales of relief paid under the Means Test to full unemployment benefit rate.

Quickly after Birkenhead came spirited demonstrations and street battles in Liverpool, West Ham and North Shields. In the early days of October 2,000 unemployed in Belfast, who were being compelled to do relief work in exchange for outdoor relief so meagre that the maximum for a man, wife and family of more than three children was only 24s. a week, organised a strike on the relief scheme. There was general sympathy for the strikers and the working-class neighbourhoods of the city began to simmer. On the night of October 10th bonfires were lit at many street corners and around these the unemployed gathered to hear speeches from representatives of the relief strikers and to voice their general grievances. The police, revolver-armed according to normal Northern Ireland practice, turned out in armoured cars to disperse these bonfire demonstrations. Ferment rose still higher and on the following day as workers gathered in groups to discuss the events of the previous night, and these groups coalesced into crowds, the police charged without warning and armoured cars were driven into the masses of demon-strators. On the workers' side stones were soon followed by pick-shafts, spades and shovels taken from the relief work sites and there were furious mêlées, especially in the Falls and Shankhills districts. At length the police opened fire with their revolvers; five workers fell seriously wounded, while others sustained lesser injuries. Rough barricades were hastily erected at the ends of certain streets and the police kept at bay.

HT

Next day, despite the drafting into the city of detach-
ments of Fusiliers armed with machine guns, the fighting
continued. Again the police resorted to their firearms and
there were numbers of casualties; but more barricades
appeared and in the Falls district flagstones were torn up
and trenches dug across the streets. That night the Belfast
Trades Council passed a resolution in favour of a General
Strike. The police guns had cost the workers 50 casualties,
of whom two died of their wounds and were buried on
October 14th, tens of thousands marching in a great
funeral demonstration. Tom Mann, who had come from
England that day to attend the funeral and with a view to
speaking at big demonstrations that had been arranged,
was arrested and deported immediately after the ceremony.
Yet on that same day the Northern Ireland Government
surrendered, making substantial concessions to the unemployed whose maximum relief was now raised from
24s. to 32s. a week, while the scale for man and wife was
raised from 8s. to 20s. a week. Again, militancy and determination had won.

Meantime the National Hunger March to London was
getting under way, encouraged by the fact that the petition against the Means Test had obtained over one million
signatures. On the road the marchers succeeded in most
places in welding the local movement into united welcome,
despite central official displeasure. Where the official ban
was locally observed, as at Stratford-on-Avon, the contingents met with hostility from the authorities; indeed, in
the instance named, the Lancashire men had a nasty
tussle with police in the workhouse under circumstances
which called forth strong protests.

As the army of marchers, totalling some 2,500, was
steadily converging on London along the main roads
north, east, south and west, the unemployed of the metropolis battled through two successive demonstrations to
County Hall on October 18th and 24th. Assembling in
St. George's Circus the demonstrators, who numbered
many thousands, had running fights with the police all

along the neighbouring streets. Batons were used very freely, the mounted men being well to the fore. Casualties and arrests alike were extensive. On the second occasion the police, evidently alarmed by the severity of the fighting on the 18th, barricaded off strategic points surrounding County Hall. The deputation of the unemployed was received by the General Purposes Committee of the L.C.C. who promised to consider the demands made for extra winter relief, etc., and specifically agreed that the Council would undertake to find accommodation for the Hunger Marchers.

In an atmosphere of considerable excitement, aided by the widest Press publicity, ranging from the mildly sympathetic to the provocatively hostile, the marching columns entered the capital on October 27th and proceeded to Hyde Park. There a vast crowd of 100,000 Londoners had gathered to welcome them. The enthusiasm of that demonstration was clear evidence, both of the solidarity with their aims that the marchers had evoked and of their success in rallying popular feeling against the Government. The events of that afternoon turned that feeling into intense indignation; for the Government had taken the unprecedented step of mobilising the Special Constables to take over for the day as much routine police duty as was practical in order to concentrate the regular forces of the Metropolitan Police, both foot and mounted, in the Park. Without warning or provocation baton charges were made on an entirely peaceful demonstration, as large numbers of eye-witnesses testified in letters and interviews in the columns of progressive newspapers and journals during the ensuing days. Typical was the description by a correspondent of the *New Statesman & Nation*:

"Suddenly, for no apparent reason, the mounted police, accompanied by foot police, began to charge the crowd right and left . . . both unemployed and innocent spectators and passers-by. People were forced to run for their lives in order to escape being trampled upon by the police horses or beaten by staves. There was no kind of disorder at any of these meetings, and no reason at all for the police to charge into them in the wanton way they did."

The following Sunday, October 30th, many years' records for Trafalgar Square demonstrations were broken when 150,000 demonstrated in support of the marchers. It was said that the police mobilisation was the most extensive known. There was a good deal of skirmishing on the outskirts of the crowd and in the streets adjoining the southern side of the Square where the police were mainly concentrated. The biggest battle, however, followed on Tuesday, November 1st, when large demonstrations sought to accompany to Parliament the deputation which was carrying the national petition. As far afield as Gray's Inn Road and Farringdon Street the police sought to divert and break up marching demonstrators. These preliminary clashes preluded an astonishing series of running fights from Parliament Square up Whitehall as far as the Haymarket and Piccadilly, when eventually crowds, estimated at 80,000, had managed to find their way through to Westminster. So great was the press that all traffic in the neighbourhood of Parliament was brought to a standstill. As the tide of struggle surged to and fro cars were overturned, and on the Embankment workers snatched destination boards from tramcars for use as weapons. The toll of injured ran into hundreds. There were fifty arrests and next day sentences ranging as high as six months on charges of assaulting the police were handed down.

On the morning of that day Wal Hannington had been arrested (newspaper editorials had proclaimed that " the Communist organisers of the march should be laid by the heels "). He has recounted how, on the previous day, at a meeting of the Marchers' Council he received a suspicious anonymous letter proposing the commission of acts of terrorism against Ministers and of arson in public buildings. On his arrest the police ransacked the headquarters of the

National Unemployed Workers' Movement without a warrant; and their action was subsequently declared illegal as a result of a High Court action. Hannington, charged with inciting the police to disaffection, received a three months' sentence, while his colleague, Sid Elias, arrested shortly after him, was sent down for two years on a wider disaffection charge.

Militancy among the unemployed by no means lacked its parallel among the workers in industry. During 1932 the strike tide surged upwards; by far the mightiest breaker was the strike of the Lancashire weavers in the summer. Here the industrial movement reached its highest point since 1926—and for Lancashire it was in many ways the most remarkable event since the insurrectionary General Strike of 1842. The Master Manufacturers, following their 1931 defeat on the more-looms issue, once more adopted the guerilla tactics of endeavouring to introduce the system at isolated mills. These mills were struck, but the policy of the weavers' officials was to confine the fight to them and to reduce strike activity to the formality of placing paid union pickets at the mill gates.

A ballot was taken by the Central Board of the Northern Counties Textile Trades Federation; it was a double-barrelled affair, put in a confusing way—for or against a strike, and for or against negotiations (it was not stated that negotiations could only proceed on the basis of wage reductions). The result was a four-to-one vote for a strike and a two-to-one vote for negotiations. The only practical result of this ballot—apart from its demonstration of the will of the weavers for action—was to enable the officials to defer action while the millowners pressed home their guerilla attack with redoubled ferocity. Notices of reductions varying from $6\frac{1}{4}$ per cent to $12\frac{1}{2}$ per cent, and in some cases 18 per cent, were posted in mills all over Lancashire, and a special concentration was made in Burnley, which had all along been the cockpit of the struggle. A number of new mill strikes took place.

By the middle of July breaking point was reached. A few

days after the Central Committee of the Weavers' Amalgamation had decided in favour of reopening negotiations (knowing that these meant wage cuts), the Nelson Weavers' Committee called for " all out " ; and the Burnley Weavers' Committee, after two mass marches on their offices demanding an immediate strike of the whole town, called the strike for July 25th. The first stage of the general battle had begun : though Burnley was to fight single-handed for a month.

In issuing the strike call the Burnley Committee urged the weavers to keep away from the mills; their advice was conspicuously disregarded. Never had such mass pickets been seen; thousands of strikers rallied on the streets leading to the few mills which endeavoured to keep working; the demonstrations were so spirited that the whole atmosphere became electric, charged with enthusiasm for the strike, hatred for the employers, and fierce contempt for the " knob-sticks " (blacklegs)—who, despite the efforts of the police, both home and imported, were in instance after instance chased right through the town. In three days Burnley was solid as a rock, and 25,000 weavers were out on strike. The response to the strike call was immediate, startlingly complete, and tremendously militant.

At the beginning of August the General Council of the Weavers' Amalgamation met and by the narrow vote of 78 to 71 decided to leave matters in the hands of the Central Committee (meaning negotiations); a week later the same body recommended the Central Board of the Textile Trades Federation to call a Lancashire strike. The Board agreed, but fixed August 27th as the day for the strike, in order, to quote one of the leaders, to " leave the door open." Meantime the Master Cotton Spinners had given notice to their 200,000 workers of a wage cut of 2s. 9d. in the £, and the Spinners' and Cardroom Amalgamations decided to take a strike ballot.

Events were now to bang the open door in the face of the weavers' leaders. On August 20th the Weavers' General Council, following a heated discussion, decided against immediate strike action by a majority of a handful of votes, and in favour of another week's delay. A last-minute mediation was hastily initiated by the deputy Lord Mayor of Manchester, but it broke down. By Monday the 27th, the vast majority of the weavers' army went over the top in support of the Burnley battalions. The experience of the first week of the Burnley strike was now repeated on a Lancashire scale. The weavers' blood was up. To the Press— from the *Daily Herald* to the *Daily Express*—the strike was a " tragedy," " calamity "; to 150,000 weavers it was an inspiring triumph of united working-class struggle. In a couple of days the big northern weaving towns were closed right down. In a week mass pickets of thousands, marching out from the big centres, were " wiping up " the weak spots. Buses conveying knob-sticks were stoned. Mill managers had to be escorted home under strong police guard, followed by booing crowds. Tradesmen whose relatives went to blackleg were boycotted.

A persistent campaign for Government intervention in the dispute had been conducted in the *Daily Herald* since June. The cat was neatly let out of the bag when the *Daily Herald* asked: " What of the Prime Minister ? Three years ago he intervened dramatically in a similar situation. Why does he not do so to-day ? " The only comment needed is that the intervention of 1929 cost the cotton workers a $6\frac{1}{4}$ per cent wage cut; and the Government intervention which now began had wage cuts as its aim, as was evident from the language used by the Minister of Labour in a letter to the employers and the Union leaders. The opening of negotiations, under Government auspices, coincided with the announcement of the spinners' ballot—no less than 20 to 1 for strike action. The cardroom ballot showed 15 to 1 in favour of a strike. The Master Spinners promptly post-dated their notice, which was due for immediate operation.

But Government intervention did not begin with the Minister of Labour. From the beginning of the Burnley strike, police were imported by the hundred from Liverpool, Manchester and the West Riding. Baton charges were an everyday affair. Young and old, women and girls as well as men, were clubbed. Repeated occurrences of this kind enraged every worker in Lancashire, called forth protests by Trades Councils, and forced discussions at Town Council meetings. Typical was the battle between a mass picket of 5,000 and a large force of police outside Hargher Clough Mill, Burnley, on August 16th. In a baton charge many workers were injured and several arrests made; but the workers fought back, injuring one policeman and releasing some of those arrested.

The Trade Disputes Act of 1927 was constantly invoked. To be out on picket at all, even to boo, was sufficient for charges of obstruction, disorderly behaviour and assault. One Burnley weaver, taken to court in this way, said, " we are fighting for our rights and for our bread and butter. I always thought this was a free country." Even the secretary of a local weavers' union, Mr. Ashworth, a Justice of the Peace, was jailed for " intimidation," though the particular case was so grotesque that he was speedily released.

Government intervention produced the Midland Hotel agreement of September 24th, which conceded a wage cut of 1s. 8½d. in the £, accepted the six-looms system under certain conditions, provided for a system of conciliation to provide " peace " for three years, and inserted a reinstatement clause which proved to be purely pious. A special correspondent of a newspaper as reactionary as the *Daily Express* was early in 1933 to sum up the operation of this agreement in these words:

" The Lancashire weaver has been betrayed. . . . With the exception of a handful of manufacturers it is safe to say that the agreement has been honoured more in the breach than in the observance. . . . Weavers in Burnley are in open revolt. . . . They were promised 42s. a week when the six-loom system was introduced. To-day many of them are going home with not more than 25s. a week. . . . No changes were made in the machinery as promised. . . . Promises to give better weft and warps to decrease the number of breakages and the stoppage of looms have not been observed. Machinery was not slowed down as agreed, and weavers found the conditions heart-breaking. . . . I did not meet a single operative who has been reduced to four looms from the accepted standard of six who had drawn a penny from the manufacturers to make his wages up to the minimum of 28s. as promised in the agreement."

Exceptional tenacity distinguished the lesser strikes of this period. The Thames lightermen, a small but important section of London port workers, struck under the leadership of their own craft union against the modified cuts that the Transport and General Workers' Union had accepted for the dockers. The strike was doggedly fought from January 4th–February 17th, 1932. In the coalfields there was no falling off in the crop of pit and local strikes; at Ryhope Colliery in Durham, for instance, the men remained out for sixteen weeks. A bitterly contested strike of trawler men at Milford Haven immobilised for some time the fishing fleet of that port in the summer of 1932. The steadily growing numbers of young women workers in industry, and the adoption of new methods of speeding-up, lent particular interest to the strike of 4,000 hosiery workers employed by the Wolsey Company, Leicester. This strike arose out of the introduction of the notorious Bedaux system and it lasted from December 1931 to February 1932. Of the strikers the great majority were girls and the remarkable solidarity and the fighting spirit they displayed gave their dispute far more than local significance.

The developments that have now been described were not without their effect on trade unionism, both at the top and at the bottom. At the Newcastle Trades Union Congress the debates and decisions on three major questions of policy showed a rapid rise in the opposition to the General Council's now somewhat less confident development of the line of Mondism. A report on tariffs, justified by Mr. Bevin on the grounds that " I do not think that free trade and protection is a thing that a Socialist can get over-enthusiastic about " and apologised for by Secretary Citrine on the grounds that it simply said "wait and see," met with general criticism, led by so conservative a personality as Mr. Naylor of the London Compositors. The reference back mustered 934,000 votes against 2,125,000. Opposition was keenly voiced to the General Council's reported collaboration with the Federation of British Industries in preparing a joint memorandum to the Ottawa Conference. Sir Walter Citrine, referring to the position of the F.B.I. and the feeling that it " cracks the whip and the Government obey," asked " surely if there is something the General Council desire to get done, it cannot be a bad thing to get the support of the people who crack the whip ? " Again the motion for the reference back of the relevant paragraphs rallied a substantial minority—842,000 against 1,649,000. Third came the report on the control of industry, which was of such a character that Mr. Bevin's own union moved the reference back, its spokesman, Mr. John Cliff, saying: " If we are to get anything out of socialised industry, it must mean that we are going to have greater freedom for the workers in industry, and there is nothing of that brought forward in this report." So sustained was the criticism in the debate that the General Council, in order to avoid the carrying of the reference back, announced that the report should be considered " merely as a statement for information," and not as adopted policy.

Within the unions themselves there were signs of some abandonment of the extreme line of disfranchising and even expelling Left members whose critical attitude had been dubbed " disruptive." In the Amalgamated Engineering Union, for instance, the expulsion of certain members of long-standing who were well-known Communists was followed by the setting up of a Members' Rights Committee which succeeded in securing the reinstatement of those excluded. At the same time there could be no doubt that trade unionists were desirous that a more forward industrial policy should be displayed; in various forms the old drive for wider rank-and-file participation in the direction of affairs, and particularly in the active conduct and leadership of disputes, made a new appearance. This was seen in the cotton strike, among the dockers, on the railways. Movements like the Railwaymen's Vigilance Movement sprang up as definitely militant groupings of union members. But the potential significance of these trends was greater than their actual achievement, with the important exception of the London busmen.

In the summer of 1932 it was generally known among London busmen that the officials of their union (the Transport and General Workers) had been negotiating the terms of a new agreement, though no report was made at their July delegate conference. When the promised circularisation of a written report failed shortly afterwards to materialise, the men of the bus fleet began to feel alarmed, especially since information began to trickle through indicating that the Company was making very drastic demands. On August 1st came the long-promised report, and the men found that their fears were fully justified. Mass meetings at the garages emphatically rejected the proposed terms. The Central Bus Committee of the union nevertheless decided to take a ballot, declaring : " We are convinced that these are the best terms obtainable, and the alternative to the acceptance of these terms is strike action." By a four to one majority the ballot went against the terms.

At this stage the busmen, feeling that their official leadership needed strengthening, responded to the initiative of one garage which convened a meeting of delegates at the Memorial Hall on August 12th. Thirty-four bus branches were represented and the London Busmen's Rank-and-File Movement came into being. The movement organised a series of mass meetings, culminating in demonstrations in Hyde Park and Trafalgar Square at which the turn-out of busmen was unprecedented. Outside the official delegate conferences at Transport House large rallies of busmen were gathered ; and to the most important, that of August 30th, a rank-and-file deputation was admitted. There could be no doubt that the men were ready to fight. Their preparedness had its effect. In September definite gains were secured when the Company withdrew its demands for wage reductions, made concessions in regard to Sunday duty payments and the guaranteed week.

In January 1933 came an unofficial strike, led by the Rank-and-File Movement, provoked by the operation of new speeded-up route schedules. The number of men out reached a total of 12,500, and the strike secured an understanding, after one week, that the grievances caused by speed would receive immediate attention and that there would be no victimisation. The union and the company regarded the issue solely as one of the observance of agreements. A statement was issued intimating that the Executive Council of the Transport and General Workers' Union " is not per- pared to support the action of the members in withdrawing their labour and is unable to recognise the strike . . . the Council requires that the members of the union should observe agreements made on their behalf." " On this issue " ran a parallel statement signed by Lord Ashfield, " the Company must take the same view as the T. & G.W.U." Following the strike the Rank-and-File Movement continued to strengthen and extend its influence which was reflected in the circulation (some 10,000 copies) of its monthly journal, the *Busman's Punch*. That this movement among the busmen struck an echoing chord among other sections of London transport workers was suggested by the fact that tramwaymen at two depots came out in sympathy during the January strike.

It was to be expected that the great break of 1931, and the sharpened struggle that was a natural accompaniment of the more intense crisis, would result in important develop- ments on the political side of the movement. A brief factual summary, by no means complete, will show how the social conflict had increased in range and vehemence from the formation of the National Government up to the end of 1932. There had been over one hundred baton charges on mass demonstrations. More than 1,300 working men and women had been arrested for alleged offences in connection with their political activities, and of these, 421 sentenced to a total of 923 months imprisonment. Whereas in 1925 Communists charged with sedition (actually " incitement to mutiny ") received sentences of six or twelve months, those found guilty on similar charges were now visited with sentences of two years hard labour or three years' penal servitude. In a case of the latter kind, two Communists were jailed on the evidence of *agents provocateurs*, the judge impressing on the jury that such evidence was admissible—although a century before a select committee of the House of Commons had declared that the use of *agents provocateurs* " was most abhorrent to the feeling of the people and most alien to the spirit of the Constitution." Resistance to an eviction brought heavy sentences (up to nine and fifteen months' hard labour) on Arthur Horner and twenty-eight workers of Mardy in the Rhondda in February 1932; great scandal was caused by the preposterous police report at the Assizes on those convicted, described in the *Manchester Guardian* as " unsupported and crudely prejudiced tittle-tattle." The Tom Mann case, in December 1932, imported into England the continental principle of " preventive arrest "; for by invoking an Act of Edward III and the Seditious Meetings Act of 1817 the veteran leader was sent to jail without any charge having to be preferred against him.

Of such were the circumstances in which the Labour Party had to face up to the task of revaluing its old values. Within its ranks the cry was now, most understandably, all for a " bold Socialist policy," " no more gradualism." Declaring that " social reform under capitalism has limitations," Mr. Herbert Morrison said that it was necessary " to put Socialism first." Miss Susan Lawrence told the Labour Women's Conference that " the time has come to abandon palliatives . . . to replace the old system instead of trying to amend it." Mr. Clynes announced: " Socialism had not failed. We had never yet begun to try even a little part of it." That statement by Mr. Clynes was perhaps of more significance as a confession by one who had occupied a prominent place in both Labour Governments than as a practical contribution to future policy; but so far as the Party leadership was concerned it was noteworthy that the whole emphasis was laid on the future. There was a natural uneasiness about any searching examination of the past, although clearly such an examination would have enabled a much clearer perspective to be drawn. To take one point only; the fact that members of the Labour Cabinet had been prepared to agree to some form of Means Test, together with the statements to this effect made by them from the opposition benches in the autumn of 1931, considerably compromised the Party's prestige in the initial fight against this inquisition. It was not till April 1932 that the position was rectified by statements in the House of Commons that the Labour Party was opposed to the Means Test.

Desire for a clear-cut Socialist policy and the preventing of any possible repetition of 1931 dominated the many resolutions from the constituencies submitted to the Labour Party Conference at Leicester in October 1932. The Executive Committee, for its part, criticised previous election programmes, including *Labour and the Nation*, on the grounds that they were " too nebulous " and did not " commit leaders to a specific course of action." It did not appear, however, that the leadership had made the decisive break with the past that alert opinion in the Party was expecting. Mr. Arthur Henderson averred that " nothing has happened either to the Party or to the electoral position to warrant any scrapping of our programme or policy or the revolutionising of our methods." In face of strong opposition from Mr. Henderson the Conference carried a resolution, moved by Sir Charles Trevelyan, that " the leaders of the next Labour Government and the Parliamentary Labour Party be instructed that on assuming office, either with or without power, definite Socialist legislation must be immediately promulgated, and that the Party should stand or fall in the House of Commons on the principles in which it had faith."

Four important policy resolutions were submitted to the Conference by the Executive. They related to (1) currency, banking and finance; (2) agriculture; (3) transport, and (4) electricity supply. Moving the first resolution, Dr. Hugh Dalton made it clear that in the Executive's view it was the pivot on which all the others turned. The essence of this resolution was that the Bank of England should be turned into a central bank under State control (assimilating the venerable institution of Threadneedle Street, that is to say, to what is the normal practice in most capitalist countries), with its Governor appointed by the Government and the Bank under the general direction of a Cabinet Minister. There was a good deal of criticism of this proposal from the floor of the Conference. " I suppose we shall call in Montagu Norman to manage the Bank of England for us " drily remarked Mr. Bromley of the Locomotive-men. From the Conference itself came the demand that public ownership and control should be extended to the Joint Stock Banks, an amendment to this effect, moved by that noted financial expert the late Mr. E. F. Wise, being accepted by 1,141,000 votes to 984,000. There was no doubt that the Party was uneasy over the Executive's timid handling of this question. There were not a few who took to heart the wry comment of Mr. J. M. Keynes that " with the personalities the same, and knowledge no greater, it might not have made much difference if the machinery which the Labour Party desires had been in operation during the last ten years."

The other resolutions showed that the Party leaders' conception of nationalisation still ran along the lines of the establishment of public utility concerns directed by Boards " appointed on appropriate grounds of ability." These Boards were to administer the transport and electricity services of the country after their purchase by the issue of Government stock; the terms of acquisition, according to Mr. Herbert Morrison, would be calculated on " a basis of the capital value of the reasonable net maintainable revenue of the undertakings." It was a little hard to see that these plans for the construction of a brave new world at Fixed Rates of Interest were other than a continuation of the policy adumbrated in the MacDonaldite *Labour and the Nation.* Conference criticism was directed against the composition of the proposed Boards. Mr. Clay, on behalf of the Transport and General Workers' Union, urged that at least certain members of the Boards should be appointed only after consultation with the trade unions concerned. Claiming that the official proposal showed a distrust of Labour's ability to govern, Mr. Clay had the support of the majority of the Conference and the resolution, together with that on electricity, was referred back for further consideration.

Meanwhile the Independent Labour Party reached the last critical stage in its relations with the Labour Party, whose adoption in October 1931 of the new standing orders directly aimed at the I.L.P. the previous chapter has outlined. The majority of the National Administrative Council were unwilling to force an issue although the sentiment of the membership was unquestionably hardening in the direction of disaffiliation. A special conference had been promised to consider the position arising from the Labour Party's decision. This was called off, and at the Annual Conference at Easter 1932, the N.A.C. were able to secure endorsement for what was described as " conditional affiliation." Such a state of unstable equilibrium could hardly be other than short-lived. A definite Left Wing had now taken shape in the Party with the formation of the Revolutionary Policy Committee early in 1932. This committee, whose most active spirits were the younger London leaders of the Party, proclaimed the need for a complete break with the Party's theoretical traditions and the substitution of a new revolutionary policy on a Marxist basis; while sharply critical of the Communist Party they urged the need for a united front with it.

When the special conference eventually met at the end of July 1932 in Bradford, the Revolutionary Policy Committee stood out in sharp opposition to the majority of the N.A.C. While the Conference carried disaffiliation from the Labour Party by 241 to 142 votes, an amendment expressing the view of the Revolutionary Policy Committee was defeated by 117 votes to 53. The lack of definition in the Bradford decisions therefore produced much uncertainty throughout the Party. The rank and file felt that they had broken with the Labour Party on the issue of revolutionary policy. Some leaders, such as Secretary Paton, claimed that the break was over " technicalities." The chairman of the London Divisional Council claimed that the Party had abandoned its traditional reliance on Parliamentarism and now advocated revolutionary Socialism. A leading member of the N.A.C. declared, on the contrary, that the I.L.P. philosophy was contained in the belief that Parliamentarism in Britain still held great possibilities.

As the I.L.P. set itself to argue out these points, the minority, who had opposed disaffiliation, seceded and planned the formation of a new Socialist body to work within the Labour Party. A brief campaign preluded the summoning of a national conference at Leicester immediately prior to the Labour Party Conference in October and here the Socialist League was established. Though small in numbers the League embodied an impressive array of intellectual talent, including former I.L.P. thinkers of the calibre of the late E. F. Wise, H. N. Brailsford and others and outstanding public figures like Sir Stafford Cripps; it absorbed the Society for Socialist Information and Propaganda which had been formed the previous year by Mr. G. D. H. Cole, with the interesting participation of Mr. Ernest Bevin. Special emphasis was laid by the League on the importance of research to secure informed propaganda. " Members of the League are pledged to work within and through the wider movements, and to place all their talents, their energies and their devotion at the disposal of the movement for one specific purpose, the making of Socialists," ran its statement of objects.

During this period the Communist Party was making

efforts to overcome its isolation from the mass of the working class. Sectarianism had been rife in the application of the " new line " and as a result Communists found themselves in a weaker position in the trade unions and among the organised workers in general than they had been before. Special stress was laid on these points by the Party's Central Committee in January 1932, and when its Congress met at the end of the year there were achievements to record. Communists had played a big part in the fight of the unemployed against the cuts and the Means Test and the *Daily Worker* had achieved its first significant increase in circulation since its foundation. While with their customary candour the Communists were facing up to their short-comings in winning authority and influence among the organised workers in industry, the fact remained that at that time the Communist Party was still predominantly a party of unemployed. Nevertheless the Communists sounded a call for unity in action against the National Government, responding to the experiences of the past year. They urged that to carry through the fight against the Government successfully there was a need to organise " the united front of struggle embracing the widest masses of the workers in the factories and trade unions, and including the working women and housewives."

Certainly as 1933 opened there were plenty of signs of new life and vigour pulsating through the Labour move-ment despite the uncertainties and difficulties necessarily connected with the continued groping for a new policy, a new path forward. The Municipal Elections of 1932 recorded substantial gains for Labour, offsetting the disastrous losses of the previous year. More than half the 869 successful candidates in the largest towns were Labour candidates. Side by side with these changed trends among the masses there were signs that those who had inspired the traditional outlook of the British Labour movement were being compelled by events to criticise all that they had stood for. Thus a new edition of the famous Fabian Essays was published with a preface entitled " Fabian

Essays Forty Years Later—What they Overlooked."
Referring to the " resolute constitutionalism " for which
the Fabian Society had stood since its foundation in the
'eighties, the preface said: " When the greatest Socialist
of that day, the poet and craftsman William Morris, told
the workers that there was no hope for them save in revolution, we said that if that were true, there was no hope at
all for them, and urged them to save themselves through
Parliament, the municipalities and the franchise. It is not
so certain to-day as it seemed in the 'eighties that Morris
was not right," for " the Treasury Bench has been filled
with Socialists. Yet, so far as Socialism is concerned, it
might as well have been filled with Conservative bankers
or baronets." And in a discussion in January 1933 the then
leader of the Labour Party and the ex-editor of the *Daily
Herald* made the following revealing statements, according
to the *New Clarion*:

" George Lansbury said he had lived to see all that Dr.
Aveling, Eleanor Marx and H. M. Hyndman had
personally taught him come true. The present collapse
of capitalism had come about precisely as they had
prophesied. There was need to-day for an absolute belief
in Socialism. After the war we had rejoiced in a swing
back to Socialism, but we had been deceived. The gospel
of Socialism had not been sufficiently spread. Hamilton
Fyfe disagreed. Socialism after the war, he declared,
had been killed by the Labour Government in 1924."

Within a few weeks of the fiftieth anniversary of the death
in London of Karl Marx it was surely notable that such
public recognition of the long-denied truth of his teachings
should come from the lips of a respected veteran of the
movement. At the same time the moral pointed by the
remark of the more detached observer of men and things
suggested once again the need for a break with the fatal
heritage of disruption and defeat that Mr. MacDonald
had bequeathed to the movement and that remained even
after his going.

CHAPTER X

THE ROAD TO UNITY

January 30th, 1933, the placing in power of Hitler in Germany, marked an epoch. Every political and social issue was henceforth transcended by the twin menace of Fascism and war. During the next three years the rapid increase of antagonisms, both internal and international, showed that mankind was entering a new period of revolutions and wars. The rise of the Fascist menace in France, instanced in the critical days of February 1934, the Fascist triumph in Austria at the same time after a week of civil war, the strengthening of monarchist and Fascist reaction in Spain and its savage suppression of the Asturias rising in October 1934, the new armaments race following German rearmament, the Italian war on Abyssinia and the crisis in the League of Nations in 1935—all these events had profound repercussions in Britain and presented the Labour movement in this country with a new and urgent situation.

Nor were these significant international factors unconnected with the trend of events at home. The most reactionary Government that Britain had known for generations was gradually and unobtrusively making inroads into the traditionally democratic fabric of the Constitution, paving the way for a possible future Fascist dictatorship. Characteristic was the passage into law, with certain modifications induced by the nation-wide protest campaign conducted by the newly formed Council for Civil Liberties, of the Incitement to Disaffection Bill; this measure was described by legal authorities like Sir William Holdsworth, Vinerian professor at Oxford, as a complete reversal of the accepted principles of English law. The

Government also began to budget heavily for rearmament, while handing out millions in subsidies to capitalist vested interests in shipping and agriculture. Though the slump had passed rock bottom the state of industry as a whole remained one of deep depression. By the end of 1935, with unemployment down by nearly a million, there were still some 2,000,000 workless registered at the Labour Exchanges. Profits recovered and began to soar steadily upwards, while industrial output climbed back to its 1929 level, though the fact that this was taking place with a million more unemployed than there were in that year indicated the increase in exploitation of the workers in industry.

" Prosperity," it became clear, had nothing to offer the working class save what they were strong enough to take. More profits were squeezed out of labour by rationalisation and speeding up of all kinds; where wage increases were conceded they did not compensate for the far greater intensity of labour. Output per head was greater by 30 per cent and more in mining, steel smelting, building. On the railways, train-miles run per employee had risen by 25 per cent. In woollen textiles, according to *Labour Research*, " the profits of eleven important concerns more than trebled from 1931 to 1934; in those same years both the number of workers earning, and the weekly wages drawn, remained almost stationary." These phenomena were common both to the heavy industries, now picking up with the beginnings of rearmament, and to the so-called " new " light industries, whose rapid development had attracted more than half a million workers to the London region alone in the space of seven years. Meantime the problem of the distressed areas, the derelict slums of industry, grew still more horrifying. The appointment of Government Commissioners, so limited in their powers that they could do no more than report the facts and make trifling suggestions, was only toying with the situation; and by the end of the period under discussion, nothing more had been done other than the introduction of a Bill so hollow that it was described in the House of Commons, by an experienced social administrator like Dr. Addison, as " a pretentious imposture."

It was symptomatic that more than at any time since the critical years of the 'eighties the condition of the working class became the centre of intensive theoretical and practical inquiry. Social surveys in great industrial centres like Sheffield, Newcastle, Hull, Merseyside and elsewhere revealed the degree of want existing among large masses of the working population. The British Medical Association appointed an expert committee to determine nutrition levels, and though the level fixed by this committee was below that officially prescribed for Scottish convict prisons, it was estimated that some 20 per cent or roughly ten millions of our people were compelled to exist near or below this barely adequate minimum. The Ministry of Health entered into controversy with the B.M.A. on the remarkable grounds that its standard was too high; but ministerial complacency did not accord with the reports of the local Medical Officers of Health. Prolonged research by Sir John Orr, the country's principal nutrition expert, and by Dr. M'Gonigle of Stockton, the leading field-worker in the study of the relation of poverty and public health, was already suggesting that malnutrition was a social evil and problem of the very first magnitude. Further, the marked increase in industrial accidents and in the incidence of sickness among industrial workers suggested the increased physical and nervous strain of working conditions.

The general unrest produced by this state of affairs was reflected in the large number of small strikes which were a feature of 1933–34. These strikes, sometimes lasting only a few days and at other times continuing for months, were particularly marked in those new industries, hitherto largely unorganised, to which reference has already been made. Many of these strikes were unofficial, though they normally resulted in substantial increases in union membership. Mr. Ernest Bevin, after a fortnight's unauthorised strike of 2,000 dockers at Hay's Wharf in London, issued a

warning to his members against such strikes and their
" unofficial " advisers, whom he stigmatised as " very often
agents provocateurs for somebody." Yet in two of the most
important strikes of the kind, that at the Firestone Tyre
Factory at Brentford in July 1933, and that at the Pressed
Steel Works at Oxford in July 1934, the *agents provocateurs* were Communists and militants who offered their
assistance to spontaneous movements of unorganised men
and were instrumental in recruiting strikers in large
numbers into Mr. Bevin's own union, the Transport and
General Workers. Of the 900 Firestone men, for instance,
800 joined the T. and G.W.U. within a few days of the
beginning of their determined strike against speed-up.
Similarly an eleven weeks' strike against the Bedaux system
at Hope's Steel Window Works, Birmingham, in the spring
of 1933, not only ended in victory but brought an increase
in union membership from 35 to 430.

These strikes testified to the determination of the workers,
irrespective of age or sex, to resist any worsening of conditions, and, more, to go forward for improvements. There
were many girls among the 1,200 strikers against the
Bedaux system at the Venesta Plywood Factory in East
London in the spring of 1933. The strike was fiercely fought,
blacklegs roughly handled, and busmen on one route, much
used by workers proceeding to the factory, refused to allow
blacklegs to board their buses. A speed-up system described
as " disguised " Bedaux was the cause of a one-day protest
strike by 10,000 workers at the great Lucas Motor Acces-
sories Works, Birmingham. Trade union organisation in
the vast Ford Motor Works at Dagenham was greatly
strengthened following a three-day strike of 8,000 men
which took its beginning in resistance to wage cuts in the
tool-room. Two prolonged strikes for union recognition,
both ultimately successful, were fought in London clothing
factories in 1933-34; that at Coleman's Mantle Factory
lasted four months, that at Fairdale's three; the latter was
described as " historic " by the London Trades Council,
which likened it to that famous strike of the Bryant & May

match girls in 1888 which was the forerunner of the tidal wave of the " New Unionism."

Unrest, coupled with wage movements on a wider scale, prevailed in the ranks of the miners, engineers and railway-men. In March 1933 a delegate conference of the Miners' Federation agreed to give the Executive power to seek a simultaneous ending of all district agreements in order to further a national movement for wage increases. Long-discussed plans for reorganising the South Wales Miners' Federation resulted in the adoption in June 1933 of a scheme generally supported by the militants in that coal-field; this recast the out-of-date and largely ineffective constituent districts of the Federation and introduced a wider democracy in the conduct of its affairs by such devices as the election of the Executive by ballot vote in place of district nominations; the new order in South Wales was symbolised by the election of Arthur Horner, most noted of Communist miners' leaders (who had previously been expelled, with his lodge at Mardy, for opposition activities) to fill the vacancy for an agent in the important anthracite district.

The S.W.M.F., which in many areas had shrunk to a shadow of its former self, began to win membership again (the figure soon rose from 57,000 to 109,000) and the South Wales coalfield once more became the cockpit of the miners' struggle in this country. On three occasions during the period we are now discussing, strikes of the whole of the South Wales coalfield were but narrowly averted; the first arose out of the many weeks' strike at the Bedwas Colliery against the employment of " outsiders," the second over a strike at the Taff Merthyr Colliery against employment of members of the Non-Political Union, and the third over the general demand for wage increases which was only partially met by concessions made in an arbitration award by Lord Bridgeman. In August 1933, the miners employed by the Amalgamated Anthracite Combine struck for a week over a dispute concerning wages and the application of their traditional seniority rule. Of the temper of other coalfields the five months' strike at Boldon Colliery, Durham, gave witness; while in Scotland, and especially in Fife, the efforts of the active militants who had constituted the United Mineworkers secured the election of several of their number as independent workmen's inspectors at some of the largest collieries, the resultant improvement in safety conditions making a deep impression.

A new award of the Railway Wages Board made certain concessions on the 1931 cuts, but the men were still largely dissatisfied. On the Northern Ireland railways a strike took place at the end of January 1933, against a wage reduction of 10 per cent; it was vehemently fought and lasted for more than two months, a marked feature of the struggle being the solidarity of the dockers and other workers. The eventual settlement revised the cut to 7½ per cent, but the general dissatisfaction, not only of the railmen in Northern Ireland but throughout Britain, was seen at the annual meeting of the N.U.R. in July, when the Irish settlement was repudiated by 79 votes to 1. The engineers were restive over the conciliation machinery operated for many years in that industry under the terms of the instrument known as the York Memorandum. A ballot vote of the Amalgamated Engineering Union showed a majority for amending this agreement; that Union's membership, which had long been declining, began to rise again, and a campaign was launched for a wage increase of 8s. a week; in the course of 1935 the employers grudgingly conceded an advance of 2s. a week.

In the cotton textile industry the aftermath of the weavers' strike of 1932 and the Midland Hotel agreement, described in the previous chapter, was sheer chaos. The Master Manufacturers sought to extend the six-loom system far beyond the limit prescribed in the agreement, embarked on wholesale cutting of price lists and reduced the provisions for reinstatement to a farce. So serious did the situation become that the Ministry of Labour had to undertake an investigation, the results of which were highly unfavourable to the employers. The Government's solution was the passage of an Act under which the Minister of Labour was enabled to make an order legalising a new consolidated agreement arrived at between the manufacturers and the Weavers' Amalgamation. Officially hailed as a " charter " for the weavers, the real point was neatly put by the Manchester correspondent of the *Daily Telegraph*, who said that " the net effect will be to level out wages, and the wage bill of the industry is not expected to be materially altered." Wages were stabilised at a low level, that is to say (in some cases reductions amounted to 10s. a week or even more), and that low level was given the force of law; it was no wonder that many of the weaving districts began to demand that the Amalgamation reconsider the whole position.

From the industrial situation which has now been described there arose one obvious commonsense conclusion. That conclusion was the need for a gathering of the working-class forces, for united action to achieve a real advance throughout industry. The point was clearly put by Mr. A. Conley in his presidential address to the Weymouth Trades Union Congress in 1934. Noting that " piecemeal wage movements are on foot," he urged that " these sporadic and unco-ordinated movements should be linked together in a disciplined and ordered effort to carry the unions forward as a united body." Unfortunately that remained a verbal recognition of an urgent need. While on every issue it became more and more apparent that only through unity could attacks be resisted and retreat turned into advance, while the realisation of this fact took deeper and more decisive root throughout the movement, most of the main leaders, alike on the trade union and political sides, set their faces against unity.

The point made in the preceding paragraph was well illustrated in the continued struggles of the unemployed during this period. A London demonstration against the National Government's treatment of the unemployed was officially called by the General Council of the T.U.C. for Sunday, February 5th, 1933. Two things made that demonstration remarkable. One was that 200,000 London workers, employed and unemployed alike, came on to the streets at their leaders' call; convincing proof that an immense response awaited any official lead for action. The other was that the General Council's attempted ban on the participation of Communist and militant organisations in the demonstration was brushed on one side by the unanimous will of the demonstrators for unity in action. Much resentment had been aroused throughout the London Labour movement by Transport House's reiterated proclamation of this ban. Only a week before the demonstration, a Press statement issued by the General Council said: " We have received evidence that the Reds are desirous of making the occasion their own. They will be disagreeably, if not painfully, surprised. . . . The authorities whose duty it is to keep order on the march, will see that their banners are conspicuously absent."[1] But the demonstrators themselves saw to it that the banners of the " Reds " were conspicuously present—billowing and streaming in the wind beside those of trade union branches, Co-operative Guilds and every other section of the movement, as the masses marched to Hyde Park on that notable Sunday.

February 5th did not convert the leaders. When, in accordance with what was now annual custom, unemployed marchers assembled outside the Trades Union Congress in session at Brighton in September 1933, it was recommended by the General Purposes Committee, who interviewed their representatives, that they should not be admitted to state their case. Secretary Citrine announced his objection to " allowing people to advocate a united front by a back-door method." To judge from this Congress it did not appear that the General Council had any positive alternative policy to realise the unemployed's immediate demands. While it had refused, very properly, to be associated with the semi-governmental National Council of Social Service, it was prepared to leave participation in local Social Service schemes to the discretion of the Trades Councils, although the annual conference of these latter

[1] *Daily Telegraph*, January 31st, 1933.

bodies had urged that all such schemes should be repudi-
ated. A resolution demanding the abolition of the Means
Test, the Anomalies Act, etc., moved by the Transport and
General Workers' Union, was referred to the General
Council for consideration, and the official resolution on
employment and industrial recovery consisted mainly in
praise of President Roosevelt, plus adjurations to the British
Government to follow his example.

By the latter part of 1933 it was clear that further action
was essential both to win back the cuts in unemployment
benefit and to resist the Government's new Unemployment
Bill. This Bill had many sinister features; the whole
machinery for dealing with unemployed who had exhausted
their statutory benefit was recast in a dictatorial and
bureaucratic mould, operating through local Unemployment Assistance Boards with a central statutory commission
advising the Minister of Labour, a form of administration
frankly adopted in order to be remote from the public
pressure to which an elected body might be subject; the
plans for training schemes and camps for youthful unemployed had an unpleasant ring, the Press quoting the Home
Secretary as referring amiably to " concentration camps."
There was good ground, evidently, for the tag " the Slave
Bill," which soon stuck to the measure. Once again the
National Unemployed Workers' Movement stepped to the
front in organising appropriate action. A new National
Hunger March got under way in January 1934, and
succeeded in rousing the country more even than any of its
predecessors.

Some 2,000 marchers took the road, including a contingent of women. While Transport House repeated its
usual warning to local Labour organisations to have nothing
to do with the march, the response of Trades Councils, local
Labour Parties, and trade union branches to the march was
exceptionally wide. When the marchers reached London
at the end of February they succeeded in making the
unemployed and their treatment a first-class political issue.
Despite preliminary bluster by the Home Secretary, there

was no repetition of the 1932 police attacks on Hunger March demonstrations. The strength and dignity of bearing of the marchers created a profound impression on all sides. Public interest and sympathy had been exceptionally aroused; and the Government's refusal to meet a deputation of the marchers or allow them to be heard at the Bar of the House of Commons aroused a storm of criticism, both in debates in the House and in the Press. Mr. Ramsay MacDonald, then Prime Minister, pleaded the refusal of the Trades Union Congress to receive unemployed marchers as a precedent for the Government's action, and alleged that the N.U.W.M. was " doing its best to disrupt organised labour."

The march climaxed in a National Congress of Unity and Action which met in Bermondsey Town Hall over the week-end of February 24th–25th. In addition to the marchers themselves, there gathered at this congress some 1,500 delegates, including representatives from 245 branches of over 50 different trade unions, prominent among them being 81 delegates from 43 branches of the Transport and General Workers' Union. Much excitement was caused by the arrest on the eve of the congress of Harry Pollitt and Tom Mann, who were charged with making seditious speeches in South Wales; they were subsequently acquitted at the Swansea Assizes. The Congress planned action, not only for the specific demands of the unemployed; it included as planks in its platform the forty-hour week without wage cuts, non-contributory social insurance, and the guaranteeing of full rights of meeting, etc. The Communists presented to the Congress a detailed and practical programme of work schemes of definite social value to be carried out by employing labour at trade union rates, it being claimed that these schemes would provide work for $1\frac{1}{4}$ million unemployed, work that would last two years.

Government complacency was severely shaken by the march. When the demand for the restoration of the cuts was publicly voiced by the Archbishop of York, by hundreds of ministers of religion and M.P.s, when even the British

Chambers of Commerce urged public works schemes, the solid front of reaction began to crack. Before the march, Chancellor of the Exchequer Neville Chamberlain told the House of Commons that there was no need to restore the cuts since the fall in the cost of living meant that the unemployed were better off than in 1931 anyway. Two days after the marchers had left London the same statesman admitted at a Conservative banquet that he was being overwhelmed with communications from organisations and individuals of all kinds urging that the cuts be restored. In April, when he introduced his Budget, he announced to the Government that he had decided to restore the cuts. The march had won. No doubt it was with a fine sense of irony that the *Daily Herald* thereupon captioned a picture of a Labour Exchange queue: " These unemployed men will benefit by the concession which Labour, by its campaign, has won from the Government."

What now of the British Labour movement's reaction to the Nazi earthquake in Germany ? The Communists were early off the mark. They approached the I.L.P., proposing the establishment of a united front for joint action ; this was agreed to and the two Parties set up appropriate machinery to co-ordinate their efforts, at the same time approaching the Labour Party and the Trades Union Congress with the proposal for a joint meeting to make united action movement-wide. Unhappily Transport House was not mollified by the new direction of the Communist International to its affiliated parties " during the time of a common fight against capitalism and Fascism to refrain from making attacks on Social-Democratic organisations." A meeting with the Communists and the I.L.P. was refused on March 22nd, 1933, and the National Council of Labour instead issued a manifesto entitled " Democracy *versus* Dictatorship."

Declaring that " British Labour must reaffirm its faith in democracy and Socialism," avowing that " British Labour stands firm for the democratic rights of the people," and that " a working class, united in its fundamental faith [described as " the attainment of Socialism by peaceful means "], can stem and reverse extremes of reaction in our midst," this document hardly touched the realities of the situation. In passing, the manifesto indicated that disunity of the working class had brought Fascism to power (" masses of the working-class electors—divided between Communism and Social-Democracy—had fallen victims to Fascism "), but it nowhere suggested the need for all-embracing unity. On the contrary it treated the dictatorship of Fascism and the dictatorship of the working class (called " reaction on the ' Left ' ") as interchangeable equivalents, under either of which the workers " will go down to servitude such as they have never suffered." The final plea was that the workers " should strengthen the Labour Party—the spearhead of political power against dictators, Fascist or Communist," while they were told that their " historic task to-day is to uphold the principles of Social-Democracy."

From the tone of this manifesto it appeared that the " principles of Social-Democracy " which British workers were adjured to uphold were those which had brought the German working class to disaster; those of which Paul Faure, secretary of the French Socialist Party, wrote— " Fascism is installed in Germany. By forgetting Socialism, by forgetting the class struggle, our comrades permitted this to happen "; those which had led to the débâcle described by the Socialist *Arbeiter Zeitung* of Vienna in these words—" The loss of prestige of Social-Democracy is so great that for millions the Party has just ceased to exist." Germany had indeed provided the supreme example of whither the " principles of Social-Democracy " led. Not only did the Social-Democratic Party and the trade union leaders retreat without striking a blow; they even sought a niche for themselves and their machine in the new gangster order. This was particularly the case with the two outstanding union leaders, Herren Leipart and Grassmann. *The Times* reported that " Herr Leipart had expressed his willingness to co-operate in the work of the Hitlerist State." But this final abasement availed nothing.

A Nazi manifesto of May 2nd, 1933, proclaimed with jeers that "the Leiparts and the Grassmanns may pretend devotion to Hitler, but they are better in custody." On that day all trade unions, their offices and property throughout Germany were expropriated by the Nazis and fifty of the principal leaders, including Leipart and Grassmann, arrested. Nine days later the entire property of the Social-Democratic Party was likewise confiscated, and a week after that the same fate befell the Co-operatives.

The alarming thing was that the passivity and lack of resistance which had drugged the German leaders appeared to be at work among our Labour leaders here. In a considered statement presented by the General Council to the Brighton T.U.C. in September 1933, and spoken to by Secretary Citrine, Fascism was presented as an automatic and inevitable product of deepening crisis and growing unemployment. " In Great Britain, just as in Germany," said Sir Walter, "we have a serious unemployment problem. If unemployment gets more desperate neither myself nor any member of the General Council will be prepared to answer for the consequences." In line with the March manifesto Sir Walter linked together the Soviets and Fascism, although this aroused objections from delegates. Referring to the collapse and surrender of the German leaders, he summed up the General Council's attitude with the pious exclamation : " I hope to God we are never put into a similar position."

Apart from the more significant trends of governing class policy operating through the National Government, the movement now had to face Sir Oswald Mosley's Blackshirts, whose activities and strength were beginning to increase. The official line was to ignore Mosley, and when the British Union of Fascists staged a mass demonstration at Olympia on June 7th, 1934, as their first big London turn-out, it was suggested that to do nothing about it was the best way to discourage the Mosleyites. Communists and the men of the Left generally, with wide support from London's rank and file, thought otherwise. The counter-demonstration at Olympia, together with the blackguard-ism and brutality displayed by the Fascists, made a national sensation of the very first order, shook the whole country, and roused a wave of strong anti-Fascist feeling that spread far beyond the ranks of the working class.

When the Blackshirts sought to retrieve their tarnished reputation by a mass rally in Hyde Park on September 9th, it was from the Left again that the call and the campaign came " to drown the Blackshirts in a sea of organised working-class activity." The sun blazed on a glorious September afternoon and contingents marched from all parts of London, stepping out briskly and gaily under their scarlet banners. I shall never forget my elation when the contingent of which I was a member wheeled into the Park from the Bayswater Road. As we looked to the right across the gentle declivity that lies just the other side of the avenue of trees along the drive, we could see nothing of the open sward, which was entirely covered by what looked like a solid bank of people. There were 150,000 Londoners there to greet the demonstrators and to show their hatred of Fascism and its works. So immense was the anti-Fascist crowd that its very size induced a gaiety and enthusiasm, born of the confidence of numbers. In face of the detailed and somewhat awed reports which appeared in the news-papers next day—the Tory *Daily Sketch* headlined the demonstration " the largest ever seen in Hyde Park," agreeing with the Liberal *Manchester Guardian's* description of the " largest crowd that has gathered in Hyde Park within memory "—the *Daily Herald* hardly added to its reputation by solemnly declaring that " the Mosley fiasco was mainly owing to splendid police organisation and the good sense of the London workers, who observed the direction of the T.U.C. *and took no part in the counter-demon-stration* " (my italics). Was it not more to the point for Transport House to consider the *Manchester Guardian's* query—" On what scale would the opposition have been had it had behind it the whole force of organised Labour and of the other parties who hate Fascism as strongly ? "

IT

Now take the rising menace of war. At the beginning of March 1933 over 1,500 delegates gathered at a national anti-war congress in the Bermondsey Town Hall, following on the World Congress against War which had met in Amsterdam with the late Henri Barbusse as its president and inspirer. Co-operative organisations and peace societies were widely represented at this Congress in addition to trade unions, Trades Councils and the Communist Party and I.L.P. The presence of 110 delegates from Student societies was a sign of the times; the rise of a militant temper at Oxford, for instance, had just been illustrated by a debate in which the Union Society at that University had scandalised reaction by adopting a motion " that this House will under no circumstances fight for King and country." The Bermondsey Congress showed that there was powerful feeling ready to be mobilised against the Government's war plans; it was noteworthy that some 200 wirters had gone on record in support of the Congress.

At the Hastings Conference of the Labour Party in the same year a resolution was carried unanimously and with great enthusiasm pledging the Party " to take no part in war and to resist it with the whole force of the Labour movement . . . including a General Strike." Dr. Hugh Dalton announced for the Executive that it " accepts the resolution. . . . We rejoice to see the rising flame of the hatred of war." At the Trades Union Congress at Brighton the previous month similar sentiments had been voiced in a resolution moved by the Locomotive-men. A report of discussions on war resistance by the International Federation of Trade Unions was given and the whole matter referred to the General Council to report further to a special congress or a specially summoned conference of trade union executives. No such special meeting was held. The question ultimately went before the National Council of Labour, which appointed a joint committee who discussed the whole problem for some months from February 1934 onwards, and upon whose report the National Council based a statement which it eventually issued at the end of June.

In the interim there had been several signs that the policy of resistance to war was to be reversed: certainly its maintenance, implying uncompromising hostility to the Government's intensive preparations for war, would have involved the abandonment of the still dominant official line of accommodation to the existing order. Sir Walter Citrine had declared that a General Strike against war would be illegal; this was hardly a discovery, and indeed the fact had been publicly stated in the Hastings debate. It was learned that " from the discussions [on the Joint Committee] emerged the fact that it would be impossible to lay down a definite line of action for all future emergencies." Yet the National Council's statement prescribed quite definitely the " duty of supporting our Government unflinchingly " in the event of war, presented as " circumstances under which the Government of Great Britain might have to use its military and naval forces in support of the League in restraining an aggressor nation." It was further argued that there could be no General Strike of workers in Fascist countries and that in any case the sole responsibility of resistance to war should not rest upon the trade union movement. Equally it was argued that the policy of refusing to handle munitions must be rejected since it would also lead to a General Strike.

This new statement of policy was duly endorsed at the Weymouth T.U.C. and the Southport Labour Party Conference in the autumn of 1934. At the latter the Hastings policy for a General Strike secured a vote of 673,000 against 1,519,000. Mr. Gibson, the General Council's spokesman at Weymouth on the war question, claimed in apparent contradiction to the new policy that " there is no question of abandoning the possibility of a General Strike." Mr. Ernest Bevin went further and said, " What they did was to keep the weapon of the General Strike." Or perhaps Mr Bevin was really suggesting no disagreement with the new policy at all; after all, a weapon can be kept purely as a museum piece.

The fact that emphasis was now laid on support for the

Government in the event of war aroused keen criticism from many delegates at Weymouth, including those from the Locomotive-men, the Distributive Workers, Painters, etc. Mr. Rowlands, delegate of the last named union, averred that " the Labour leaders in 1914 waited until war broke out before going over to the support of their Government. In this report they were going over before the war started." Nevertheless there was evidence that the new policy was not the last word on the matter. In the new official programme which was adopted at the Southport Conference the Labour Party declared that to achieve peace " nothing short of a mass movement will suffice." What were the prospects for the development of such a movement ?

If it be conceded that a mass movement cannot be developed successfully without combining a unity of forces with a clear-cut and rousing forward policy, then the auguries could hardly be described as favourable. The official line on socialisation and control of industry was in 1933 modified to include the principle of trade union representation; but even so trade union opinion was unsatisfied. The General and Municipal Workers moved at the T.U.C. and Labour Party Conference in that year to amend the Executive proposals in order to secure that 50 per cent of the membership of the Controlling Boards in socialised industries should consist of direct trade union representatives. Rejected by a small majority at the Brighton T.U.C., this amendment carried at the Hastings Labour Party Conference by 1,223,000 to 1,083,000.

By 1934 official policy had hardened still further in a " safe " rather than in a Socialist direction. Informed outside comment on the Weymouth T.U.C., for example, deduced that that body " stands for safety, for marking time " (*New Statesman & Nation*), or referred to its " subdued and uneasy temper," concluding that " the trade union wing of the Labour Party is not really interested . . . in destroying the so-called capitalist system " (*Economist*). The new Labour Party programme *For Socialism and Peace* spoke of advancing to " a Socialist reconstruction

of the national life " by means of " persuasion " and with
" fair compensation to existing owners," the level of wages
and prices to be " reasonable." On this the Socialist League,
who had constantly protested their loyalty to the Labour
Party, and had, in 1933, agreed not to press their proposals
on the constitutional procedure for a Labour Government,
joined issue with the Executive. They were overwhelmed
by over 2,000,000 votes to less than 150,000; yet when
their spokesman, Mr. William Mellor, declared that " the
phrases used by the Executive would be acceptable on every
political platform. It was not a plan for socialism, but a
repetition of the 1929 attempt to work within declining
capitalism," somehow the description stuck.

And what of unity ? The leaders persisted in their efforts
to construct a 100 per cent *cordon sanitaire* between their
mass membership and the small but active militant leaven.
The incurable predilection of the wicked Communists for
initiating or taking part in various organisations which
they conceived might assist the working-class cause was
unmasked in 1933 in a statement entitled *The Communist
Solar System*; and at the Hastings Conference of the Labour
Party a general anathema was formally pronounced against
any association by Labour Party members with any
organisations of this kind. That the Executive meant
business was seen at the Labour Party's Southport Conference in the following year. Here an Executive ban on the
Relief Committee for the Victims of German Fascism,
which though conducted on non-party lines included
Communists among its number, was upheld. At the same
time the Conference, by 1,820,000 votes to 89,000, granted
powers to the Executive to take disciplinary action against
Party members who infringed any ban of this order.

Yet it was clear that the hostility aroused in the working
class by the actions of the National Government was producing a kind of elemental swing towards the Labour
Party. At the Municipal Elections of 1933 net Labour
gains totalled 242 and 25 Councils had Labour majorities.
In 1934 Labour achievement in the municipal field broke

all records. For the first time the Labour Party won a majority on the London County Council; they increased their representation from 35 to 72, while the Municipal Reformers declined from 83 to 52, the increase of over 123,000 in the Labour poll giving a clear majority of votes over all other parties. That was in March. In November the municipal elections gave 457 Labour gains in London, with majorities in 15 metropolitan boroughs, surpassing the hitherto untouched high water mark of 1919. In the provinces the gains were 241 and there were now 41 provincial boroughs under Labour control. It may be wondered whether these brilliant successes were not too dazzling for the Labour Party leaders. For example, Dr. Hugh Dalton wrote:

> " In 1934 we have regained confidence in ourselves, and as the by-elections and the local elections show, we have regained the confidence of at least as large a number of the electors as in 1929 . . . Those who speculate on the results of the next General Election are only divided as to whether we shall win a clear majority in the next House of Commons, or, falling a little short of this, shall constitute a powerful Parliamentary Opposition, needing for that majority only a relatively small access of further strength."

Those words were written in January 1935. The General Election in the following November belied the speculation. Something had happened which showed that the confidence of Dr. Dalton and his fellow members of the Labour Party Executive was sadly misplaced.

The tragic thing is that that confidence might so easily have been triumphantly justified; for 1935 opened with a united working-class offensive which put the Government to rout, for all its inflated Parliamentary majority. The story is worth telling at some length. The appointed day for the operation of Part II of the new Unemployment Act was January 7th. During the preceding months there had already been signs that a new wave of resistance to this part of the Act was rising; for, apart from its clamping of a new bureaucratic system on the unemployed, the Act made the hated Means Test even harsher, and it was generally anticipated that a new drive would be made against the already meagre relief scales. Accordingly the National Unemployed Workers' Movement, meeting in conference at Derby in the early days of December 1934, passed a resolution for united action against the Act which it addressed to the General Council of the Trades Union Congress, urging their co-operation and requesting a meeting between representatives of the two bodies. They received the following reply:

DEAR SIR,—I am in receipt of your letter of the 13th December, forwarding the resolution passed by your organisation at its conference held in Derby from the 8th to 10th December. Acting under instructions, I have to inform you that I cannot in future reply to communications from your organisation.

(*Signed*) WALTER M. CITRINE, *Secretary*.[1]

Before this exchange of correspondence—on December 11th to be precise—the new relief scales had been officially made known. They involved reductions ranging from 2s. to 9s. per week, a cut so heavy that it surpassed even the most pessimistic anticipations.

Protests began to pour in as the House of Commons debated and endorsed these scales against the opposition of the Labour Members. From the public authorities themselves in Glasgow, Norwich, and elsewhere, came demands for the withdrawal of the scales. As the appointed day drew near the feeling in the localities strengthened and plans were laid to resist attack. On January 3rd, 1935, the Communists and the I.L.P. jointly issued a call for united struggle. Two days later the Executive Committee of the South Wales Miners' Federation decided to call an all-in conference of

[1] Quoted in Wal Hannington: *Unemployed Struggles, 1919–36*, p. 303.

trade unions and all working-class organisations to organise
the defeat of the Act in that great industrial area, where
demonstrations and marches constantly mounting in magnitude were soon to be the order of the day. From the
anthracite miners and the men of the Cambrian Combine
in the Rhondda came the call for a 24-hour strike of
protest; the will to action electrified the 1,600 delegates
who gathered in Cardiff on January 26th at the all-in
conference. The tale of angry demonstrations was now
spreading to Scotland and the North-East coast; and on
January 28th the Government, beginning to waver before
the storm which was starting to blow even through the
enervating air of St. Stephens, nervously announced certain
slight concessions. These were merely trifling; and the
gale rose to a hurricane.

South Wales was the centre of the storm. There Communists, Labour men, co-operators, trade unionists, all
were now banded together in a single impregnable working-
class front, which drew around it the warm support of the
small middle class folk represented by the churches and
chapels, the shopkeepers, etc. February 3rd was an historic
day for South Wales. There were demonstrations everywhere, no less than 300,000 people attending them; in many
places up and down those straggling valleys that day saw
what amounted to a general turn-out of the whole population. On the following day a huge demonstration stormed
and wrecked the premises of the new Unemployment
Assistance Board at Merthyr. The ruling class were flung
into what Mr. Baldwin called, perhaps a little apologetically,
a " curious state of hysteria and panic." The Government,
in short, was clearly on the run. On February 5th it issued
a " standstill " order declaring that the new scales would be
suspended at the end of a further week and announcing
that reduced payments made under the scales would be
made up.

That did not satisfy the unemployed, who were fighting
for the immediate cancellation of the scales. On February
6th a resounding blow was struck by Sheffield where a

demonstration of 30,000 raged round the City Hall and for three hours fought the police, determined that the Council should receive a deputation (" the march of the unemployed was organised by the National Unemployed Workers' Movement and the I.L.P. and had not the sanction of the official Labour organisation," reported the following morning's *Daily Herald*). Next day the Ministry of Labour hastily sanctioned an immediate cancellation of the scales and restoration of the cuts in Sheffield. Government panic was suggested by the fact that the Prime Minister confessed on February 8th that he knew nothing about the granting of the sanction to Sheffield.

Orders sanctioning the immediate restoration of the cuts were now being hurriedly despatched to London, Manchester, and the other principal towns. For some reason Cumberland was omitted. On February 11th an unemployed demonstration stormed the relief offices at Maryport and immediate restoration of the cuts was granted. What then happened was typical of those hectic days. Somebody in the grim and hard-hit little town must have decided to strike back; for at 11 o'clock that night the police arrested the local unemployed leaders. Then out over the cold air of that bleak winter night there clanged the tocsin—the echoing and re-echoing peals of the fire alarm. Out poured the people on to the streets and by midnight a further huge demonstration had gathered, surging along towards the police station and securing the immediate release on bail of the arrested men. Next day the passage of the special legislation required to regularise the Government's complete capitulation marked the achievement of one of the most decisive victories of the working class in this country during the whole of the post-war period.

What part did the official leadership play in this tremendous movement? An appeal for united action, addressed to the Labour Party Executive and the General Council on January 30th by the Communists and the I.L.P. met the fate of previous appeals (it had been occasioned by the declaration made the day before by Mr. George Lansbury, then the Party leader, that " we hope all sections of the British Labour movement will unite " against the scales). Indeed, it appears from correspondence that passed at this time between the Abertillery Trades Council in Monmouthshire and Transport House that the leaders were singularly ill-advised as to the scope and significance of the mass movement then in progress. The Abertillery Trades Council alleged that the Trades Union Congress " never gave a lead to the workers to fight and resist this attack. . . . Take our local position; before the Council took an official part in this present movement, 7,000 employed and unemployed demonstrated to the Unemployment Assistance Board on this matter. The N.U.W.M. initiated this movement and it gained mass support. Then the Council associated itself with the united front, which embraced all organisations, including ministers of the church and shopkeepers. This movement has extended right throughout the country. . . . We call upon the T.U.C. to get on with the fight. . . . All we ask for is action." To this letter the following reply was sent, signed by the secretary of the organising department of the General Council:

> " I have your letter informing me that your Council consider that the actions of the General Council over the regulations issued by the Unemployment Assistance Board have been slack and without vigour and that your Council have consequently allied themselves with the united front. It appears that your Council feel that the action taken by a few Communists in South Wales is of more importance than the deputation to the Minister of Labour and the debates in the House of Commons—a point of view with which I can only express surprise. . . .
> " The fact that your Council are connected with the united front will be reported to the appropriate committee of the General Council at their next meeting."[1]

A call was indeed issued by the National Council of Labour on February 1st; this manifesto was entitled " an

[1] Quoted in Hannington, *op. cit.*, p. 311.

Appeal to the National Conscience," and was concerned to urge " all leaders of public opinion . . . in no partisan spirit " to concern themselves with the " lamentable state of affairs." A week later, when victory had been won, a further manifesto announced that demonstrations would be held.

It might have been thought obvious that if the united working-class front defeated the Government on the Unemployment Act it could also defeat it in the coming General Election. As it happened, a by-election at this moment in the Wavertree division of Liverpool emphasised the point; in the general atmosphere of united struggle the poll of the successful Labour candidate, 15,611, exceeded the 1929 high level of 13,585. At the same time it was evident that the campaign against the Government to enforce the entire repeal of Part II was far from being damped down by the surrender over the scales. In the last week of February the Durham Miners' Association held a conference on the Act. All over the country tens of thousands rallied for further demonstrations, from Aberkenfig to Aberdeen, from London to Tonypandy. " The spirit of 1926, which produced the General Strike," wrote *The Times*, " is showing itself again."

These signs of the times seemed unmistakable. They suggested one practical conclusion. That was to consolidate the unity which had brought initial success, to sharpen the attack against a retreating enemy—in short, to open the throttle and roar forward to victory. Instead the leaders addressed themselves to the task of flinging the gear lever into reverse. This feat seemed all the more unaccountable since the rising ferment was by no means confined to the unemployed and their grievances against the new Act. The general movement for wage increases and improved conditions, whose growth has already been noted, continued to gather strength. The crop of local strikes showed no signs of abating; in the Hawker Aircraft factories there were successful strikes for trade union recognition and during the summer union recognition was also won by a series of bus strikes in provincial towns.

Most important was the fact that the miners were on the move. In February a delegate conference of the M.F.G.B. discussed plans for a campaign to win a general increase of two shillings a day and a national agreement. Launched in the summer, this campaign soon showed that the miners were " determined that the present intolerable conditions must not be allowed to continue," as Secretary Ebby Edwards said. A national ballot taken in November showed the impressive majority of 93 per cent for strike action in favour of these demands.

National attention was attracted in October when miners at Nine Mile Point Colliery in Monmouthshire adopted the novel weapon of a " stay-down strike " as a protest against the employment of non-Federation men. Rapidly the movement spread. Miners in other pits stayed down or else struck in sympathy. Railwaymen refused to man trains carrying blacklegs. At Nine Mile Point itself there was hand-to-hand fighting underground when officials sought to compel the strikers to ascend the pit. After a week of electric excitement in South Wales, the most amazing and moving strike the coalfields had known ended with victory for the strikers; and they had not only won recognition for the Federation, they had lit a train that was later to flash round the world with the great " stay-in " or " sit-down " strikes in France and America.

Certainly, so far as the miners were concerned, the Trades Union Congress and Labour Party passed resolutions in support of their campaign. But the general line of the Labour leaders was on the one hand to perpetuate disunity in the movement by carrying the attack on the Communists still further and on the other hand to find more points of agreement with their enemy, the Government, than points of conflict. The strange thing was that the leaders in Britain were continuing just that policy of disunity which had proved fatal in Germany at a time when their own colleagues in leadership abroad had come to see the need to abandon this policy of disaster. Both in France and Spain the establishment of a united front between the Socialist and Communist Parties was showing that here was the way to stem the tide of Fascism and reaction, here the means by which the masses of the middle class could be drawn into a general People's Front to storm the citadel of power and privilege. By the summer of 1935 it was clear that the developments of unity in France were of the first importance for the cause of democracy and progress everywhere; not least in significance was the achievement in September of trade union unity in the land where, for a decade and a half, the organised workers had been split in two.

At the same time the forces of the Left in this country were undergoing considerable changes. The I.L.P. was passing through a period of internal struggle and confusion. Its 1933 conference had voted in favour of an approach to the Communist International, but its 1934 conference decisively rejected the proposal for affiliation to the C.I. as a sympathising party. The Party leadership fell more and more under the influence of the supporters of Trotsky and accordingly began to manifest a rigid sectarianism, combined with bitter attacks on the Soviet Union and the Communist Party. Eventually the Revolutionary Policy Committee, who led the opposition within the Party, and included the bulk of its London leaders, felt that they could not avoid a break; with very few dissentients they seceded and in the autumn of 1935 applied *en bloc* for membership of the Communist Party.

The Communists themselves had grown in numbers, though these still remained small. Yet they had undergone important qualitative changes. No longer were they mainly a party of unemployed. At their Congress in February 1935, out of 294 delegates 205 were employed workers. Increased standing in the trade unions was witnessed by the fact that 234 delegates were trade unionists, of whom nearly two-thirds held official positions in their unions. It was of moment, too, that for the first time a detailed and realistic programme for the Socialist revolution in Britain, entitled *For Soviet Britain*, was adopted at this Congress.

Nor could the relation to Britain of the proceedings of the Seventh World Congress of the Communist International in the summer of 1935 be ignored. The point was summed up by Dimitrov himself in his report to that Congress. He said:

" The growing hatred of the working class for the National Government is uniting increasingly large numbers under the slogan of the formation of a new Labour Government in Great Britain. Can the Communists ignore this frame of mind of the masses, who still retain faith in a Labour Government ? No, comrades. We must find a way of approaching these masses. We tell them openly, as did the Thirteenth Congress of the British Communist Party, that we Communists are in favour of a Soviet Government, as the only form of government capable of emancipating the workers from the yoke of capital. But you want a Labour Government ? Very well. We have been and are fighting hand in hand with you for the defeat of the National Government. We are prepared to support your fight for the formation of a new Labour Government, in spite of the fact that both the previous Labour Governments did not fulfil the promises made to the working class by the Labour Party. We do not expect this Government to carry out Socialist measures. But we shall present it with the demand, in the name of the working-class millions, that it defend the most essential economic and political interests of the working class and of all toilers. Let us jointly discuss a common programme of such demands, and let us achieve that unity of action which the proletariat requires in order to repel the reactionary offensive of the National Government, the attack of capital and Fascism, and the preparation for a new war."

In contrast to this plain exposition of the line of militant unity stood the General Council's adoption in March of the notorious circulars 16 and 17, generally referred to as the " Black Circular," ordering Trades Councils to ban delegates who were Communists or had any associations with Communists, and requesting trade unions to modify their constitution and rules to exclude Communists from any office. The issue became an important one throughout the trade unions. The Miners, the three Railway Unions, the Transport Workers, Woodworkers, Engineers, Distributive Workers, Painters, Electrical Trades, and many smaller societies went on record against the " Black Circular."

When Mr. Baldwin contrived the celebration of the royal Silver Jubilee (a thing quite without precedent) as a monster piece of patriotic propaganda and creation of the " national unity " war atmosphere, Transport House circularised instructions to all local Labour bodies to participate in the celebrations. In the Jubilee honours Mr. Arthur Pugh received a knighthood and upon Mr. Citrine there was conferred the star and purple ribbon of Knight Commander of the Most Excellent Order of the British Empire. The Tory *Daily Telegraph* gracefully commented " that those also serve who oppose the Government of the day is generously admitted in the titles conferred upon Labour statesmen, and in the specific honour offered to the trade union movement." Had the Tory organ in mind the Weymouth–Southport policy of " supporting our Government unflinchingly " in the event of war ? It was certainly the case that, during this critical year, the Labour leaders " also served " by supporting the Government's foreign policy, including rearmament, not merely unflinchingly but uncritically.

That came to be the vital point. The Labour Party Executive recommended co-operation with the Home Office in the air-raid " precautions " which the highest scientific authorities have since shown to be farcical. " The Labour Party, no less than the Government parties, recognised the necessity for maintaining defences at the highest point of efficiency," said Sir Walter Citrine. Though during the Abyssinia crisis and the Italian aggression it was so soon to be seen that the Government was merely posing in its apparent support of the League and was in reality allowing the aggressor an almost free hand, the leaders stood solid with Mr. Baldwin. " Irrespective of party, irrespective of domestic conflict, the overwhelming majority of the nation is firmly behind the Government in the stand that it has now taken on this dispute " ran a *Daily Herald* leader, entitled " The Voice of Britain," on Sir Samuel Hoare's Geneva speech in September. Blindness could go no further. Three months later the revelation of the cynical Hoare–Laval pact was to arouse a spontaneous outburst of popular indignation, so widespread that Sir Samuel had to resign the Foreign Secretaryship.

By-elections might have served as alarm signals. Two contests in Aberdeen in May showed the Government's candidates considerably exceeding the 1929 Conservative level, while the Labour Party vote was in both cases markedly below the 1929 figure and in one case (West) over 2,000 less than that recorded in the 1931 débâcle. In July the West Toxteth (Liverpool) by-election, while registering success for the Labour candidate on a very low poll, showed a Labour vote not exceeding that of 1931. There is no evidence that heed was paid to warning signs of this kind. Nor did there seem to be any sense in the highest Labour circles that in the coming General Election they were out to win power. An astute commentator like Mr. A. J. Cummings, the political editor of the *News Chronicle*, wrote: " One must deplore the shameful spirit of political defeatism which has overtaken the Labour Party in this country. One day last week a group of Labour leaders in London were discussing with an air of patient resignation the prospect of returning 170 Labour representatives to the next Parliament. That was the maximum calculation."

At the Margate Trades Union Congress in September and the Brighton Labour Party Conference the following month reaffirmation of the official policy on war was carried by large majorities. The T.U.C. likewise rejected a resolution instructing the General Council to act with all organisations hostile to war and Fascism, and calling for international trade union unity. Debate, none the less, was keen at both assemblies. At Brighton the official policy was opposed by Sir Stafford Cripps, who claimed that to support sanctions meant to support imperialism, while Mr. George Lansbury opposed from the pacifist angle and shortly after the conference decision resigned the Party leadership. At Margate several union delegates took the opportunity to point out that it was not only necessary to attack the Italian Fascist aggressor by enforcing sanctions, it was also necessary to expose the aims of the British Government. It was notable that Mr. W. Kean, in his presidential address to the Margate Congress, went out of his way to pay tribute to " that great working-class power, the Soviet Union," which he described as " one of the powerful factors operating against international Fascism." This surely implied a reversal of the official line of bracketing together Fascism and Communism; though two months later, at the height of the General Election campaign, the *Daily Herald* was to repeat that " equally towards the dictatorial ideas of Fascism and the dictatorial ideas of Communism, Labour's attitude has been one of unremitting hostility."

Against the endorsement of the " Black Circular " at Margate 1,274,000 votes were rallied against 1,869,000 for the General Council; and the result might have been different if it had not been for the reported swing-over of the near half a million votes of the Transport and General Workers' Union. Over the question of honours there had been much scandal in the movement and a flood of protests, which found reflection at the T.U.C., where a resolution of regret that honours had been accepted was moved by the Women Clerks and Secretaries. Sir Walter Citrine made a personal statement, claiming that this was a question on which the movement had never made any declaration for guidance; on a show of hands 125 votes mustered against 237 to oppose the carrying of the previous question.

From what has now been said the result of the General Election of November 1935, profoundly disappointing though it was, cannot be considered surprising. Both in strategy and in propaganda, defeatism, passivity and scepticism did their work only too well. It was not until the last week before the poll that the *Daily Herald*, for instance, changed its tone and declared that Labour " is out to win power. It is ready to take office." Unfortunately the sentence continued : " To-day Labour is as ready for office as in 1929." But it was not a repetition of the MacDonald Government of 1929–31 that the working-class electorate wanted. Nor could the workers be expected to rise like lions at the call of leaders who, as did Mr. J. R. Clynes in his election address, sought to recommend themselves by quoting a statement of Mr. Baldwin that " the Labour Party as a whole has helped to keep the flag of Parliamentary Government flying in the world in the difficult periods through which we have passed. From the first day they had taken their part as His Majesty's Opposition."

Yet, while the Labour Party only increased their representation to 154—considerably below even the 1923 figure—it spoke well for the solidity of the working class that their poll reached $8\frac{1}{2}$ millions. Despite official rebuffs the Communist Party flung its weight wholeheartedly into the election campaign in support of the Labour Party, withdrawing all its candidates except Harry Pollitt (Rhondda East) and William Gallacher (West Fife). Transport House disapproval could not prevent an unofficial united front operating in many constituencies. Whatever the General Staff thought, the Labour men in the front line, even when they were hesitant at first, were not long in welcoming the assistance of their Communist brethren. Not least striking among the election results was the ignominious defeat of Mr. MacDonald at Seaham and the victory of Wm. Gallacher in West Fife. Yet nothing could offset the fact that reaction had received a further mandate. This was the result of the refusal to tread the path of unity.

CHAPTER XI

THE MOVEMENT TO-DAY—AND TO-MORROW

It is impossible to record the latest stage of this eventful history and not be sensible of a compelling, an overwhelming urgency. The factors of sensational change in the world situation, described at the beginning of the previous chapter, are operating at a constantly increasing pace. A frontier and a battle-line is being carved across the face of the earth. On either side of it there stand over against each other the forces of barbarism and retrogression, the forces of civilisation and progress. The future of mankind, nothing less, depends upon the issue of the struggle between Fascism and Democracy. Indissolubly connected with this issue, and depending upon its decision, are the issues of war or peace, capitalism or Socialism.

Fascism has continued to take the offensive. Encouraged by the Anglo-German Naval Treaty Hitler carried German rearmament to its farthest point, reintroduced conscription and completed the destruction of the Versailles Treaty by the military reoccupation of the Rhineland. In the west, co-operation between Germany and Italy was strengthened. In the east the conclusion of the German-Japanese Pact " against Communism " marked another step in the Nazis' anti-Soviet drive. Of the intervention in Spain more will be said below.

At the same time, 1936 witnessed significant developments on the other side of the frontier. There were the striking victories of the People's Front in the Spanish and French general elections of February and May. In the

Soviet Union the introduction of the new Constitution, cornerstone of the edifice of Socialist democracy, marked the most important stage in the growth of Socialism since the Revolution itself. On the other side of the Atlantic the almost unanimous will of America's millions for change was symbolised in President Roosevelt's spectacular re-election, while the emergence of new trade union forces around the Committee for Industrial Organisation, led by John L. Lewis, with their successes in the automobile and steel industries, indicated the approach of a new era both in the Labour movement and in the political life of the United States.

In Britain Premier Baldwin unsealed his lips to reveal that the General Election of 1935 had been a gigantic confidence trick. The Government, as we have seen, had secured the uncritical support of the Labour leaders for their supposed backing of the League and collective security, had won the election on that issue, and then had abandoned the convenient camouflage for their real policy of wholesale rearmament. It was not surprising that Mr. Baldwin described his revelation, made in the House of Commons twenty-four hours after the solemn celebration of Armistice Day, as one of " appalling frankness." He said :

" From 1933, I and my friends were all very worried about what was happening in Europe. You will remember at that time the Disarmament Conference was sitting in Geneva. You will remember at that time there was prob-ably a stronger pacifist feeling running throughout this country than at any time since the war. I am speaking of 1933 and 1934. You will remember the election at Ful-ham in the autumn of 1933, when a seat which the National Government held was lost by about 7,000 votes on no issue but the pacifist. You will remember, perhaps, that the National Government candidate who made a most guarded reference to the question of defence was mobbed for it. That was the feeling in the country in 1933. . . .

"I asked myself what chance was there—when that feeling that was given expression to in Fulham was common throughout the country—what chance was there within the next year or two of that feeling being so changed that the country would give a mandate for rearmament? Supposing I had gone to the country and said that we must rearm, does anybody think that this pacific democracy would have rallied to that cry at that moment? I cannot think of anything that would have made the loss of the election from my point of view more certain."

Even before this cynical confession, Mr. C. R. Attlee, the new leader of the Labour Party, referring to the Labour movement's declaration of its readiness to support the Government in operating the Covenant of the League, said, "the Government used our declaration in order to win the general election. Then they betrayed us." Could it be denied that the Communist warning had been justified? It was in November 1935 that a leading Communist, J. R. Campbell, had written " now this Government is coming out for a rearmament programme—a programme for enriching the private arms trusts in this country. It is coming out with a proposition for a defence loan, so that the rich can avoid paying for the defence of their Empire and can enrich themselves not only as armament shareholders but also as subscribers to the defence loan. We must see in this Government not the defender of the League, but its enemy, not the enemy of the main Fascist powers, but their supporter." The launching of the £300,000,000 rearmament programme, swollen in February 1937 to the staggering figure of £1,500,000,000, drove home, after the event, Campbell's conclusion that " all who wished to fight Fascism and war must level the barriers and unite the forces of the working class and of all friends of peace for the complete destruction of this Government."

Meantime, the political and social background in this country had not changed; events had etched its outlines more sharply. The golden rain of rearmament was pouring in still heavier and more refreshing showers upon 1 per cent of the population—they also serve who only sit and speculate. The other side of the " prosperity " medal was authoritatively revealed in the summer of 1936 when the separate investigations of Sir John Orr and Dr. M'Gonigle demonstrated that no less than one-half the population of this island is prevented by its enforced economic standards from maintaining the requisite level of nutrition. Of the reactionary home policy of the Government there was sufficient evidence. The long-overdue Factory Bill made no decisive step forward ; the wide demand for a 40-hour week, especially for young workers, was flouted. As for the distressed areas, despite still more reports and debates, and the resignation in disgust of the Government's Chief Commissioner, Mr. Malcolm Stewart, they remained where they were ; the monarch who last November created some stir by his visit to South Wales and his shocked protestations that he would see that something was done, was a month later driven into abdication.

Intensified activity by the Mosleyites did not move the Government. Indeed, when the British Union of Fascists held a big rally at the Albert Hall in March, the conduct of the police in breaking up a counter-demonstration of anti-Fascists in Thurloe Square, some distance from the Albert Hall, provoked much scandal and led to a debate in the House of Commons. Though Home Secretary Simon was ultimately driven to confess that his " blood boiled " at the outrageous campaign of anti-Semitism that the Blackshirts let loose in the East End, accompanied by incidents as near to pogroms as anything ever seen in this country, the Government took no steps, despite numerous public appeals made to it, to ban the provocative Blackshirt march through East London that was planned for October 4th. It was the working-class movement of the East End, united in its determination to bar the way to the Fascists, that settled matters. On that Sunday the people of the East End boroughs turned out into the streets literally in hundreds of thousands. They were reinforced by masses of anti-Fascist workers from all over London. The tension was tremendous. In Cable Street barricades were erected. If the Fascists had attempted to march they would have been annihilated, admittedly at the cost of heavy street fighting and violent disorder. The Commissioner of Police thereupon took the responsibility of banning the march when the Fascists had gathered at their place of assembly. Still the Government policy remained equivocal. The Public Order Bill banned the wearing of political uniforms, but gave the police extended powers which would be as valuable for dealing with the working-class movement as against the Fascists; it had been claimed by many legal authorities that the existing provisions of the law were ample to deal with the provocation to disorder of which so many complaints had been laid at Fascist doors.

In the industrial world ferment grew. Wage movements affecting the majority of workers in industry were able in a number of cases to win certain increases. Generally these did not go further than tending to restore the wage levels prevailing before the cuts of 1931–32, although the cost of living was beginning to show an upward trend. The dissatisfaction of the railwaymen, for instance, was reflected in the pledge of the N.U.R. to reopen negotiations on the basis of the 1936 figures and in the continued fight of the locomotive-men for wage adjustments, for a 6-hour day and holidays with pay. Unrest was marked in the Civil Service. The postal workers launched a national campaign for a 5-day week of 40 hours; while the Civil Service Clerical Association sought counsel's opinion as to the legality of a stay-in strike. Busmen continued active. There were local strikes in Northampton and the Thames Valley, while in London itself eleven garages were affected by strikes in October over the introduction of the winter schedules and the union pledged itself to advance negotiations for a 7-hour day for London busmen. It was also announced that the T. and G.W.U. was aiming at the conclusion of a national agreement for provincial busmen, no fewer than 85,000 of whom are employed by local companies controlled by the Tilling-British Electric Traction Combine.

The armaments industries, with increasing employment, saw increased determination of the men in the works and the factories to strengthen their own organisation and win concessions. In Glasgow and Barrow, for instance, the engineers were driving for a complete embargo on overtime. There were further strikes in aircraft factories, frequently around the question of the recognition of shop stewards. Such vital concerns as de Havilland, Fairey, Handley Page and Parnall were affected. In December, the Amalgamated Engineering Union held a special national conference of delegates from 40 aircraft firms and decided to press a claim for a national aircraft agreement with wage increases; delay in pressing this claim was criticised by the rank and file Aircraft Shop Stewards' National Council.

Boom periods are normally accompanied by general trade union activity and industry-wide movements for higher wages and improved conditions. There has been a lag in this usual reaction so far as the rearmament boom is concerned. The union leadership has rather given the impression of holding back; and the strikes that have taken place have generally been unofficial, a circumstance which has incurred the declared disapproval of the Trades Union Congress General Council. Here it may be of interest to record the view of so well-known a Labour publicist as Mr. Hamilton Fyfe, who wrote in *Reynolds News*: " Unofficial strikes are unfortunate. They ought not to be necessary, but the people who ought to make them unnecessary are Trade Union officials. It will not do for these officials, whether branch or headquarters, to blame ' Communist propaganda ' for what are clearly acts provoked by harsh treatment or a feeling that those who do the hardest part of the work are getting the dirty end of the stick. To order them back and not to inquire carefully into the reasons for their coming out is the way not to end unofficial strikes, but to make them more frequent."

Among the miners interest was particularly concentrated on the fight for the right to organise and the smashing of company unionism. In South Wales, where Arthur Horner was elected president of the Federation by a large majority, stay-in strikes on this issue took place at the Taff Merthyr and Bedwas collieries. The Taff Merthyr strike was accompanied by collisions with the police which led to the trial of 69 men and 6 women, of whom 33 were sentenced to terms of imprisonment ranging from three to fifteen months; countrywide protests were aroused. At Bedwas a ballot of the men showed 1,177 for the Federation against 309 for the " non-political " union. The obduracy of the owners, continuing right up to the last moment, almost precipitated a coalfield strike.

Widest national attention was drawn to this issue by the dispute at Harworth Colliery in Nottinghamshire. Here a ballot last November had a result even more striking than that at Bedwas—the Spencer Union was rejected by 1,175 votes to 145. Thereupon the continued attempts of the colliery company to force the men to subscribe to the Spencer Union resulted in a strike which continues unshaken at the time of writing (April 1937). Despite the sentencing of six miners (including the Union branch chairman) to terms of hard labour for offences against the Trade Union Act of 1927, the heavy fining of ten others, the attempted eviction of miners from their company-owned houses, the local membership of the Notts Miners' Association has increased from 200 to 1,200. On January 20th a special National Conference of the Mineworkers' Federation of Great Britain instructed the Executive to take a national ballot for strike action in support of the Harworth men and also to approach the Trades Union Congress to enlist the backing of the whole movement in this vital fight. In April, after the rejection of a scheme of fusion with the Spencer Union, the ballot was being taken.

Just as in January and February 1935, so in 1936 the will to united struggle against the Government found expression in the fight of the unemployed. The announcement by the Unemployment Assistance Board of new scales revealed that while these were an improvement on the scales of 1935 they were still well below benefit level; while the Board were discreetly vague as to the numbers that would suffer actual reductions under them, there was no doubt that these would be extensive. A new Hunger March was planned for the autumn, its aim being directed especially against the Means Test. The march surpassed even the 1934 record. Initiated, as before, by the National Unemployed Workers' Movement, it gained wider support than ever from all sections of the Labour movement in the localities. In London for the first time the Reception Committee was formed under the official auspices of the London Trades Council. When the 2,000 marchers, coming from as far north as Aberdeen, from the Clyde and the Tyne, from Lancashire and South Wales, assembled in Hyde Park on Sunday, November 8th, they were welcomed by a united demonstration variously estimated at 150,000 to 250,000 strong. The contingents were accompanied from the different parts of London by impressive processions in which the banners of local Labour Parties, trade unions, Co-operative Guilds, Communist Party and I.L.P. branches, student and youth organisations, peace councils, etc., testified to a new and wider unity.

The spirit of that remarkable day was symbolised in the appearance of Mr. Attlee, leader of the Labour Party, to speak on the same platform as Wal Hannington. Another Labour speaker, Mr. Aneurin Bevan, M.P., said " the Hunger Marchers have achieved one thing. They have for the first time in the history of the national Labour movement achieved a united platform. Communists, I.L.P.ers, Socialists, members of the Labour Party and Co-operators for the first time have joined hands together, and we are not going to unclasp them. This demonstration proves to the country that Labour needs a united leadership." In its annual report for 1936 the London Trades Council observed that " the most significant feature of the march was the support given by people of all classes, creeds and politics . . . this wave of sympathy should serve as an impetus to the Labour movement to seek ways and means of harnessing the great forces of public opinion in the fight." The point of view of the marchers was put in extensive mass lobbying of M.P.s. The Government refused to see a deputation, but after a sharp debate in the House they gave way and the Minister of Labour received the marchers' representatives. A further blow had been struck for the just demands of the unemployed.

During the year that had preceded the Means Test Protest March there had been ample evidence throughout the whole of working-class politics that the urge to unity was growing steadily more imperative. Significant discussions had developed in the local Labour Press immediately after the General Election. Thus the Birmingham *Town Crier* opened its columns to rank and file contributors under the general heading " What is Wrong with the Labour Party ? " Here was voiced the demand that the Labour Party should " attack more," should " cease to fear its friends and apologise to its enemies," should abandon heresy-hunting; on the subject of apathy it was contended that " apathy comes from the top," " apathy is due to lack of leadership and to vagueness," while it was claimed that the membership " had little opportunity for voicing opinion on policy. The Rotherhithe *Labour News* outlined proposals for a fighting programme in its issue of January 1936 and called for " unity—leadership and struggle through unity."

The application of the Communist Party for affiliation to the Labour Party, made at the end of November 1935, soon became the test issue for supporters and opponents of unity alike. In forwarding the Communist application Harry Pollitt wrote that his Party was prompted to take this step for the following reasons: (1) the many far-reaching changes in the political situation at home and abroad with the advent of Fascism in Germany and Austria; (2) the bitterest opponents of Communism in Britain, leaders of the fight against Communist affiliation in 1922, had now gone over to the enemy; (3) the General Election had shown that only a united Labour movement could overthrow the National Government. The reply of the National Executive of the Labour Party, transmitted by Secretary Middleton, was that " no circumstance had arisen to justify any departure from the decision registered by the Annual Conference at Edinburgh in 1922." The Labour Party added that nothing had taken place to reconcile the " fundamental difference " between " the democratic policy and practice of the Labour Party " and the Communist Party's " policy of dictatorship." It contended that the Communist Party only desired affiliation in order to use the Labour Party's platform and Press in the interests of its own Party propaganda. Rebutting these claims a further letter from Harry Pollitt contrasted the successes of the united front in France with the disasters of disunity in Germany, asked whether British Labour was " to remain apart from this great movement towards unity that is now taking place in every capitalist country " and remarked:

" During the General Election there was a united front between branches of the Labour and Communist Parties all over the country. Your National Executive chose to ignore that this was taking place. Yet many of your own candidates and successful members of Parliament publicly testified that this united front was of considerable help to them in winning a victory against the National Government, or a substantially increased vote.

" We have not heard of a single complaint that during this united campaign any attempt was made by the Communist Party to exploit this position for any other aim but that of defeating the National Government.

" The united activity that was carried out during the

General Election was warmly welcomed by all your rank-and-file members and local organisations. But if it was good and useful to have unity in action in the General Election, how much more necessary is it now with the National Government in power again."

Pollitt concluded by suggesting a meeting of Labour Party and Communist Party representatives. " We are ready at any time for such a meeting, believing that it is possible for us to reach agreement and thus take the first steps along the path that alone can lead to Socialism—the path of working-class unity." No answer was given by the Labour Party to these further points. Mr. Middleton wrote that " the Executive Committee were unanimously of the opinion that no good purpose would be served by the joint meeting proposed. I have also to intimate their decision that our correspondence should now be concluded."

Accordingly the Communist Party took steps to have its proposals discussed throughout the movement, and organised a petition advocating Communist affiliation which members of the Labour Party and its affiliated organisations were asked to sign. The response was widespread. By the summer, reports published in the *Daily Worker*, which did not claim to be complete, indicated that over 1,200 organisations had gone on record in support of Communist affiliation. They included 765 trade union bodies, national, district and branch, 360 Labour Party bodies and 80 Co-operative bodies. National unions supporting affiliation included the Mineworkers' Federation and the Locomotivemen, while the Scottish Women's Co-operative Guilds, the Socialist League and the Fabian Society itself also went on record in the same sense. Other unions, including the Engineers and the ordinarily conservative London Society of Compositors, expressed themselves in favour of unity in general terms without specific reference to the Communist Party.

At the beginning of May the French elections had registered their remarkable triumph for working-class unity, while later in the same month the elections in Belgium, where unity had been refused, underlined the moral; for there the Labour Party lost seats while the native Fascists (Rexists) scored sensationally. The moral appears to have been lost on the Labour Party Executive; for in a statement entitled " British Labour and Communism," which it combined with its associates in the National Council of Labour to issue in mid-July, it argued against any emulation of the French example, claiming that the Popular Front was simply " an electoral device " which " has served Communist purposes." Making play with the fact that Communist Party membership had been reported (summer, 1935) as being about 7,000, the statement asserted that " it is this abject failure to secure a substantial membership that has dictated the more subtle tactics of the united front," contending that Communist strength in Britain was " negligible " and that " the Communist Party represents no substantial part of British public opinion." It was concluded that the proposals for unity and Communist affiliation were put forward " for the purpose of subjecting the Labour and trade union movement of Great Britain to the dictation of the Russian Government." The Communist Party was accused of receiving " Soviet subventions," given to it " with the object of destroying existing democratic industrial and political Labour movements, and of bringing about the overthrow of the present social system by violence."

It may have comforted the Labour Party leaders to emphasise the small membership of the Communist Party. But the point was quite misconceived. As the editor of the Rotherhithe *Labour News* wrote: " The unity of the working class has been presented as a matter of simple arithmetic (x millions of affiliated members of the Labour Party plus y thousands of Communists). If that were so, we might conceivably agree with the official Labour view that those odd thousands of Communists could safely be left outside the Labour Party. But unity is not a matter of x plus y: it is a matter of leadership. To-day it is a matter of leading the workers and such allies as they can find in the struggle against war and Fascism."

Indeed, the Labour leaders' attempts by a formal and quantitative evaluation of the Communist forces to suggest their insignificance, contrasted curiously with the simultaneous suggestion that unity with the Communists would swamp the Labour Party and bring frightful disasters. Surely this formal approach bore no relation to political reality? No one would contend, because the tiny nucleus of leaven bears only a fractional relationship in weight to the lump of dough, that yeast is therefore " negligible " in the baking of bread. From the previous descriptions of working-class activity during the preceding two or three years, it will have been seen that the Communists and the militants grouped around them had played a big part, alike through their display of initiative and in the energy and drive which they brought to the carrying out of campaigns. Their newspaper, the *Daily Worker*, had doubled its size and far more than doubled its daily circulation during this period; while its achievement of a circulation of over 100,000 for its week-end edition marked the highest point ever achieved by any revolutionary Socialist journal in this country. Nor could it be denied that there was meaning in the greatly increased sale of Communist propaganda pamphlets and literature of all kinds; from January 1935 to March 1937 the sales of Communist publications were in excess of 900,000 copies.

The case was no better with the claim that the Communists represented " no substantial part of British public opinion." On the contrary, the Communists were attracting into their ranks or into whole-hearted participation in the drive for unity against war and Fascism the most significant and able elements in the intellectual life of the nation. The decisive forces among the younger scientists of eminence stand firmly on the Left. Among writers and journalists, in the academic and technical worlds, among artists and intellectuals of all kinds, the same trend is to be perceived.

Within a few days of the issue of the National Council of Labour's statement against Communism there took place the counter-revolutionary military uprising in Spain. The Spanish Civil War was rapidly transformed into a war for the defence of national independence against the German and Italian Fascist invader; and it is not necessary to labour the point that the war in Spain and its successful issue for democracy was, as Stalin put it, " not the private affair of the Spaniards, but the common cause of all advanced and progressive mankind." What was the British Labour movement's reaction to this supreme test? From the beginning the Labour leaders correctly summed up the issues of the Spanish struggle in public statements. A fund was opened. Yet from last July to the time of writing these lines seven months later there has been no sort of national campaign as there was in defence of the Soviet Republic seventeen years ago. Except for the fund, solidarity has remained verbal. And the fund itself, which was incorporated with the international fund established under the auspices of the International Federation of Trade Unions and the Labour and Socialist International, has naturally not produced a tithe of the amount that could have been raised, as everybody knows, given a country-wide platform campaign.

In a declaration issued on August 28th, the National Council of Labour proclaimed that " it was clearly the right of the Spanish Government by the rules of international law to obtain arms for its defence," and added that the embargo on arms to Spain that was being operated required that " the utmost vigilance would be necessary to prevent these agreements being utilised to injure the Spanish Government." Yet the concern of the leadership was to prevent the movement from opposing the considered policy of the British Government, namely the giving of a free hand to the Fascist Powers to overwhelm democracy in Spain. The fact that the abandonment of international law by the democratic Powers was screened by the use of the term " non-intervention " was used by the leadership to imply that any contrary policy would be one of intervention, that is to say, of immediate war against the Fascist Powers who were intervening in Spain. At the same time it was repeatedly stressed, both by Mr. Ernest Bevin and by Sir Walter Citrine, at the Trades Union Congress at Plymouth last September, that the non-intervention agreement had been initiated by the Blum Government as a kind of " lesser evil " and that any opposition to the agreement was therefore an attack on the Socialist Government of France. Sir Walter Citrine declared that from the Communist side in France " a campaign was raging against the Government to make it change its position," while Mr. Bevin declared that " we of the National Council of Labour, while we come to a British decision, are not going to be made a catspaw in order that a decision of this Congress may be used in France to bring down the Blum Government."

Neither of these two responsible leaders mentioned this fact ; those sections of the working-class movement in France that were campaigning for the Blum Government to change its Spanish policy had repeatedly made it clear that there was no intention of bringing the Government down. Nor did Sir Walter and Mr. Bevin indicate that it was not the Communists alone but the whole of the French trade union movement who were concerned in this agitation. The very day before they spoke the Confédération Générale du Travail, the French counterpart of the Trades Union Congress, had concluded a two-day discussion of the Spanish problem and had passed a resolution which, while reaffirming loyalty to the People's Front and the Blum Government, asked it " to reconsider, in agreement with the British Government and the other democratic countries, the whole policy of neutrality." But indeed the whole Bevin-Citrine argument about France was soon to go completely by the board when, in November, a delegation of representatives of the Front Populaire, headed by the veteran Socialist Jean Longuet himself, came to London with the express knowledge and approval of Léon Blum to see whether British opinion could be mobilised in support of

KT

a French denunciation of the non-intervention agreement that was now seen by all to be a cruel mockery.

Informed circles were aware from the start that it was the attitude of the British Government that forced Blum to adopt his position on non-intervention. To accept this point of view, however, would have involved a reversal of their policy; so the Labour leaders denied its validity, apparently preferring to accept the word of the Baldwin Government. In a reference to this contention Mr. Bevin said at the T.U.C., " our delegation to the Foreign Office tested that by every means at their disposal, and I think they are satisfied that there is no truth in it at all." Yet in August the *Manchester Guardian Weekly* had written : " When the Spanish war broke out, the French Government was sharply split, not knowing whether or not to let the Spanish Government have its full legal rights ; the British Government urged non-intervention on it." One of the best informed foreign correspondents living, Mr. Robert Dell, referred in the New York *Nation* at the end of October to the July visit of Blum and his Foreign Minister, Delbos, to London. He said " it was during the visit to London that the British Government proposed the policy of non-intervention in Spain—that is, the policy of intervention against the Spanish Government. Delbos was won over to it at once, but Blum was strongly opposed to it. Soon afterwards the British Ambassador in Paris informed Delbos that if Germany attacked France because the Spanish Government obtained war material from France, the British Government would not consider it an ' unprovoked attack ' within the meaning of the Treaty of Locarno and would not therefore go to the aid of France." The same facts emerged clearly in the speech of Delbos himself at the League of Nations Council in December, while at the Conservative Party conference at Margate in October, Chancellor Neville Chamberlain openly boasted of the influence brought to bear on Blum by the National Government.

At the Trades Union Congress speeches by many

delegates testified to the depth of feeling on the Spanish issue. It is doubtful whether the official policy would have got through if it had not been for the specific pledge given to reconsider it in the event of the non-intervention agreement proving ineffective. Typical was the statement by President J. C. Little of the Amalgamated Engineering Union that he supported the official resolution with all his inclinations in favour of the amendment moved by the Furnishing Trades calling for the launching of " a great international campaign to force the democratic countries to abandon the deceptive policy of neutrality which the Fascist dictators are not observing." In the event, the amendment was defeated by 3,029,000 votes to 51,000.

Before proceeding further it will be appropriate to dispose of the argument that " the choice before us is whether or not we would take a step which in our view would lead to war " (Bevin). With this may be coupled the statement from the same source that " we have not to throw our weight about and threaten war on the Fascist Powers, but I feel sincerely the time has come when the whole of the democratic Powers have to say to Hitler and Mussolini ' do not take us too cheaply.' " In the light of the French experience last January over the German infiltration into Spanish Morocco it is clear that to call the bluff of the Fascist Powers does not involve war; it is also clear that the apologetic " do not take us too cheaply " needs to be replaced by a firm " get to hell out of it." That was precisely what happened over the Morocco incidents. The French Government told the German Government bluntly that any German troops that landed in Spanish Morocco would be " chucked out " (the phrase was actually used) by the French. Immediate preparations were made to implement the threat; and with uncanny haste the Führer registered his first diplomatic climb-down.

It has been suggested above that the official policy was far from representing the true sentiments of the movement. Former Labour Cabinet Ministers like Mr. Herbert

Morrison and Sir Charles Trevelyan denounced the non-intervention policy. On the Left, immediate initiative was displayed in organising a nation-wide drive to aid Spain. It was alleged by Mr. Bevin at Plymouth that the Communists " scarcely said a word about intervention until the National Council had issued its decision; then they thought it well to issue their attack. Those are their usual dishonest tactics." Actually the Communists had set themselves from the start to develop the most intensive campaign in the whole of their history in support of Spain, endeavouring to persuade the Labour leadership to do likewise.

The National Council of Labour's statement had been issued on August 28th. As early as July 25th, in an appeal issued by Harry Pollitt on behalf of the Communist Party, the Labour movement was urged to demand that the British Government supply the Spanish Government warships and planes with the oil they needed, which was the immediate issue at that time. On August 1st a Communist Party manifesto demanded that the British Government supply the Spanish Government with arms and medical requirements. A big demonstration in Hyde Park on August 9th, organised by the Communists, demanded " every facility and help to the legal Spanish Government to obtain the aeroplanes and arms it requires to defend democracy." A few days before the meeting of the National Council of Labour, Harry Pollitt in a speech at Wigan urged that it was the Council's duty to present an ultimatum to the Baldwin Government to force it to accord the Spanish Government its normal international rights.

By the time the Labour Party Conference met at Edinburgh on October 5th there could no longer be any doubt that the non-intervention agreement was operating disastrously against the Spanish Government; in addition the Baldwin Government had set the seal of its approval on the official Labour policy. Sir Samuel Hoare, no less, had told the Conservative Conference at Margate on the eve of Edinburgh that " the wise attitude adopted by the Trades Union Congress over the Spanish crisis shows that in the ranks of Labour there is a solid force of patriotic responsibility." The first debate on the Spanish situation took place on the opening day of the Labour Party Conference. It was evident that the temper of the delegates had hardened very much in the month that had elapsed since the Plymouth Congress. In moving the official resolution supporting non-intervention Mr. Arthur Greenwood admitted that he had a difficult task and described the policy as " a bad second best." There was difficulty in obtaining a seconder for the resolution and opposition came from all quarters of the conference.

Sir Charles Trevelyan, for example, said that he wanted the Labour movement of Britain to lead the world, but there was no leadership where people were thinking chiefly of playing for safety, adding that " playing for safety to-day means the creation of another Fascist State in Europe which will inevitably bring war." He concluded: " I say you are beggared of policy at this moment . . . when the war that is looming comes and Japan and Germany crash in to try and destroy Soviet Russia, I hope the Labour Party will have some other policy to offer than sympathy, accompanied by bandages and cigarettes." Defending non-intervention, Mr. Ernest Bevin said that he and his colleagues had taken their lead from the French Government which was probably saving France from the deluge of Fascism. In so saying, incidentally, Mr. Bevin contradicted his own speech at Plymouth, where he said that they had come to a British decision without taking their lead from anybody, and the speech of Sir Walter Citrine, who had told the T.U.C. that " in France Fascism to-day has not been materially weakened as a consequence of the change in the electoral front."

The official resolution was carried by 1,836,000 votes to 519,000; but two days later the position was entirely altered by the powerful speeches of the Spanish fraternal delegates, Señor de Asua and Señora de Palencia. The conference was moved to its depths by the bitter reality of " non-intervention " as exposed by the Spanish delegates, whose

appeal for a reversal of this policy and for the fullest aid
for Spain called forth thundering ovations. All observers
agree that another vote taken at that moment would have
overwhelmed the leadership and its policy. On behalf of
the National Council of Labour, Mr. C. R. Attlee and
Mr. Greenwood were therefore despatched to London to
interview Mr. Chamberlain, who was acting as Prime
Minister in Mr. Baldwin's absence; on their return they
reported to the Council and a statement demanding
investigation of breaches of the non-intervention agreement, and its abrogation if the breaches were proved, was
unanimously accepted by the conference. It was also
pledged that constant pressure would be maintained on
the Government (the leaders would " sit on the Government's doorstep " was the phrase) to see that this modified
policy was carried out.

Not till October 28th, when the Fascist forces were near-
ing Madrid, did the National Council of Labour finally
abandon its support of " non-intervention." Of the promised pressure on the Government the only overt evidence
was a couple of deputations that went to visit Mr. Eden
in January and in March to protest against the flood-
ing of German and Italian Fascist reinforcements into
Spain. There was still no sign of a national campaign. The
Socialist and trade union movements of every other important democratic country in Europe could send official
delegations to Spain; not so the most important movement
of all, that of Britain. This act of solidarity was left to the
trade unionists of London to accomplish. While the Communists took the initiative in raising a British battalion for
the famous International Column—as Mr. H. N. Brailsford, who came in to give invaluable assistance in this work,
has borne witness—this most practical form of aid was not
turned into the mighty movement that it could have been
had the official leadership taken it up. In the early days of
the war in Spain the *Daily Herald* had written " armed
struggle, not of their seeking, has begun and must be
carried through." Brave words in Long Acre are hardly as

effective as a British machine-gun squad in stopping a charge of Moorish mercenaries or Italian conscripts at the gates of Madrid.

By the beginning of the present year the demand for action, for the calling of a national conference of the Labour movement to rouse the whole country with a campaign in aid of Spain, became more and more insistent. It was voiced on January 14th in a resolution adopted by the Executive Council of the Amalgamated Engineering Union; a few days later the *Daily Herald* reported that it was receiving numerous resolutions from trade union branches to the same effect; early in February the same demand was unanimously endorsed by the London Trades Council, representing 300,000 trade unionists in the capital, and by a conference of delegates from all over South Wales meeting under the auspices of the Cardiff Trades Council. It was urged by the London District Committee of the Transport and General Workers' Union (General and Transport groups); from the Sheffield and Chesterfield district council of the National Union of Railwaymen, representing forty-six branches of the union, there likewise came the call for a national campaign of action in a resolution " deploring the present passive attitude of the national Labour Party in connection with the Spanish workers' fight in defence of democracy "; a deputation from the Birmingham Borough Labour Party, representing 100,000 affiliated members, visited London in the middle of February to demand immediate action on the issue of a national united front campaign with regard to Spain. A veteran of the movement like Mr. John Hill, the former secretary of the Boilermakers and an ex-member of the General Council, noted for the moderation of his views, wrote to the *Daily Herald* urging the summoning of a special conference against Fascism and asking, in connection with Spain, " how long must we be quiescent partners with our Government in their hellish duplicity ? "

After long agitation by the Spanish Labour movement for an all-in international working-class and anti-Fascist conference a gathering, limited to bodies associated with the Labour and Socialist International and the International Federation of Trade Unions, assembled privately in London in the second week in March. The Spanish delegates demanded a break with the policy of non-intervention, urging that as a last resort the working-class forces in the democratic countries should organise an international protest strike to compel their Governments to raise the ban on arms for the democratic Government of Spain. Support for, or at least sympathy with, this demand was general among the continental delegates. And Britain ? The answer was given by Mr. Ernest Bevin in a speech to which no reference was made in the columns of the *Daily Herald*[1] but to which the national Press generally referred. It was summarised in the *Daily Telegraph* as follows:

" Mr. Bevin said he was speaking in the name of the entire British Socialist movement when he frankly told the Spanish delegation that the movement refused to accede to its demands. The decision and policy of the British Socialist leaders, he said, must not be allowed to be influenced in any way by the war in Spain."

This speech was described by Emile Vandervelde, Belgium's veteran Socialist and the old chairman of the Second International, as " brutal " and as a " cold douche " thrown on hopes of effective action for Spain. The indignant and cruelly disappointed Spanish delegates immediately announced their withdrawal from the Conference Commission; and they abstained from voting on the final resolution, whose sentiments were admirably expressed but which stopped short at *immediate* action.

Reverting now to the proceedings of the Edinburgh Conference, it has to be noted that not only on the issue of Spain but on the issues of unity and rearmament the underlying question was the same. Was the Labour Party to lead

---

[1] On the *Herald's* attitude, see also the appendix on p. 317.

a united advance of the working class and of all democratic forces in the country against the National Government or was it by refusing that unity, by refusing to have confidence in the response of the masses of the people to a fighting lead, to paralyse effective opposition to the Government and reduce the Labour movement to impotence and a fatal co-operation with those who would turn and rend it when the time came ?

The arguments put forward against Communist Party affiliation were those of the July statement, to which detailed reference has already been made. Debate was drastically curtailed on the scarcely convincing pretext that the Spanish delegates were due to speak; this procedure evoked considerable protest which on a show of hands rallied 258 votes against 367. Thus there were only five speeches in all on this key issue. None the less the affiliation resolution received the substantial vote of 592,000 against a majority vote of 1,728,000. Later in the conference the unity issue was again raised on a resolution from the Engineers instructing the Executive " immediately to meet representatives of all working-class bodies to bring about a united front." In the debate a number of delegates from Divisional Labour Parties, supporting the resolution, stressed the urgent importance of following the French example and closing the ranks against Fascism. This resolution was defeated by 1,805,000 to 435,000 votes.

It was worthy of note that the leaders had already employed their handling of the Spanish problem to suggest the need for supporting rearmament. In the Spain debate at the T.U.C., Sir Walter Citrine had advanced as one of the reasons for not pressing for a firm policy against the Fascist Powers the fact that " in our movement there were those who for years have been burking this issue, who every time there has been under consideration the question of force to be exercised against aggressors, had evaded facing it." Mr. Bevin had said, " there is a lot of confused thinking on the whole problem of defence in this country, and a failure in our movement to realise the real situation. That is what I meant when I said earlier in my speech that some of our cherished beliefs . . . may have to be revised and the whole situation reviewed." It may be remarked that the speech by Sir Samuel Hoare approving the Spanish policy of the Labour leaders, which has already been quoted, had continued, " responsible leaders of Labour can give invaluable help. They came forward with their assistance in the war. Let all who believe in liberty and ordered progress join with the Government in bringing the rearmament programme to a swift and successful fulfilment."

At Edinburgh Dr. Hugh Dalton moved an emergency resolution on behalf of the Executive stating " that in view of the threatening attitude of dictatorships . . . the armed strength of the countries loyal to the League of Nations must be conditioned by the armed strength of the potential aggressors." That clause, on the face of it, was an endorsement of the Government's rearmament plans; but the resolution went on to refer to the function of the country's armed forces as " the preservation of the people's rights and liberties, the continuance of democratic institutions and the observance of international law," adding that " the Labour Party declines to accept responsibility for a purely competitive armament policy. It reserves full liberty to criticise the rearmament programme of the present Government, and declares the continuance of vested interests in the private manufacture of arms to be a grave contributory danger to the peace of the world."

The debate that followed was the most confused and contradictory that a Labour Party Conference has known. Executive members were at variance one with another. Did the resolution mean the abandonment of opposition to the rearmament programme or did it mean, as Mr. Morrison claimed, that since the Government's policy amounted to a competitive arms race, " we cannot vote for it in the House of Commons " ? Ought the Opposition to trust the National Government to resist the menace of Fascism, and in that case ought it to support rearmament, or ought it to say that unless given certain guarantees it " declined," in

Mr. Attlee's words, " to give the Government a blank cheque " ? Even in the voting, when the resolution was adopted by 1,738,000 to 657,000, confusion continued; for, as the *Daily Herald* reported, supporters and opponents of rearmament were both included in the majority. And the confusion itself was a danger signal, an indication that the resolution could be used to harness the Labour movement to the Government's war chariot.

The other decisions adopted by the Edinburgh Conference were also retrogressive. Widespread opposition had been aroused in the Party by the Executive's memorandum on the League of Youth, to whose militancy official exception had been taken. While the Executive proposed to circumscribe the League's activity by reducing the maximum age from twenty-five to twenty-one, by disbanding its National Advisory Council, closing down its journal the *New Nation*, and suspending its annual conference, the conference agenda carried pages upon pages of resolutions from constituency parties proposing on the contrary that the constitutional powers of the League should be extended, so that it could become a really strong youth movement along Socialist lines. Though this was an issue affecting the local parties only the block vote was brought in to win the day for the Executive, whose opponents claimed that the striking down of the League of Youth meant that " Sir Oswald Mosley was going to be presented with a great opportunity to get the youth of this country into his own hands." The questions of unemployment, malnutrition and the depressed areas were telescoped into one debate, despite a strong protest by Miss Ellen Wilkinson, M.P., who urged support for the Means Test Protest March; but a ruling from the chair prevented any discussion of the march— whose great success has been referred to above—and also barred any discussion of plans of action on these long-standing problems.

Not the least important feature of the conference was the testimony it afforded of the unrest among the constituency parties. It was later revealed by the Glasgow *Forward* that over 200 delegates had wished to speak on matters affecting the Party constitution. On the last day of the conference the question of constitutional reform was raised and there were loud protests when it was announced that the problem would be referred to the Executive. The local temper was revealed when a Manchester delegate, seconding the reference back of the Executive's non-committal report on ceremonial events and honours (the reference back was carried by 185 votes to 174) said, " I think I am voicing the opinion of every Divisional Labour Party in the country when I say we do not get a fair deal from the Executive. I hope they realise our dissatisfaction." After the conference some 250 delegates from constituency parties met under the chairmanship of Sir Stafford Cripps and decided to appoint a committee to collect evidence to further their claim for a reform of the constitution to give the local organisations a more equitable voice in party governance.

Edinburgh administered a severe shock to the whole movement, Right and Left alike. On the last day of the conference itself a trade union delegate opposed to unity (Mr. J. Howarth of the Railway Clerks) had nevertheless said : " Nobody can leave this conference with any feeling of hope about the future of our movement. He was profoundly disturbed about the way the movement was being run." Mr. Herbert Morrison declared that the conference was " by no means as good as it might have been." Dr. Dalton, the new Party chairman, admitted with qualifications that " it was not a good conference," and Dr. Addison, a former Labour Minister, added sharply, " indeed, no ! it is possible that another conference of the same kind would destroy the Party as an effective force for a long time to come." Mr. J. R. Leslie, the former general secretary of the Shop Assistants, wrote that " even the most perfervid Labour Party supporter must have left with a feeling of discontent. There was something lacking, something indefinite. If delegates and visitors came expecting inspiration, they went empty away." *Reynolds News* declared editorially that " the bold imaginative leadership for which the nation looked to Labour's Edinburgh Conference is still to seek." Sadly Mr. H. N. Brailsford wrote, " thirty years ago as a young man I joined the I.L.P., for under Hardie it had courage and faith. Were I, as a young man, to read the record of this Edinburgh Conference, would anything it had done fire me with a wish to join the Labour Party ? This slouching leadership, this parasitic attitude towards the Government of the other class would attract no young man." Professor Harold Laski described Edinburgh as " the worst annual conference in the post-war history of the Party." Sir Stafford Cripps reported that " wherever I have been since the conference I have heard dismay expressed at its temper and results. There is the great danger to-day that a defeatist attitude may spread through the Divisional Labour Parties."

Further events were soon forthcoming to heighten the sense of alarm running through the opinions cited above and summed up in the declaration of the Communist Party at its national conference in Sheffield, immediately after Edinburgh, that " the Labour movement is facing the most serious crisis in its history." The Municipal Elections of 1936, when Labour was defending its gains of three years before, resulted in a net loss of eighty-one seats. Commenting on the results the *Daily Herald* confessed that " the fact had better be candidly faced that Labour's dynamic drive forward as a national force stopped in 1929. Since then it has just on balance held its ground but no more." By-elections told a similar tale. Averaging the results of the by-elections from the General Election up to the Clay Cross poll on November 6th last, the Government vote was seen to have fallen by 23 per cent, but the Labour vote stagnated —it rose by only 1 per cent. While a vigorous candidate with a united movement behind him could win, as Mr. Noel-Baker did at Derby, the outstanding thing was that important seats which had been won by Labour in 1929 were not regained. This was the case at Preston (November 25th, 1936) where the Government candidate dropped 4,600 votes and the Labour candidate 1,300 votes as compared with 1935; but compared with 1929 the Government candidate had gone up 3,500 votes whereas the Labour candidate was down by nearly 7,000. The moral of North St. Pancras (February 1937) was similar. While the poll was admittedly low and the Government candidate polled 5,100 less than in 1935 to the Labour candidate's drop of 1,800, the comparison with 1929 showed a Government decline of 2,600 compared with a Labour fall of almost 6,000.

Throughout the country the rank and file responded with quick concern to the crisis that they felt was upon them. A critical analysis of the Labour Party conference by Professor Harold Laski in the *Labour Monthly*, urging the need " to reshape the movement into a fighting movement " on the basis of unity, brought no fewer than 143 letters of comment, mainly from trade unionists and local militants generally; of these letters only 18 were unfavourable to the criticisms made, 81 were generally favourable, while 44 were in entire agreement. The reaction of the local Labour Parties was early evidenced at a conference of the Home Counties Labour Association in London in November. This conference, which was largely attended by the constituency parties around London, was highly critical of the party leaders (" it is time Transport House was scared stiff," said one speaker) and at the same time was keenly alive to a danger of a split in the Party, was conscious of the need to make the Labour Party the supreme political force in the country. A resolution was adopted condemning the " present vacillating policy of the Labour Party leadership " and demanding a strong militant lead for the abolition of the Means Test, full support for Spain, and the uniting of the whole working class. At a similar conference in Manchester, attended by delegates from 33 constituency parties in the North Western area, Mr. Ben Greene, secretary of the committee which had been set up at Edinburgh, said that the divisional parties had been treated by headquarters with a contempt and neglect which had virtually killed the spirit inside the movement, and if this state of things continued the situation for the Labour Party would be very serious. He added:

" I am simply appalled at the break-up of our local Party organisations. There are divisional parties that have returned Labour Members to the House of Commons that have not had a meeting since the last General Election. I believe I am right in saying that there are dozens of other constituencies which should have Labour Members where the Labour parties have had only one meeting, or perhaps two, since the General Election."

Revealing, too, was the discussion that filled the correspondence columns of the *Daily Herald* during January of this year, following the publication of articles by Professor Laski and Dr. Dalton. Professor Laski's article laid stress on the two irreconcilable class interests in society to-day and said: " That understanding is the keystone of the central arch of all Socialist policy. Recognise that and the divisions in the Party would vanish rapidly. Fail to recognise it, and the policy of the Party is bound to be indistinguishable from that which, under Mr. Ramsay MacDonald, led us to disaster in 1931." The country, he went on, " wants to feel that the Labour Party has the initiative in its hands "; " to that initiative unity is the road ; and the path to unity lies through a fighting policy." In his reply Dr. Dalton referred to the need for a short programme, tilted at " our professional grumblers," dismissed the united front as " windy verbiage " and made the following constructive contribution to political leadership—" I have left the international situation till the end. It is very black. We were lucky to get through 1936 without a European war. May we have equal luck in 1937 ! " He did not mention Spain.

From all over the country came letters supporting the viewpoint of Professor Laski, overshadowing those few that supported the Executive attitude expounded by Dr. Dalton. Local Labour stalwarts such as Party chairmen and secretaries and town councillors were represented. The general note struck was the need for united action against the Government. A Norwich councillor objected to Dr. Dalton's " bland optimism," while from the other side of England a Wigan councillor criticised the " present inept leadership of the Party " and said plainly that Dr. Dalton " must be blind or easily satisfied." From Coventry came the demand that " the Labour leaders must come out of Baldwin's pocket and take an independent line on questions of foreign policy." A Labour candidate declared that the action of the Socialist League (discussed below) was symptomatic of the temper of all active members of the Party, adding " they are not content to be a faint echo of the Baldwin Government." Nor was the criticism confined to working-class representatives. A B.Sc. wrote in to explain how he and many of his middle-class friends were " staggered " by Dr. Dalton's failure to mention Spain.

Obviously, expression of opinion alone could not resolve the movement's crisis. It was also clear that the campaign needed to rescue the movement from impotence, surrender and wholesale defections must have unity as its central point. Dr. Dalton's reference to " windy verbiage " looked cheap enough when contrasted with the achievements of unity in arms on the battlefields of Spain and its achievements in both the political and trade union movements of France. It was not a matter of words, but of membership statistics. Before the " windy verbiage " of the united front the combined memberships of the Socialist and Communist Parties in France totalled 110,000; to-day they total 485,000. Similarly the combined memberships of France's two trade union centres before the achievement of unity totalled 800,000—to-day the membership of the united C.G.T. is 5,000,000. In England we have one significant example, small, it is true, but suggestive. It is that of the University Labour Federation, of which Mr. Arthur Greenwood is president and with which Dr. Dalton himself has long been associated. In January of last year that Federation united with the Federation of Student Societies, led by Communists, to form one University Labour Federation affiliated to the Labour Party. Before unity the membership of the two bodies aggregated 1,500. To-day the membership of the united Federation is 3,100; at its annual conference in January 1937 it was reported that the establishment of unity had brought the Federation " the record year of its existence " since its foundation.[1]

With these facts in mind the Socialist League, the Communist Party and the Independent Labour Party announced in the Press on January 18th that they were combining to launch a unity campaign " for action, for attack, for the ending of retreat, for the building of the strength, unity and power of the working-class movement." In their manifesto the three parties emphasised that they stood for " unity of all sections of the working-class movement . . . in the struggle against Fascism, reaction and war, and against the National Government . . . in the struggle for immediate demands, and the return of a Labour Government as the next stage in the advance to working-class power." It was emphasised that the objective was " unity within the framework of the Labour Party and the trade unions . . . to-day is no time for defections or for breakaways." Urging that " the fight for peace demands unbending hostility to a National Government that can in no circumstances be trusted to use armaments in the interests of the working class, of the peoples, or of peace " the manifesto proclaimed—" Let the movement not wait for General Elections, but now . . . win organised support for:

    (1) Abolition of the Means Test.
    (2) T.U.C. scales of unemployment benefit.
    (3) National work of social value for distressed areas.
    (4) Forty-hour week in industry and the public service.
    (5) Paid holiday for all workers.
    (6) Higher wages, the abolition of tied cottages, for agricultural workers.

[1] It is now reported that the Labour Party Executive contemplates taking disciplinary action against the U.L.F. (*Reynolds News*, April 4th, 1937).

(7) Co-ordinated trade union action for higher wages in industry, especially in mining, cotton, and sweated trades.

(8) Non-contributory pensions of £1 at 60.

(9) Immediate rehousing of the workers in town and countryside in houses that are homes.

(10) Power to get back the land for the people.

(11) Nationalisation of the mining industry.

(12) Effective control of the banks, the Stock Exchanges, with their gambling and private profiteering—profiteering accentuated by the armament boom.

(13) Making the rich pay for social amelioration.[1]

Launched amid keen enthusiasm at a mass meeting in the famous Free Trade Hall at Manchester on January 24th, the message of the unity campaign has been carried far and wide during the weeks that have followed. Mass meetings at Cardiff and Swansea, at Birmingham and Plymouth, at Bristol and in the Rhondda, at Glasgow, Dundee and Edinburgh, at Leeds and Stockport, have shown the extent of the rank-and-file response. Thousands upon thousands of the most active workers in the Labour movement have signed pledge cards to work for unity around the programme of the campaign. From Manchester came a statement endorsing the campaign from nineteen of the principal leaders of the Labour Party in that great city —councillors, executive members, chairmen and secretaries of divisional parties. From Nottingham came a similar declaration signed by the presidents and secretaries of district unions, the Trades Council and the Co-operative Party. The tale of local Labour Parties and trade union branches going on record in support of the campaign is impressive, including Mr. Attlee's own Divisonal Party in

[1] These points may be compared with those of the Labour Party's Short Programme for the next Labour Government, summarised as follows in *Reynolds News*, March 14th, 1937: Public control of the Bank of England; large public schemes of housing, electrification and transport; public ownership of railways, coal, and power; power to take over any armament factories; extension of Rent Restriction Act; abolition of the Means Test.

Limehouse. Whole-hearted support likewise has come from outstanding intellectual figures in the movement like Mr. H. N. Brailsford, Mr. G. D. H. Cole, Professor Laski, from Labour M.P.s like Mr. Aneurin Bevan and Mr. G. R. Strauss, the right-hand man of Mr. Herbert Morrison.

In face of this campaign and its declared purpose, the Labour Party leadership employed the weapon of misrepresentation. Despite the emphasis laid by the three parties, an emphasis reiterated constantly throughout the campaign, on their desire to secure unity *within* the Labour Party, the *Daily Herald* described them as a " triple alliance " which " lines up against Labour." Dr. Dalton referred to those " who are tempted to prefer a spurious unity with small forces outside the Party to a real unity with great forces within it." A manifesto issued by the Labour Party Executive on January 13th carefully quoted the figures of the " disciplinary " vote at the Southport Conference in 1933 (1,820,000 to 89,000), while concealing Edinburgh's more than six-fold multiplication of the minority favouring unity under the phrase " overwhelming majorities." The manifesto proclaimed anew a ban on organisations " which do not share the Party's determination to achieve our democratic Socialist objective " (what else does the unity campaign propose ?) and urged the members to " place Party loyalty in the forefront of their political activities." In accordance with this attitude the Socialist League was expelled from membership of the Labour Party on January 27th; there was a not insignificant minority on the Executive, as it turned out, the voting being reported as 23 to 9.

Additional evidence of the frame of mind of the dominant leaders was afforded by Mr. Ernest Bevin in a speech at Bristol on February 13th when he likened the leaders of the unity campaign, Sir Stafford Cripps, Harry Pollitt and James Maxton to MacDonald, Snowden and Thomas, and in a more particular reference to Cripps compared him with Mosley. And apparently it seemed quite proper to Transport House that Sir Walter Citrine should enter into a united front with Mr. Winston Churchill, speaking with him on a joint political platform. Yet Mr. Churchill's contempt for democracy in the event of it failing to protect property—when, he said, " no Parliamentary system can endure "—had emerged clearly in a reference made by him to the Spanish situation. He had said that " it is idle to claim that a constitutional and parliamentary régime is legally or morally entitled to the obedience of all classes, when it is actually being subverted and devoured from day to day by Communism."

Shrewd and objective appreciation of the whole position was afforded in an editorial in the *New Statesman & Nation,* which asked " what is to become of a movement which, having rightly shed one set of leaders who have turned into open reactionaries, is now busy shedding or threatening to shed anyone who will not obediently sit down and do nothing at the orders of Transport House ? " Stressing the danger of driving out the most active Labour workers (" some no doubt into the Communist Party, but far more to sulk in their tents and stop working for any political party at all "), the country's leading progressive weekly added—" If this is what Transport House achieves, it will avail it nothing to be buttered with laudatory leading articles in *The Times*; the people who will most loudly praise it for its devotion to the cause of democracy will be those who have no belief in democracy themselves, or who interpret democracy as including anything that leaves things pretty much as they are. Leading articles in *The Times* will not help Labour to win elections."

" There are moments (the *New Statesman* went on) when it is criminal for democrats to wait for General Elections— moments when the fate of democracy is hanging in the balance. But the Labour Party seems only half aware that this opportunity is here now, that the battle it is supposed to be fighting has begun in Spain. Instead, it wastes its thunder on a few thousand British Communists for all the world as if it wished to rally the British people behind Hitler's anti-Bolshevik crusade." Transport House would do well to ponder the final warning that the " loss of vitality " through exclusion of the Left must be " disastrous " —" German Social Democracy ceased to appeal to the young, cautiously followed in the wake of its Conservative opponents and finally dried up into a party incapable of inspiring enthusiasm in resisting Fascism. It is not yet too late for the British Labour Party to avoid that fate, but the danger is real."

In January Mr. H. N. Brailsford, long one of the movement's most esteemed thinkers, pointed out in *Reynolds News* that the official short programme could not differ greatly from the programme of the unity campaign (and it does not). " Then why in the name of reason," he asked, " should the official Party reject the aid of three groups who wish to work for the same urgent measures ? " Can any programme rouse the people when a " jealous boycott of the Left impoverishes and narrows the Party " ?

In January, too, the *Daily Herald* had prophesied of the unity campaign that " by next Easter, after a series of revival meetings, the evangelists will find themselves without any effective lead to harness the enthusiasm to their purpose." By Easter the unity campaign actually had close on 30,000 pledged signatories ; the Easter conferences of the Distributive Workers and Shop Assistants Unions had gone on record in support of the campaign—and together they represented some quarter of a million trade unionists ; general support for the conception of working-class unity was voiced from the chair at the Easter conference of the Co-operative Party. The Labour Party Executive maintained its diehard attitude, ruling that as from June 1st members of the Socialist League would be expelled from individual membership of the Labour Party, and damning anew " the so-called [*sic*] unity campaign " in a statement issued in April. No account was taken of the fact, stressed by the *Manchester Guardian*, that the campaign's " very success . . . is proof of the widespread unrest inside the Labour movement."

There had already been ample evidence of a deepening

of political consciousness throughout the movement, suggesting the increasing extent to which people were ready to respond to straightforward and progressive guidance. One instance was the striking growth of the Left Book Club to a membership of over 40,000, together with some 400 local discussion circles, in less than a year from its foundation in May 1936. The modernised *Reynolds' News*, launched in March 1936, added speedily and without effort 100,000 to its circulation at a time when the *Daily Herald*, for all its immense resources and heavy expenditure on circulation-pushing, was unable to advance its figures; the one paper was prepared to have the problems of unity and a forward policy freely discussed in its columns, while the other continued rigidly as the Transport House organ. That Sidney and Beatrice Webb, founders of Fabianism, should produce their monumental *Soviet Communism*, virtually refuting the politics of their past, was an historic event; the querulous and ill-informed public attack which Sir Walter Citrine launched on this great work only served to emphasise its importance. It was also notable that the serialising of Sir Walter's own anti-Soviet travelogue in the *Daily Herald* produced a formidable volume of highly critical correspondence.

Of importance in this connection is the steady growth of the Co-operative Party, which now comprises an affiliated membership of 5,000,000 co-operators, exceeding the Labour Party's affiliated membership of under 2,000,000. This powerful organisation continues to work in association with the Labour Party, but as an independent ally and not an affiliated section, a state of affairs which has produced a disagreement between the two Parties, ventilated at the Edinburgh Conference; and while the organisational problems involved have been straightened out the impact of the growing Co-operative Party on Labour policy will inevitably produce future heat as well as light. It is no secret that Transport House does not relish the independence of an associated body with the resources of a wealthy trading movement behind it and access to its own Press (Mr. Alfred

Barnes, M.P., the chairman of the Co-operative Party, is also the chairman of the Co-operative Press, Ltd., publishers of *Reynolds' News*). The Co-operative Party has also shown that it has a mind of its own; and here there may be significant potentialities. At its conference at Glasgow in 1934, for example, Mr. Barnes pronounced from the chair in favour of " full and complete nationalisation " rather than the public ownership and control through expert Boards which the Labour Party was advocating.

Parallel with the growth of political consciousness, of keener and more general awareness of the problems facing the movement, there are many signs of a wide and active rallying of the working-class forces. Reference has been made above to the mass mobilisation of the East End against the Blackshirts and to the great success of the Means Test Protest March in the autumn of 1936. There has also been a quickening increase in trade union membership, which had already begun to show itself with the passing of the worst of the slump. In 1935 the Trades Union Congress was able to report an increase of 94,000 in its affiliated membership (the first since 1930) while in 1936 the reported increase was 225,000. True, the number of trade unionists affiliated to the T.U.C. was still below the pre-slump figure; it had over 600,000 to go to reach the 1926 level and over 2¾ millions to reach the post-war peak. But the increase won, indicated what might be achieved by a national trade union drive, especially in the newer and largely unorganised industries.

Possibilities of a big response were further suggested, both by the continuance of keenly fought local strikes and by the desire of trade unionists for closer unity, which found expression in the opening of a new and important series of union amalgamations. Thus in April of last year nearly 70 per cent of the memberships of the principal unions in woollen textiles—the National Union of Textile Workers and the two unions of Dyers—took part in an amalgamation ballot, 90 per cent of these voting in favour of amalgamation. The four district unions of Hosiery

Workers in the Midlands have likewise gone on record in favour of fusion. These two moves affect respectively 100,000 and 40,000 workers. In view of the rapid development of the distributive trades in recent years, exceptional importance attaches to the forthcoming amalgamation of the Distributive Workers and the Shop Assistants, which will result in the establishment of an amalgamated union with 250,000 members; plans are already being made for a big organising drive, of whose results the negotiation of a union agreement with the large multiple store concern of Lewis's offers a foretaste.

Symptomatic alike of the rallying of working-class and democratic forces, and of the power of unity, was the remarkable result of the London County Council election this March. After three years' rule the Labour Party was returned with an increased majority of 22 in spite of the most violent anti-Labour campaign known in metropolitan politics and the mobilisation of the whole Tory electioneering machine. While the Municipal Reform vote was pushed up by 28 per cent the Labour vote rose by 31 per cent. The Labour Party had a good record, had shown that they really got things done; their election publicity was first-class, perhaps the best ever seen in an election campaign in this country; and for the first time for many years the working-class forces were united. The London Communist Party flung its whole weight into the campaign behind the Labour Party. Let Mr. G. R. Strauss, M.P., the lieutenant of Mr. Herbert Morrison, tell the story:

" Opponents of Working-Class Unity have always told us that it would be disastrous to Labour's chances at the polls. This argument has been shattered by the L.C.C. elections. . . . Throughout London they [the Communists] held meetings attacking the Conservatives and supporting Labour. They sold and distributed much excellent literature, sent loud-speaker vans to the marginal constituencies, and, wherever they were allowed to, did an immense amount of canvassing, envelope addressing and other election donkey-work in the Labour Party offices. . . . It is noteworthy that it was just in those constituencies where such co-operation was practised that Labour's best electoral results were achieved, and it was in those areas where Communist support was rejected that Labour did less well.

" I can speak from personal experience of the good effects of such co-operation in my constituency of North Lambeth. There the Party received the help of many Communists and other progressive people. They were of the type of young, keen worker who, unfortunately, is not being to-day attracted to the Labour Party. I am sure that every one of our members will agree that the Party's efficiency as a fighting unit has never been greater. The energy and enthusiasm of these new workers was unbounded, and their hard work and the spirit in which it was done created an atmosphere of confidence and victory so infectious that it raised the whole level of the Party and radiated outside the Party to the people of the area. And what were the results of the election ? In a poll of 40 per cent. our clear majority was nearly 3,000 as against some 600 three years ago. . . . North Lambeth was by no means exceptional in this regard. In Hampstead, for example, similar co-operation took place. In spite of a barrage of scare propaganda, the Labour vote was more than doubled.

" The L.C.C. elections have established two important truths. First, that the scare value of Communists is practically negligible. Secondly, the effect of such co-operation, even in the imperfect and limited form in which it was practised at this election, with the constant opposition of headquarters, is to raise the spirit and efficiency of the Labour Party electoral machine, and secure striking results at the poll."[1]

It has to be added that, in Mr. Strauss's words, " the London Labour Party co-operated with the Conservatives

[1] *The Tribune*, March 12th, 1937.

in maximising the scare-value of the Communist support."
Mr. Morrison himself has persisted in alleging that " a
Tory quarter put up £5,000 for the Communists on the
understanding that they would damage Labour by 'supporting' it," has said that the Communists " deliberately
played the Tory game " to " perfection " (the Tories
can hardly think so!), has averred that Communist intervention " on exactly the line the Tories wanted *may* have
cost us " the four losses that were recorded (what about
the gains, Mr. Morrison?). Mr. Morrison has not answered
the claim by Mr. Strauss in a speech at Blackburn that
" for every vote the Conservatives gained by their use of
the Communist threat Labour got 100 by unity of the
working-class movement." Mr. Strauss, however, has not
been reappointed to his offices as chairman of the High-
ways Committee and vice-chairman of the Finance Committee of the L.C.C.

Our story ends—or, rather, breaks off—at a time of
grave crisis, as the opening of this final chapter has already
indicated. It has been seen to what an extent that gravity
is rallying the movement of Britain's working men and
women for the supreme effort that the times demand. The
great army of Labour is mobilising. Not yet has it caught
up with the pace of the enemy's mobilisation: but this is
no ground for pessimism; rather should it serve as the
keenest spur to redoubled activity on the part of everyone
aware of the magnitude and urgency of the issues.

Those issues are in essence plain and simple, though their
manifestations are often complex, since life is after all
a varied and elaborate thing. In an article quoted above,
Professor Laski stressed that the underlying fact we all have
to reckon with is that we live in a society cut in two by
class divisions; the interests of the wealthy men of property,
the capitalists, and the working and lower middle class,
are irreconcilable. In the Britain of 1936, shown by the
researches of Sir John Orr and Dr. M'Gonigle to have at
least half of its people below proper nutrition standards,

the Inland Revenue authorities record 49 more millionaires than the previous year. The very rich, the real rulers of the country, amount to less than 1 per cent of the population. The working class and the middle class together amount to some 95 per cent, the working class alone being not less than 80 per cent.

Does not daily practice make it clear that the interests of the vast majority of the British people who live by working can only be advanced at the expense of the interests of that infinitesimal minority who live by owning? But this does not involve the issues which are so often dragged in as distractions—violence or non-violence, evolution or revolution, etc. The problem to-day is: how are the demands and desires of the working people of Britain for a better life, for an end to insecurity, want and frustration to be satisfied? Can that be done by a policy of accommodation to a social order which nowadays is always on the brink of slump, of war, of grinding democracy under Fascism's iron heel? Surely the whole course of the British workers' post-war history has shown the folly of any such policy; has, on the contrary, proved conclusively that the only hope lies in a straightforward, consistent and unequivocal working-class policy, setting forth what the workers want and leading them boldly and unitedly forward to win it.

The policy of accommodation to capitalism was that practised by Mr. MacDonald. It led inevitably to the catastrophe of 1931. The militant policy beat the Government in the railway strike of 1919, stopped the war on Russia in 1920, won respite for the miners on Red Friday, defeated the Lancashire cotton employers in 1932, reduced Mr. Baldwin's hosts to " hysteria and panic " and compelled the withdrawal of the new unemployment relief scales in 1935, won the London County Council election in 1937.

Which path is the movement to tread? Let us not deceive ourselves. The army, we have said, is slowly mobilising; but its principal generals are not anxious to lead it to war.

On foreign policy, on rearmament, in their general attitude and actions, they continue to take the old disastrous road that Mr. MacDonald trod before them. They maintain the disunity, the emotional and uncontrollable hatred of unity, which was the hallmark of the MacDonaldite line. That way, as experience shows, defeat and ruin lie.

Is it that the leaders of the movement are insincere men, dishonest men, men who deliberately ignore the lessons of experience ? Nothing of the kind. They are men whose point of view has been shaped by the circumstances of their personal and political lives; and that point of view may be summed up by saying that they have a profound lack of faith in the working class and an equally profound, almost a superstitious, awe of what they feel to be the almighty and unshakable power of the capitalist class. Hence they take the accommodating course. Hence Black Friday, hence the General Strike surrender, hence 1931, hence the line-up with the Government over Spain.

To overcome this point of view will not be easy; for it is held with the vehemence of emotion, of a subconscious urge, rather than with the assurance of reason. Yet overcome it must be, if the movement is to save itself, if victory is to be won. Patient, tireless, energetic work lies to the hand of every conscious individual in the mighty Labour movement of Britain in order to ensure—and that speedily —the triumph of unity and a forward fighting policy. I believe that the history of the past vital twenty years, as set down unadorned in this book, can lead to one commonsense conclusion and one only. That was bluntly put by Frederick Engels, one of the greatest of all Socialists, one of the profoundest students of Britain and the British, when he wrote: " There is no power in the world which could for a day resist the British working class organised as a body."

APPENDIX

On April 14th, 1937, the House of Commons debated a vote of censure on the Government, moved by the Labour Party, in respect of the refusal to protect British vessels trading to Bilbao from the pirate ships of General Franco. The following extracts appear worth exhuming from the limbo of the Official Report:

MR. NOEL-BAKER: Have we ever recognised the right of an insurgent Government to make a blockade? I do not believe the Foreign Secretary could find a case. . . .

MR. CHURCHILL: There are a number of cases recorded in the *Daily Herald* this morning.

MR. NOEL-BAKER: With great respect, I believe that every one of those cases is open to doubt. This is a highly technical matter, to which I have given a good deal of attention, and I do not believe that the writer in the *Herald* had done so. . . .

MR. EDEN: If the non-intervention scheme were torn to pieces, who would benefit? Not the Spanish Government. I have here some very wise words which were written on this subject: " It is suggested that non-intervention should be thrown over . . . that the Spanish Government should be provided with arms. . . . But in view of what has actually happened these last eight months, can it be reasonably doubted that the results would not be these, but the very reverse? . . . And if non-intervention were now abandoned, is it not certain that the Fascists would pour men into Spain until a Government defeat were assured? " That is the *Daily Herald* of March 15th.

MR. COCKS: He will get a peerage for that.

MR. EDEN: It is very sound sense; whether that deserves a peerage I do not know.

The reader will observe that the Labour Party organ was repudiated by the Party's principal expert on foreign affairs; its endorsement came from the Foreign Secretary of the National Government.

INDEX